MATERNAL PERSONALITY, EVOLUTION AND THE SEX RATIO

Do mothers control the sex of the infant?

Valerie J. Grant

London and New York

First published 1998
by Routledge
11 New Fetter Lane, London EC4P 4EE

Simultaneously published in the USA and Canada
by Routledge
29 West 35th Street, New York, NY 10001

© 1998 Valerie J. Grant

Typeset in Baskerville by Routledge
Printed and bound in Great Britain by Creative Print and Design (Wales)
Ebbw Vale

British Library Cataloguing in Publication Data
A catalogue record for this book is available from the British Library

Library of Congress Cataloguing in Publication Data
Grant, Valerie J., 1937–
Maternal personality, evolution, and the sex ratio: do mothers control the
sex of the infant? / Valerie J. Grant.
p.   cm.
Includes bibliographical references and index.
1. Sex determination, Genetic. 2. Sex ratio. 3. Dominance (Psychology).
4. Pregnancy–Psychological aspects. 5. Human evolution. 6. Testosterone.
7. Mothers–Psychology. I. Title.
QP278.5.G73 1998
612.6'2–dc21   97–14825
CIP

ISBN 0–415–15879–6 (hbk)
ISBN 0–415–15880–X (pbk)

P

MATERNAL PERSONALITY, EVOLUTION AND THE SEX RATIO

Ever since Aristotle, people have wondered what determines the sex of the infant. There have been many suggestions from folklore and false leads from science. Most educated people have been taught that it depends on whether an X- or Y-chromosome-bearing spermatozoon reaches the ovum first. Yet this may be only a small part of the picture.

Valerie Grant examines evidence that women who score highly on personality questionnaires designed to measure dominance are more likely than less dominant women to conceive sons. She argues that dominance is a core personality trait, and its biological basis, even in females, is testosterone. It is likely that the action of this hormone within the reproductive system leads to the favouring of sperm carrying male or female chromosomes. Thus the mother's personality is both relevant and appropriate, in evolutionary terms, to the sex of the child she conceives. This is the maternal dominance hypothesis.

The maternal dominance hypothesis makes sense of many puzzling findings in demography, including the fact that more boys are born following a war. Tough times mean more males. It explains research findings in developmental psychology. Mothers of boys and mothers of girls interact differently with their newborn infants. Since dominance makes the difference, it is probably advantageous, in the evolutionary sense, for dominant mothers to conceive sons. The sex of the infant may not be a matter of chance. It may depend on which sex infant the mother is more suited to raise.

Valerie J. Grant is Lecturer in Behavioural Science at the School of Medicine, University of Auckland, New Zealand.

DEDICATED
TO MY HUSBAND
KELVIN CHARLES GRANT

CONTENTS

1

OVERVIEW

'What determines whether the baby will be a girl or a boy?' Ever since Aristotle, prospective parents have been asking this question. Most educated people today have been taught that the sex of the infant is a matter of chance: it depends on whether it is an X- or Y-chromosome-bearing spermatozoon from the male that first penetrates the ovum. Yet this may be only a small part of the total picture.

This book describes the idea that the sex of the infant may be under the control of the mother through the hormones of reproduction. These hormones in turn appear to provide the biological basis for a personality trait known as dominance. Thus the mother's personality is both relevant and appropriate, in an evolutionary sense, to the sex of the child she conceives. This is the maternal dominance hypothesis.

Research shows that women who score highly on personality questionnaires designed to measure dominance are more likely to conceive male infants than less dominant women. Women whose scores are in the top 20 per cent on dominance are five times more likely to conceive a male infant than women at the other end of the scale.

At first such an idea appears to be incompatible with the knowledge that a spermatozoon from the male is responsible for determining the sex of the infant. But contemporary research in reproductive physiology has shown that several factors related to the determination (and ratification) of the sex of the infant are likely to be influenced by the mother. Individual differences in the female reproductive system may make it easier for either an X- or a Y-chromosome-bearing spermatozoon to fertilize the ovum, or the uterine environment may be more conducive to the development of a male or a female embryo depending on certain characteristics of the mother. Furthermore, these characteristics are likely to be both physical and psychological, the former providing the basis for the latter.

The link between the physical and psychological factors is almost

1

certainly hormonal. The theory is that the same hormonal influences that regulate reproductive processes and increase the chances of an X or a Y sperm fertilizing the ovum also provide the biological basis for the woman's personality, and influence the ways in which she responds to her social environment. At present most scientific evidence supports the idea that testosterone is the relevant hormone, even though it is present in such tiny amounts in women. Individual differences between women in the amount of testosterone appear to underlie both the potential to behave in a dominant way and the potential to conceive male infants.

Factors within the female which may make a critical difference to the successful access of an X or a Y sperm are variations in the uterine environment, either biochemical or mechanical, or differences in the ovum which may make it more or less difficult for an X or a Y sperm to breach the outer rim. Alternatively, or additionally, maternal factors may be operating at the level of implantation. Thus, although X and Y spermatozoa are produced in equal numbers by the male, the chances of either one or the other actually fertilizing an individual woman's ovum may not be equal at all.

A lot depends on the comparative importance of these suggested differences within the female. If molecular biologists confirm the importance of current findings, there will be enough evidence to support the idea that the predetermination of the sex of the infant is at least partly, and perhaps totally, under the control of the female. If so, the sex of the infant will not be a matter of chance, but the result of a highly complex set of factors which take into account both the physical and psychological attributes of the mother. Thus there appears to be an inextricable intertwining of body and mind at the very heart of the reproductive process.

In the 1980s it became apparent that work on the maternal dominance hypothesis in humans corresponded in a remarkable way with research by evolutionary biologists, who had been investigating maternal dominance rank and its relation to the sex ratio in animals. This in turn had arisen out of a theoretical model first offered by Trivers and Willard in 1973. They argued that animals would invest more in either sons or daughters according to what would most benefit later reproductive success. They argued that if a son and a daughter were both in good condition, the male would outbreed the female, whereas if both were in poor condition the female would outbreed the male.

To test this idea, evolutionary biologists had to find a way of measuring good condition. And, since studies of animal behaviour commonly run for several years, it would be especially helpful if this measurement could be derived from existing data. The problem was solved by assuming that, since animals high in dominance rank have priority access to the best food and mates, rank ordering animals for dominance would be equivalent to rank ordering them for condition. Between 1982 and 1984 the first studies were published using dominance rank as the measure. Several research teams found that high-ranking females produced significantly more male offspring than female offspring. The work, done with both primates and ungulates, showed that the sex ratio of the offspring was related to maternal dominance rank.

In some studies, however, the relationship between dominance and sex of the offspring ran in the opposite direction to the one predicted (that is, the less dominant animals had more male infants). Evolutionary biologists have tried to explain these findings. Some researchers have suggested that competition for local resources may play a part; others think that variations may depend on which sex disperses on sexual maturity. It is also possible that conflicting results may be explained by looking at whether or not the animals in captivity were interacting in ways which would be normal in the wild. If testosterone is the link between dominance and the sex ratio, then any additional factors that influence the production of testosterone in the female (such as stress) need to be taken into consideration. Whatever the explanation, it is clear that in many animals maternal dominance is related to the sex of the offspring.

The question of exactly how females could manipulate the sex ratio of their offspring is not usually addressed in the literature in evolutionary biology, though some workers have shown how dominance behaviours (usually in male animals) are linked with testosterone. But scientists working in agriculture and animal husbandry are particularly concerned with what the evolutionary biologists call 'proximate mechanisms' – that is, how it all works at the physiological level. They would like to be able to control the sex ratio in domestic animals, and the commercial rewards for such a discovery would be great.

Thus workers in a variety of disciplines have focused their attention on what controls the sex ratio. Some are motivated by wanting to solve the theoretical puzzle: What could possibly account for the apparently conflicting results? Some have been more interested in the technological side of the problem, and have sought ways to manipulate the sex ratio in both animals and humans. Some have approached the problems from the viewpoint of evolutionary biology, others from reproductive physiology. Researchers from both these disciplines have studied animals and humans in their search for answers.

Because the problems have proved intractable for so long, many hundreds (possibly thousands) of researchers have sought clues from disciplines somewhat removed from the core issues – for example, population statistics or demography. One of the most tantalizing aspects of sex ratio data for both humans and animals is its consistency: in animals that reproduce bisexually, the sex ratio is 100:100 – that is, for every 100 males born there are 100 females. But in humans there are more males born than females: for every 100 girls there are 105 boys. This is true for all human populations in all countries. If the numbers had been equal, study of the sex ratio would hardly have held the long-term fascination that it has. Given that the two types of human spermatozoon are produced in equal numbers, and that until now the sex of the infant has been deemed to be a matter of chance, what could possibly account for these consistent, worldwide differences?

Mathematicians, statisticians and epidemiologists have written hundreds of papers seeking to describe, analyse and explain human sex ratio data. When sample sizes exceed a million births, small effects become apparent. Birth order, race and socio-economic status all appear to have some influence, but so far the reasons for this are elusive. In smaller samples involving specific groups, particularly occupational groups, there are some curious findings which appear to indicate a departure from the acknowledged norms. There is also the well-known phenomenon of more boys being born following war. The maternal dominance hypothesis not only introduces a new dimension into thinking about these otherwise unexplained data, but it also helps make sense of many findings.

If the determination of the sex of the infant is at least partly controlled by factors relating to maternal hormones, and these in turn relate to the biological basis of personality, then there needs to be more information about the relevant aspect of personality. What exactly is dominance and what does it mean to say that a woman is more or less dominant in personality than other women?

This book gathers together all the relevant information. There is a chapter on dominance and how it can be measured (Chapter 2), which includes the most recent and successful questionnaire and how to score it, together with an account of the research done so far and suggestions for future research.

The question of how dominance affects the way the mother interacts with her children becomes both relevant and important. If dominant women conceive and bear sons, then baby boys as a group are being exposed to women whose personality, at least temporarily, is a little different from women who have daughters.

Since the early 1960s, developmental psychologists have been studying mother–infant interaction in meticulous detail. The studies have been done in different countries by different researchers. Whether they were looking for it or not, every team found that the mothers of baby boys interacted with their infants in ways that were different from mothers of baby girls, even though there were no differences in the behaviours of the babies. The data show how differences in personality are apparent in the ways mothers typically interact with their babies. Mothers of male infants tend to initiate interactions with their babies more frequently, while mothers of female infants tend to be more responsive.

When theorists in developmental psychology noticed how uniformly and strongly all these studies showed the same thing, they searched for a theory that would explain these differences in mothers' behaviours. They decided that mothers interacted differently with their infants according to the sex of the child because of the strength and pervasiveness of universally held sex stereotypes. Of course sex stereotyping plays an important role, but the maternal dominance hypothesis would suggest that, in addition, mothers behave differently because they themselves have different personalities. The differences are exactly what one would expect, given the nature of dominance in human beings.

Does this mean, then, that some women are especially suited to conceiving male infants, and others female infants? The sex of any particular woman's infant may not, after all, be a matter of chance. Each may be contributing to a kind of grand-scale, psychological homoeostasis which both sustains and limits psychological differences between men and women. Such an argument would make evolutionary sense: since dominance makes males sexually attractive to females, but only half the males find dominance attractive in females, it could pay a dominant woman to pass on her genes for dominance to male offspring.

The suggestion that a woman conceives an infant of the sex she is most suited to raise could have wide implications for a number of social issues, including adoption and the ethics of sex selection. Many couples seek to select the sex of their infant, particularly in some Asian cultures. Partly because of this strong pressure from parents, researchers have tried to oblige by offering advice on what to do to increase the chances of conceiving a child of a particular sex, most frequently a boy.

From ancient times, such advice has covered a wide range of suggestions. Today's advice may consist of recommendations to follow a special diet, instructions on pre-coital douching in an attempt to change the uterine environment, or treating the man's sperm in a sex selection clinic to provide an X-enriched or Y-enriched sample. A number of these ideas have been widely publicized through women's magazines and newspaper articles. This book points out why none have so far proved successful, as well as explaining why the figures offered by the proponents often make it look as though they are.

Throughout the book, there is an emphasis on scientific methodology. The main reason for this is that in this area of science there have been so many false claims. Some have been made by charlatans, usually in order to dupe the gullible into parting with their money. But there have also been some allegedly scientific reports which have later been shown to be wrong. False conclusions arise when insufficient attention is given to the design of the research. All scientific research has to be set up in such a way as to produce results which can be interpreted as unequivocally and accurately as possible. If results can be interpreted in several ways, they are of little use. Much research on the sex ratio has produced conflicting results, which have confused rather than clarified the issues. When these are published in reputable scientific journals and within a short time of one another, it is necessary to look critically at the design of the research to help decide how much credence to place on the findings.

Research design holds many traps for the unwary, and no proper understanding can be gained without taking it into consideration. For this reason the research studies described in this book have been selected not only because at the time of their publication they contributed important new findings, but because they are examples of excellent research design. Issues in research methodology are most clearly described in the chapters on reproductive physiology and the measurement of dominance (Chapters 5 and 2 respectively), but reference is made to them in passing throughout the book.

For many years the emphasis in the social sciences was on the nurture side of the nature–nurture question. Most psychologists studying human behaviour focused almost exclusively on the importance of learning and the power of environmental influences rather than on biological influences. The rise of evolutionary biology has made this one-sided approach impossible to sustain. The pendulum is swinging back towards a more balanced consideration of how both biological and environmental factors are intertwined in many of contemporary science's most challenging unsolved problems.

Work on the sex ratio is being carried out increasingly by researchers collaborating across disciplinary boundaries – reproductive physiologists, evolutionary biologists and social scientists. One of the features of scientific discovery is that some of the most exciting developments come at the boundaries between one discipline and another. In this case, there is a resurgence of interest in the way biological factors can influence human behaviour, and how personality and developmental psychology may provide an indicator for something physiological. Reproductive physiology in turn may provide the foundations for viewing social, political and cultural phenomena in a new light.

2

DEFINING AND
MEASURING DOMINANCE

A core component of the maternal dominance hypothesis is that a woman's personality is an indicator of whether she will conceive a boy or a girl. Thus for any particular woman the sex of the infant may not be a matter of chance, but may depend on which sex she is more suited to raise. The particular aspect of personality that appears to be relevant is dominance: the more dominant a woman is, compared with other women, the more likely it is that she will conceive a male infant.

If dominance makes the difference, it is important to define exactly what is meant by the word 'dominance' in this context. What differentiates a dominant woman from one who is not dominant, and how can it be measured? To answer these questions it is necessary to describe several aspects of definition and measurement in personality.

Dominance is one of the few personality characteristics that humans share with animals. It is also a universal attribute of humans. The anthropologist E. M. White spent years gathering cross-cultural linguistic data. He found that

> common conceptual themes underlie the meanings and uses of personality descriptors cross-culturally ... [and that] domi-nance–submissiveness is a universal schema produced by the interaction of innate psycholinguistic structures and funda-mental conditions of human social life ... for example the asymmetrical influence of one actor upon another.
>
> (White 1980)

He demonstrated not only the universality of dominance, but the fact that people everywhere vary along this dimension.

The *Concise Oxford Dictionary* defines 'dominant' as 'ruling, prevailing, most influential'. The *Shorter Oxford Dictionary* defines dominance as 'paramount influence, ascendancy, dominion, sway' and, in giving an example of how the word is used, cites psychiatrist Anthony Storr who said: 'Male therapists are often put off by dominance and assertiveness in women.'

An important aspect of definition is to exclude closely related terms. The two adjectives most frequently confused with 'dominant' are 'aggressive' and 'domineering', neither of which are the same as dominant. In a paper on 'Dominance and heterosexual attraction', Sadalla and his colleagues (1987) took care to avoid confusion between these terms. They offered the following lists, which help clarify the differences in meaning. Dominance, they said, is associated with the adjectives 'powerful, commanding, authoritative, high in control, masterful, and ascendant'. By contrast, aggressiveness is associated with the adjectives 'hostile, belligerent, quarrelsome, argumentative, angry and violent', and domineering is associated with 'overbearing, oppressive, bossy, dictatorial, arrogant and high-handed'.

Sadalla *et al.* demonstrated that, while being dominant increases the sexual attractiveness of males, being domineering or aggressive does not. Even more interesting, being dominant neither increases nor decreases a woman's sexual attractiveness. This work is discussed in more detail in Chapter 3.

When journalists report work in this area they often need to use everyday language. They balk at 'dominance', preferring something more readily understood. Often this has led to inaccuracy in reporting, but some of their words have been both useful and interesting. John Passmore of London's *Evening Standard* asked if the word 'tough' would be a reasonable substitute for 'dominant'. Later he wrote that 'easygoing, compliant women are more likely to have daughters, and the toughest women are five times more likely to have sons' (18 December 1991).

A basic working assumption of the maternal dominance hypothesis is that dominance, and the lack of dominance, are independent attributes. Even though they may be commonly found in association with other well-known characteristics, there is no necessary link between dominance and other aspects of personality. For example, a shy person may be either dominant or not dominant, just as an extraverted person may or may not be dominant. Many people, for example, will be able to think of a shy, but dominant (and prominent), mother of two sons, while in the same family there is a non-dominant, extravert mother of daughters. Just because shyness and non-dominance are found more frequently in combination, this does not mean that they *must* be. Dominance may be found in combination with any other personality attribute, and so may non-dominance. If personality is viewed as having a biological basis, with different aspects of physiology underlying the main traits, then every trait that is underpinned by a distinct physiological process is likely to be independent of the others.

DESCRIPTIONS OF DOMINANCE IN LITERATURE

Exploring personality description in literature has not been popular with psychologists. But skilled writers can illuminate the study of personality by the way they use a few carefully selected words to describe characters in novels or plays, and real people in biographies.

An illustration from literature occurs in *Macbeth*. 'We will proceed no further in this business', Macbeth tells Lady Macbeth (Act 1, scene vii), after deciding not to murder Duncan, King of Scotland. She responds with a strong speech demanding whether he is afraid to go forward with his stated plans and giving a vivid description of her own determination. In recapitulating, Macbeth says to her, 'Bring forth men-children only; For thy undaunted mettle should compose Nothing but males'. In this description, 'undaunted mettle' suggests the emotional strength and determination that appears to characterize women at the extreme end of a continuum between low and high dominance. Its association with the conception of male infants makes the quotation doubly interesting.

An example from real life occurs in Malcolm Muggeridge's autobiography. He writes that his family of origin consisted of five boys. Of his mother, he says:

> She was extremely pretty, with very fair hair, and an expression of fathomless innocence which she retained to a considerable degree to the end of her days. Only, if you looked deep into it, far, far below the pellucid surface, you came upon something steely, tough, even merciless there.
>
> (Muggeridge 1972, 32)

This description, which I did not see until 1990, was of particular interest. Not only did it illustrate the clarity of some non-psychologists' descriptions, it also reminded me of a way of viewing the definition problem that I had had many years before. In trying to come to terms with cultural changes in the manifestation of dominance, I had envisaged it (at the individual level) as being deep below the surface. I even used to think that trying to define and measure dominance was like trying to find out about some amorphous substance far below the surface of the ocean. There was no possibility of fishing it up to look at it, feel it or otherwise experience it. It was more a matter of deducing its characteristics by trying to measure its effect hundreds of metres above on the wave-tossed surface.

Even this was not as fanciful as it sounds. Like many other entities in contemporary science – for example, in molecular biochemistry or astrophysics – the attempt to describe what something is can often be done only in terms of its effects. One assumes its presence because something must be making other substances behave the way they do. My working assumption is that the biological basis of dominance is hormonal, and that it is the intricate and complex mix of both hormonal and environmental influences on behaviour which needs to be unravelled.

Although literary descriptions of the personality trait relevant to the present work are rather rare, it is surprising how often characters in classic novels give birth to infants of the 'appropriate' sex. For example three babies are born in Emily Brontë's *Wuthering Heights*. Cathy gives in, relinquishes the emotional initiative, marries Edgar and has a girl. The frivolous Isabella chooses the man she wants and has a boy; so does the shadowy – so far as the novel is concerned – but dominant wife of Hindley. In D. H. Lawrence's *Sons and Lovers*, tough Mrs Morel has much joy in her new son. In Defoe's *Moll Flanders* the heroine is perhaps one of the strongest women in literature. She is both a thief and a prostitute, and becomes pregnant either for love or for money, or both. She is not ashamed of giving birth to illegitimate children: 'I was brought to bed about the middle of the day and had another brave boy and myself in good condition as normal on such occasions.' In Doris Lessing's *A Proper Marriage*, Martha Quest, who allows things to happen to her and annoys even her friends (at least in the early part of the book) by her passivity and 'reticences', has a daughter.

It is as though good writers have such sensitivity that they convey what feels right for their characters, dare one say, almost by instinct? Of course all the above could be pure chance. In the future, if a link between maternal dominance and the conception of males were to be established, it would be interesting to conduct a thorough study of infants born to women in fiction to see if, in fact, there was a relationship between their individual personalities and the sex of the infants born to them.

THE STUDY OF PERSONALITY AND
PERSONALITY TRAITS

Although they often have a wonderful clarity, literary descriptions such as the ones cited above play only a minor part in contemporary academic psychology. Research requires concise definitions, but these are difficult because the study of personality is largely pre-scientific. Kuhn has said that the foundations of any particular science are built upon an 'entire constellation of beliefs, values, techniques and so on, shared by members of a given community' (Kuhn 1970, 175). Such is not the case in personality psychology.

In 1974, in a paper entitled 'The limits for the conventional science of personality', Fiske summarized the state of research on personality thus:

> The conventional field of personality is severely handicapped by its reliance on words and by its dependence on complex observations . . . Moreover the field still focuses on concepts with inadequate specification and tenuous linkages to measuring procedures. Substantial progress in the field requires . . . reformulations, or new approaches yet to be discovered.
>
> (Fiske 1974)

The situation has hardly changed since the 1970s. It could be argued that the only work which has furthered the study of personality in any substantial way is that which has taken physiological characteristics into account: for example, the theories of Eysenck (1967), Gray (1982) and Zuckerman (1990). The study of personality will become scientific in the true sense of the word only when more is known about the way in which body chemistry influences behaviour. To this end, theories of personality which incorporate biological concepts seem to hold more promise than those based largely on linguistic or mathematical foundations. This is not to undervalue the usefulness of both these approaches, but it now seems likely that this third, biological dimension will need to be incorporated for the study of personality to advance.

Bromley wrote one of the most satisfactory definitions of personality traits, which 'are relatively enduring dispositions . . . to behave in characteristic ways in a wide variety of circumstances and over long periods of time . . . ' (Bromley 1977, 222). Eysenck spoke for many when he maintained that there is now so much evidence to support the existence of traits that they should be regarded as 'definitely established' (1981,

3). He wrote that 'Individuals differ with respect to their location on important semi-permanent personality dispositions, known as "traits"'; that 'personality traits are importantly determined by hereditary factors', and that 'personality traits are measurable by means of questionnaire data' (Eysenck 1981, 3).

Individual traits are usually described by clusters of words which give a general idea of the aspect of personality contained within the trait. In addition, over the years personality traits have frequently been conceptualized as being characteristics with polar opposites. For example, a person may be described as either trusting or suspicious; either adaptable or rigid. For a number of traits this makes sense, but for others it may not.

CATTELL'S DEFINITION OF DOMINANCE

Viewing personality concepts as bipolar has been very influential, especially through the work of Raymond B. Cattell, one of the world's outstanding personality theorists. Cattell's determination to make the study of personality scientific resulted in a body of work which owes its structure to multivariate factor analysis. The raw material for this work consisted of approximately 3000 trait words taken from Allport and Odbert's (1936) monograph entitled 'Trait names: a psycholexical study'. As Allen and Potkay (1981) have noted, 'the monograph contains the most complete list of personality labels available in the psychology literature'. It comprises 17,953 words considered by the authors to be labels for concepts referring to personality. Cattell made decisions about which words to include in his own list of traits by analysing the ways in which they were used interchangeably.

From his mathematical analysis, Cattell found 16 personality traits. These have been widely recognized and used for diagnostic purposes in the well-known Sixteen Personality Factor Test (16PF). One of these factors was a bipolar dimension ranging from dominance to submissiveness, which Cattell labelled Factor E. He described the dimensions of this source trait as follows:

E plus		E minus
Self-assertive, confident	vs	Submissive, unsure
Boastful, conceited	vs	Modest, retiring
Aggressive, pugnacious	vs	Complaisant
Extra-punitive	vs	Impunitive, intropunitive

Vigorous, forceful	vs	Meek, quiet
Wilful, egotistic	vs	Obedient

(Cattell 1965, 90)

Cattell's trait definitions provided the basis for the questions on his personality questionnaires, so the questions that Cattell devised to determine the presence or absence of dominance (Factor E) were based on the above words. Although Cattell's definition of dominance was very close to the one required for the maternal dominance hypothesis, it did not entirely coincide with it. This meant that, although some of the items on the questionnaire were very useful, some were not quite right.

Although dominance, especially the assertiveness aspect of it, has in many countries become a valued attribute in women, it was not always so. When Cattell first described it, he was obliged to distinguish dominant personality from authoritarian personality, which had come into heavy disrepute. This was in the wake of attempts by psychologists to describe what had gone so badly wrong in the events leading up to the Second World War. Some authors had been describing the dominant personality as a person who 'kicks those beneath and bows to those above'; whereas, as Cattell demonstrated, a dominant person is more likely to be one who 'leads those below and kicks those above him!' (Cattell 1965, 91).

The debate about dominant and authoritarian personalities referred only to men. But Cattell had already noticed a significant sex difference in the range of scores between men and women. He also noted that the questions on the 16PF had more relevance for masculine behaviour. He was thus drawn to add to his description of dominance by saying: 'It appears to have a somewhat different loading pattern for men than for women. In women the dominance traits hypochondriacal, socially poised, prominent and attention-getting are more highly loaded than they are in men' (Cattell et al. 1970, 85).

Another of Cattell's traits relevant to the definition of dominance in women is Source Trait I, described as tender-mindedness vs tough-mindedness. This was further defined by Cattell as the dependent vs independent-minded characteristic.

Today the chief limiting factor on Cattell's work derives from something quite outside his control, and possibly not foreseen by him. The difficulty is that both cultural mores and the use of words change over time. Cattell's measures are gradually becoming dated. In particular, although he provided the essential tools for the first 15 years of research on the maternal dominance hypothesis, some of the items used to measure dominance in the early days are now obviously time- and culture-bound.

This is not to underrate Cattell's work. Hundreds of researchers have found his methods both interesting and useful. Much of his work was conspicuously far-sighted, as can be seen in the following paragraph.

> Dominance-submissiveness scores have shown some interesting criterion relations besides that just mentioned with creativity. Men and boys score significantly higher than women and girls . . . Firemen, airpilots and Olympic champions score high. Neurotics improving under psychotherapy show a rise in E . . . Though it is definitely affected by environment, being fed by social success (and therefore higher in high social status persons), it also has a fairly strong constitutional component. Apparently it is the same as a pattern also clear in chimpanzees, rats and other animals, and in these it responds to the level of male hormone, in either sex.
>
> (Cattell 1965, 92)

This passage contains a surprising number of associations with the research described in the following chapters of this book. There are links here with the work on dominance in animals and with population studies of the normal sex ratio (including its relation to social status and to specific occupations). Not only does Cattell mention the possibility of a biological basis for dominance, but he associates it with testosterone in both sexes. Every word of this paragraph, written more than 30 years ago, had far-reaching implications.

THE MORAL NEUTRALITY OF DOMINANCE

Because misunderstandings easily arise on this point, attention should be drawn to the fact that both dominance and lack of dominance are morally neutral. There appears to be a tendency to label attractive personality traits as 'good' and unattractive ones as 'bad'. The confusion arises when someone says 'I don't like Sam   he's too obsessive', and then, on the grounds of this dislike, declares 'obsessiveness' to be bad. This *non sequitur* is probably largely unconscious. There may be any number of things about Sam that make a particular person dislike him, but these will be partly a function of the combination of attributes, and partly, or mostly, a function of the personality of the observer. 'Obsessiveness', just as much as, say, being 'happy-go-lucky', is morally neutral. Each has its place. One has only to think which would be the preferred attribute in the mechanic who services one's aircraft, and which for a holiday camp assistant.

Most personality theorists are fascinated by the marvellous range of human attributes, and accept them all. And certainly Cattell considered source traits to be morally neutral. There could be either attractive or unattractive characteristics at both ends of the spectrum. Since at that time dominance was seen as 'antisocial', Cattell felt compelled to point out the positive side of dominance. He noted that creative scientists and artists tend to score high on dominance. He presumed that their need (on intellectual grounds) to break with convention was sustained by their tough dispositions. He showed that dominance tends to be positively correlated with social status, finding that persons high in Factor E (dominance) 'show more effective role interaction, and democratic procedure; they feel free to participate; they raise group problems; they criticize group defects'. He also noted that in younger people Factor E was 'negatively related to school achievement up to graduate school (since docility enhances examination performance)' (Cattell *et al.* 1970, 85).

Since then, dominance has come to be overvalued by society. In many cultures today the attributes which Cattell had to defend as having a socially and morally acceptable pole now have to be demonstrated as *not* uniquely claiming the moral high ground. The culture has changed in the direction of putting such value on some of these attributes that many now view them as no longer simple descriptors but as labels for desirable states. It is to be hoped that, before too long, there will be another swing of the pendulum and those attributes which are associated with a lack of dominance will come to be viewed more positively.

People low in dominance are often more cooperative, more tolerant and more accepting. They make better team members than their more dominant fellows. They may be more obliging, more flexible, and more willing to compromise. People who do not have a strong personal need to get their own ideas accepted ahead of everyone else's have an important role in settings where differing views need to be heard and settlements negotiated with delicacy. Non-dominant women who are essentially loving, accepting and nurturing may provide oases of calm where these are most needed. Such women are less attention-getting, and less prone to hypochondriasis or hysteria, than those who are high in dominance.

FISKE'S DEFINITION OF DOMINANCE

Where Cattell had relied on factor analysis to throw up clusters of characteristics that became source traits, Donald Fiske approached the problem of definition using the analysis of language. Like Cattell, he recognized that his first goal as a personality psychologist was to be able to define exactly what it was that he wished to measure. He put intense effort into 'the conceptualization of the construct' (Fiske 1971, 94). This was not done by factor analysis or any other formal technique, but by hard thinking in the manner of a philosopher struggling with a difficult abstract concept.

What, he asked, is the 'core' of dominance? What is the unique quality to which the construct refers? His definition, the result of a penetrative analysis of both his own and others' observations, was this: 'the core of dominance can be identified as acting overtly so as to change the views or actions of another' (Fiske 1971, 98).

Fiske also contributed some important observations on the way personality constructs are conceptualized. He noted that almost all measurement in psychology is relative and that this applies outstandingly to personality psychology. The definition of personality traits is always in terms of what one person is like in comparison to others.

He also described the problem of typical versus optimal behaviour. When other human characteristics are being measured, the subject usually tries for an optimal result. If height is being measured, the subject stands up as straight and tall as possible so that a true recording may be made. In intelligence tests, subjects are asked to do their best so that optimum performance may be measured. But in personality testing subjects are usually asked for a typical response. They are required to respond in the way they usually would. This means that researchers can describe typical ways of behaving, which in turn are seen as characteristic of particular personality types.

Fiske also cast doubts on the presumed necessity for personality traits to be conceptualized as bipolar. If high dominance is defined as influencing others a great deal, then what is its opposite? In one sense, it could be said that 'being influenced' was the opposite. But in another sense, 'not influencing others' could be considered the opposite. Fiske argued that 'being influenced', as in submissive, is a separate quality with features of its own, and not necessarily related to dominance or the lack of it.

This way of viewing the construct provided the impetus for change in my own work. Until about 1983, Cattell had been the chief source of information about dominance. For many years I had measured dominance–submissiveness as a bipolar trait, using items from Cattell's Factor E. Items were scored the way he suggested, consistent with his underlying hypotheses. It never occurred to me that biological dominance need not be a bipolar trait. When at last I saw that absence of dominance was not the same as submissiveness, many research problems were solved.

CHANGES IN THE MANIFESTATION OF DOMINANCE ACCORDING TO THE CULTURAL MILIEU

Cultural changes influence the ways in which personality traits are expressed at any particular time or place. In any social group there are acceptable or fashionable ways of behaving, and these change over time. In the 1970s and 1980s there were some striking changes for women in behaviours associated with dominance. For example, in the late 1960s it was possible to differentiate between dominant and non-dominant women by observing what role they took in decision-making with their husbands. At that time dominance seemed to correspond to a certain independence of mind and an eagerness to express opinions. But during the 1970s there was a change in the status of women, co-inciding with the new wave of feminism. All women were encouraged to be more assertive, and this shifted the threshold for dominant behaviours. For example, in the late 1970s it was not socially acceptable for a woman to say, 'My husband wouldn't let me do anything like that', whereas no one would have thought it unusual in the 1960s.

The change in women's dominance-related behaviours was accelerated in the mid-1980s by a sharp rise in the popularity of assertiveness-training classes. From that time on, assertiveness was no longer an attribute that discriminated dominant from non-dominant women. It had become so highly valued that everyone claimed to possess it. This was one of the most graphic illustrations of how change in the culture can influence the social indicators of dominance.

In a culture where all women were expected to behave submissively, there would be a range of behaviours along the submissive–not-submissive dimension, with those nearer the submissive end being considered the more socially acceptable. If high submissiveness were a prized attribute, then biologically dominant women would either learn and practise the submissive behaviours (as non-dominant women in some of today's cultures must learn and practise assertive behaviours) or be socially disadvantaged.

Fortunately, as Sadalla and his colleagues (1987) have shown, individual differences in men mean that some find dominant females attractive and some do not. Thus, neither high nor low dominance in women is a barrier to sexual attractiveness in any culture; it is just that one may be more fashionable at a particular time or in a particular place.

Fluctuations in the manifestation and social desirability of dominance in women lead to further problems in definition and measurement. Cultural variability means there cannot be a definition of dominance in terms of specific behaviours. As Fiske has shown, one has to think of the core quality of dominance, and then relate it to ways of behaving that are commonly found in the group one wants to measure. For example, defining the behaviours of a dominant woman living in ancient China would be very different from defining the behaviours of a dominant woman in any contemporary Western country. In every situation, indicators of dominance will fall between extremes of behaviour that are allowed or promoted by a particular culture at a particular time. In cultures where women are required to be subordinate, the admired behaviours will fall within a different framework and will be set on a totally different scale from those of a society in which women's rights are strong.

COMFORTABLE DOMINANCE

When people first hear about maternal dominance and its relationship to the sex of the infant, they usually begin to think about the women they know and whether or not their children fit the theory. Usually these quick personal checks result in the person saying, 'Yes, the theory does not seem unreasonable.' Some are more enthusiastic, especially those that know women who have had several infants of the same sex. (Of course, people who disagree would be less likely to say so, thus rendering the information valueless as a piece of evidence.)

Occasionally someone will say that everyone he or she knows fits the theory well, with one outstanding exception. Upon closer enquiry, this will often be a woman who is seen to be conspicuously dominant, and yet has daughters. The woman with the highest score ever recorded in this research also bore a daughter. This seemingly contradictory situation may come about when a biologically non-dominant woman is exposed to a social environment in which dominance is highly valued. To become acceptable or pleasing to those people closest to her (usually her parents or siblings), a young woman might feel she had to acquire a dominant style. In doing so, the style may be overcultivated. It comes out in an exaggerated way that suggests the woman has to make an effort to maintain it. The dominance thus acquired has an artificial quality to it. Shakespeare put this tricky concept neatly in his phrase, 'The lady doth protest too much, me-thinks' (*Hamlet*, Act III, scene ii).

Since both environmental and physiological factors are equally likely to influence behaviour, this refinement to the concept of dominance not only made more sense, but brought a new challenge to the problem of definition. The personality trait believed to be associated with the conception of sons might be more accurately termed 'comfortable dominance', meaning that a woman was at ease with her own behaviour, that it came naturally to her and had not been forced upon her by circumstances.

In his work on the definition of traits, Allport made a similar point, using shyness as an example. Shyness in a person, he said,

> may be due to hereditary influences that no amount of contrary pressure from the environment has been able to offset; in another person shyness may stem from an inferiority feeling built by an abnormally exacting environment. In spite of dissimilar histories, in appearance and effect, the shyness of these two persons may be very much alike.
>
> (Allport 1937, 324)

In the same way, it can be hard to discriminate between biologically based dominance and acquired dominance. This constitutes a particularly difficult problem for measurement and is one of the reasons why no psychological measures of dominance are sufficiently accurate to predict for the individual.

PROBLEMS IN PERSONALITY TESTING

If it is hard to define something, it is even harder to measure it. The problems stem from the fact that a personality trait is an abstract concept and therefore cannot be measured directly. Researchers must decide which behaviours are indicative of the particular personality trait they wish to measure, and since there is often little agreement on this a serious problem arises over construct validity. Did the test measure what it was designed to measure? By what criterion can the results be validated? For example, would measuring a person's willingness to intervene in another person's task necessarily constitute a valid measure of dominance? It might, or it might not. Generally speaking, in personality measurement it is almost impossible to answer such questions satisfactorily. There is no objective criterion against which results can be compared; hence the poor reputation of personality measurement as a scientific enterprise.

For the most part measuring personality has focused on behaviour. The reasoning here is that because people's personalities are different they behave differently even in situations which are the same or very similar. Because behaviour is objective and visible, it is possible to measure it in a way that it is not possible to measure thoughts or feelings. But already researchers are one step removed from what it is they want to measure.

In trying to solve these problems, psychologists have evolved three main ways of attempting to measure personality. The first consists of observing people's behaviour in normal settings in everyday life. The second involves observing people's behaviour in specially designed laboratories or other artificially structured settings. The third way is to ask people how they would behave or feel if they were in a particular situation. Each of these has advantages and disadvantages.

Measuring personality by observing behaviour

Some psychologists argue that the first method, observing how people behave during the normal course of events, is the only way to arrive at conclusions about their personalities. This would be especially true of observations carried out over a long period of time. People who have lived or worked together for many years come to know one another's personalities well. They can describe one another's personalities and even predict their behaviours reasonably accurately, at least for everyday situations. They can often do this more accurately than formal personality tests.

The better one gets to know a person, and the more settings in which that person is seen behaving, the more likely one is to be able to describe accurately that person's personality. This is borne out in everyday life in a number of ways, such as the value placed on a testimonial from a person who knows a candidate well. It is also seen in the way novelists make use of a number of incidents over time to build up a complete picture of the characters in their novels. Indeed, it was observations of differences in my friends' personalities over time that first alerted me to the differences that appear to underlie the conception of male and female infants.

In addition to its advantages, there are several obvious weaknesses associated with this method. First, it is totally dependent on the accuracy and objectivity of the observer: since every human being brings a unique perspective to the world, there are limitations on the consistency and reliability of the judgements made. With modern recording techniques, these difficulties can be partially overcome. One can employ several trained observers and have them come to a consensus view, though even this does not provide the scientific reliability that physicists or chemists achieve in their work.

From the researcher's point of view, another important limitation of this method is the length of time it takes to become informed about each subject's personality. Even if only one aspect of personality (such as dominance) were being measured, the observer would have to wait for examples of situations in which dominance (or lack of it) would be apparent. And what woman would want a psychologist (or two) watching her every move for weeks on end? Related to this difficulty is the fact that the mere presence of an observer – especially if this observer is a stranger to the subject – changes the way people behave.

Sheer impracticality eliminates this method of assessing personality in almost every research setting. Almost, because it is exactly this method of observation that Piaget used when studying the development of cognition. He made daily observations and recordings of his own children's behaviour. Of course young children are less self-conscious than people over 11 years, and Piaget was a normal part of their environment.

Although not usually studying personality, anthropologists have devised and developed techniques for observing people in their natural settings. Their method, known as 'participant observation', requires a large commitment of time and energy. Researchers learn the language and customs of the group they want to study, then they spend long periods, sometimes years, living among them, adopting the same patterns and ways of living as their subjects. Over time people adjust to their presence and begin to behave, for the most part, as though the observers were not there.

A well-trained anthropologist or psychologist knows how to use the techniques of unobtrusive observation in any setting. It is, after all, little more than a sophisticated form of people-watching which everyone participates in to some extent. Nor do social scientists have a monopoly in this area – any good novelist, salesperson, health worker or politician makes use of such skills.

Difficulties arise when psychologists and others apply to ethics committees for permission to use these techniques as part of their formal research protocols. Although they have devised a variety of methods for making unobtrusive or naturalistic observations of human behaviour, it is true that by the very nature of the work there is a latent or implied deceit, and this is generally less acceptable now than it was in the past.

Measuring personality in the laboratory

One way of overcoming all these problems is to adopt the second option and observe behaviour in a laboratory setting. The chief advantage of this method is that one can devise a standardized setting and thus have a better basis for comparing individuals. There are many examples of this kind of research in psychology, and in some areas (for example, the study of perception, memory or reaction times) the laboratory setting is ideal. Opinions and attitudes can also be studied in artificial settings. But for the personality psychologist it is more difficult. It is possible to set up different scenarios involving confederates or actors and to watch how people behave in different circumstances; but the knowledge that their every move is being watched and their every word recorded makes many people anxious and thus changes their normal personality. Nevertheless, such work is being done and a wide range of scenarios is used.

Subjects are invited and sometimes paid to take part in the research. Before they begin they are given as much information as is consistent with the aims of the research, and they are debriefed afterwards. The psychologist can observe their behaviour directly and record what happens. One-way glass has been used to try to overcome observer effects and, more frequently, contemporary research laboratories are equipped with video cameras and sound equipment so that subjects' responses and behaviours are recorded and available for later checking and further study.

But even the most carefully standardized laboratory task cannot control all the relevant factors. For example, if the subject arrives at the laboratory anxious and upset after a difficult morning, the results on the behavioural task might be very different to those of someone whose morning has been relaxed and pleasant. Another criticism is that laboratory situations are artificial, and will produce only artificial behaviour. Since the research is being done in a laboratory, people will know they are being watched, even if it is not obvious how this is being done. There are hardly any people who do not modify their behaviour when they know they are being watched by others.

One of the most important problems in contemporary research in psychology is the extent to which it is morally responsible to subject people to situations about which they are not fully informed. There have been instances in the past when psychologists manipulated subjects' behaviour in a way that is totally unacceptable today. The very terminology has changed and some psychologists, acknowledging the injustices of the past, now refuse to use the word 'subject', preferring 'participant' instead. These psychologists tell their subjects about every detail of the research beforehand, and afterwards invite them to help interpret the data.

This is certainly a more democratic and equitable way of going about research with human beings, and for some topics it is helpful to have people who are better informed about what is being measured. But in a number of other areas, including personality research, knowing beforehand what is being measured makes people so self-conscious that results can be distorted and inaccurate. A good example of this can be seen in the research described in Chapter 9. Researchers went to subjects' private homes to observe the behaviour of mothers and babies. To prevent the mothers from being too embarrassed and to try to ensure that they were behaving as naturally as possible, researchers told each mother that it was the baby's behaviours they were recording. In this delicate matter there has to be a balance between the amount of deception involved, the reason for the deception, and the expected value of the research. It is with such problems as these that members of contemporary ethics research committees must struggle.

Measuring personality by self-report tests

Since there are so many problems with other methods, why not just ask people about themselves? Although there are problems with this method, too, it is in fact the most common way of trying to measure people's personalities. Instead of watching to see how people behave either in naturalistic settings or in the laboratory, psychologists ask them how they would behave or feel in a particular situation, usually by means of written questions in the form of self-report personality questionnaires.

The advantages of this method are the comparative ease with which it can be done and the fact that it generates reliable data. For example, an item from a personality questionnaire attempting to measure dominance might ask, 'Do you like making decisions on behalf of the group?' Then, according to how the subject answers this and a number of other questions, a dominance score can be calculated. Anyone with access to the scoring key would arrive at the same figure.

The most serious problem is validity. If a person says they do like making decisions on behalf of the group, does that necessarily mean that they are dominant? Of course not. In addition, there are problems of individual interpretation. For example, personal association patterns determine how each individual interprets the word 'group'. If a young businesswoman answered this question, she might interpret it as meaning her work colleagues, and she might quail at the thought of making decisions on their behalf. The same young woman, without having changed her personality, might answer the question quite differently two years later, thinking of 'the group' as meaning a small number of close friends meeting to compare notes on child-rearing.

Depending on individual association patterns, any number of different interpretations of a question are possible. Researchers usually try to counteract this difficulty by having a large number of questions, so that individual differences in interpretation are less likely to obscure response trends. After a person has responded in the dominant direction on several different questions, one can be more confident that the person may be dominant.

Self-report measures have many more limitations. An obvious one is the extent to which subjects answer either with honesty or with insight. There is nothing to stop a person being blatantly dishonest. If people are annoyed about the purpose of a test, or are being asked to do it against their will, or even if they are angry for some completely separate reason, they may simply lie. Or they may misrepresent themselves, either consciously or unconsciously. If they are upset or distracted they may pay scant attention to the task and not care whether they do it accurately or not.

At a different level, they may not be able to answer the test accurately. If it is written in a language they are not completely familiar with, they may not understand it. There may be difficulties of comprehension. They may not understand written words as well as they do spoken words, or may simply misread items. They may misunderstand complex grammatical constructions. For example, a true–false item might read: 'I am not usually happy to forgo opportunities to speak out.' Unfortunately, double negatives are sometimes used in personality questionnaires, and even people whose first language is English can be confused by them.

Sometimes personality tests involve forced choices. An item might read, 'I would rather set the agenda for a meeting than have responsibility for taking the minutes (true–false)'. A perfectly normal response might be 'Neither, thank you', yet this opportunity is not available and subjects may become increasingly uncomfortable because the personality test does not offer them items that allow them to express the kind of person they really are.

Another limitation common to self-report personality inventories is the difficulty of achieving anything other than a comparatively gross measure. Personality questionnaires are blunt instruments and fine-tuning is simply not possible. In the research on dominance, it would have been helpful to be able to differentiate between dominant and domineering, but so far no way of doing so has been found. Suppose a question reads: 'Are you the one who usually has a good idea about what to do next?' A positive answer to this question may be considered an indicator of dominance. A woman answering 'Yes' to this question may also, if asked, describe herself as dominant, but her friends may see her as bossy. If confronted with this difference, she may be very hurt. She may say that her friends do not realize how much they benefit from her organizational skills. More important, the question about whether she is or is not dominant is far from clear. She may be domi-nant and impatient, antagonizing people with the latter quality, or she may be non-dominant and compensating for this by being domineering, thus earning herself the label 'bossy'.

This difficulty is one of the reasons why personality tests can give a completely false measure of dominance in some individuals. Concepts in personality are hard to pin down and are frequently criticized as being vague or soft. Buss and Craik (1983) called them 'fuzzy sets' to emphasize their unclear boundaries.

To compensate for this, a number of strategies have been developed. First, all personality tests need naive subjects. The tests should be administered only in settings where people are ignorant of the precise aims of the test. This is because it is far harder for subjects to stay neutral if they know what is being measured. In personality testing, the less people know about what is being measured the better. That means that, in spite of what some critics call 'deception', the tests cannot be carried out satisfactorily without it.

It also means that a woman who has heard or read about the maternal dominance hypothesis, especially if she wants an infant of a particular sex, cannot use the tests with the same confidence as a woman who has never heard of the theory, and the informed subject is no longer a suitable subject. (The most successful and accurate ques-tionnaire for measuring dominance in women, including the scoring key, has been included for information in the Appendix, but it will have limited usefulness for any reader of this book.)

People completing personality tests usually get a clue about what is being measured by the very nature of the questions being asked. Thus a further safeguard is to construct tests in such a way that the theme of the questions is disguised. This means that a professionally designed personality questionnaire (in contrast with the usual magazine questionnaire) will often consist of a few key items embedded in a list of questions that are irrelevant.

The way tests are administered may also influence results. Unlike other human attributes, where maximum performance or attainment is desired during testing, measuring personality dimensions is best done in a neutral setting. As far as possible there should be no pressure on respondents to act in any particular way, 'neutral' being a desirable frame of mind for the respondent to adopt. In addition, if someone is administering the test, it is important that this person is warm and accepting, and treats the test with matter-of-factness. It should be seen as an ordinary, everyday event. This helps to minimize the problems associated with having a tensed-up subject whose primary effort goes into making a good impression.

SOCIAL DESIRABILITY

Self-report personality questionnaires are further weakened by their vulnerability to 'social desirability'. This confounding factor stems from a fundamental attribute of almost all human beings, namely the wish to look good in others' eyes. It is not that we deliberately say things about ourselves that are not true; it is more a matter of being much better informed about ourselves than we are about others and seeing ourselves from a different and more kindly perspective. The information we have about ourselves is not only more comprehensive, but often contains an element of what we would *like to be*, as well as what we *are*. We are thus less able to compare our own behaviour with that of others. Most people can more accurately compare the behaviour of two people equally well-known to them than they can compare their own behaviour with that of others.

Furthermore, because perceptiveness and modesty are valued attributes, we usually try to describe some of our 'faults'. We also try to describe our virtues modestly – at least, that is what we do in the culture to which I belong. Other cultures have different rules about the extent to which it is acceptable to describe one's positive attributes.

The situation in which people are describing themselves also has an influence on how simply or how strongly they describe their personal attributes. Behaviours change depending on whether people are competing with others for a desirable job, presenting themselves as candidates in a political election, or trying to make a good impression on a possible sexual partner at an informal party. Even in trying to come to grips with some of their less attractive attributes in a confessional or counselling situation, people tend to put the best possible light on their failings.

Because of the widespread and pervasive nature of this human attribute, personality psychologists have been forced to devise ways of overcoming, or at least minimizing, the 'social desirability' factor. The most common method is to try to construct questions in which the alternative responses are equally socially desirable and, since these desirable ways of behaving keep changing, that means being alert to what is socially desirable in a particular culture at the particular time. Another safeguard is to build in a lie scale.

The social desirability factor is an important influence in all self-report personality testing. But if, in addition, one is trying to measure a socially desirable attribute, the difficulties are compounded. In the late 1960s and early 1970s, when I first became interested in the measurement of dominance, it was considered a neutral characteristic. Most women were happy to be described either as non-dominant or dominant. They were neither hurt nor complimented by either label. Had I been working twenty years earlier, I would have found, as Cattell did (1965, 91), that dominance was associated in many people's minds with the authoritarian personality and was considered a most undesirable attribute. I would have had to design my key items to make it easier for women to answer positively, by thinking of items which embodied dominant behaviour in other more socially acceptable behaviours.

In contrast, since the 1980s, dominance has become an attribute high in social desirability. In some cultures it is now so desirable that questions that tap into any form of assertive or dominant behaviour are automatically marked at the positive end by most subjects. One of my most difficult problems was to find items that measured non-dominant behaviours in socially desirable ways. Unlike some, I do not believe that subjects are necessarily misrepresenting themselves when they mark such questions inaccurately. They have been trained to be assertive and believe they are. It is not for them to differentiate between biological or comfortable dominance on the one hand and environmentally induced dominance on the other.

An example of the pressures on non-dominant people can be found in the following paragraph published in *Psychology Today* in November 1995. It implies that 'shyness' is the opposite of dominant, which I believe is wrong – there are plenty of shy but dominant people. In addition, it fails to discriminate between the sexes. However, the article does illustrate the contemporary preference for dominance. The authors say:

Shyness is un-American. We are, after all, the land of the free and the home of the brave. From the first settlers and explorers who came to the New World 500 years ago to our leadership in space exploration, America has always been associated with courageous and adventurous people ready to go boldly where others fear to tread. Our culture still values rugged individualism and the conquering of new environments whether in outer space or in overseas markets. Personal attributes held high in our social esteem are leadership, assertiveness, dominance, independence and risk-taking. Hence a stigma surrounding shyness.

(Carducci and Zimbardo 1995)

If this is indicative of the majority view in America, pity the person who is biologically non-dominant, and possibly shy as well. He or she must be as socially disadvantaged as the unfortunate endomorph in a world where naturally occurring individual differences are not valued and everyone 'should' be assertive and thin. Given this lack of acceptance, it is no wonder that people everywhere try to present themselves in the way they believe will please the researchers. Psychologists will have to go on worrying about the social desirability factor in personality tests for as long as society continues to direct unwarranted criticism towards some people's natural attributes and unwarranted praise towards others'.

MATERNAL DOMINANCE AND THE SEX OF THE INFANT

The story of this research goes back to 1966, when a small domestic incident made me wonder whether some women were more suited to raising girls and others to raising boys. I began observing young mothers, my friends and contemporaries, and found I could predict the sexes of their infants. I began to wonder what it was exactly about a particular woman that made me sure she would have a girl or a boy, writing down lists of personality attributes and characteristic ways of behaving.

Later it became clear that these early descriptors corresponded quite closely to Factor E dominance–submission, on Cattell's Sixteen Personality Factor Test (16PF). I selected a dozen items from this scale, mixed them in with a number of irrelevant items and thus constructed the Maternal Personality Questionnaire. After doing some trials on friends, I administered it to women late in pregnancy at a hospital antenatal class. The questionnaire did not predict accurately for individual women, but it did show a trend for dominant women to conceive sons. There was no correlation between fathers' dominance scores and the sex of infant, either in the trials with friends or in the trials with hospital subjects. To improve the predictive power of the questionnaire, I began to wonder if I should administer the personality test closer to the time of conception.

At the end of 1979 I had the opportunity to join a team (France *et al.* 1984) who were investigating the efficacy of the then fashionable sex selection techniques (see Chapter 4, page 65). This gave me the opportunity to test women before they became pregnant. I had always thought timing was important, but it was not until the mid-1980s that I learned it was a requirement. By the eighth week of pregnancy the male foetus is secreting small amounts of testosterone into the maternal bloodstream and this could be a confounding factor.

This new research opportunity enabled me to conduct the necessary reliability trials required to establish psychological tests. During this period I removed some items which were not contributing anything to the final results. Because I was still refining my instrument, results from the earlier groups of subjects had to be discarded, even though they had shown a strong dominance effect. The results from the studies conducted after the reliability trials had been completed were statistically significant, but never as strong as I had expected. I had yet to learn the difference between statistical and clinical prediction.

In 1982, with the help of the Family Planning Association, I began a study of normal women, not yet eight weeks pregnant. A senior staff nurse administered the Maternal Personality Questionnaire to women who came in for confirmation of pregnancy tests. If a pregnancy was confirmed, if the woman was happy about it, and if she understood English, she was invited to fill in the questionnaire. The only additional information required was the date and her clinic number to enable later follow-up. As before, there was a statistically significant correlation between test scores and the sex of the infant (see Figure 1), but not the accurate prediction for individuals that was my goal.

During the mid-1980s I began to wonder whether I should try to design a new measuring instrument. The later studies at the sex selection clinic had shown that the Maternal Personality Questionnaire was becoming less effective. The decreasing power of the questionnaire coincided with the rise in assertiveness-training classes, already described. Although I barely realized it at the time, this new, strong social desirability factor was undermining my instrument. For example, one of the questions asked: 'If you were served the wrong food in a

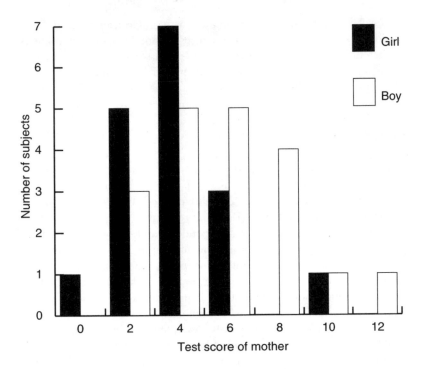

Figure 1 Family planning studies 1982–3: relationship between scores on MPQ administered 211–45 days before birth, and sex of infant
Notes: Total subjects = 36, number of boys = 19, number of girls = 17
Significance Mann-Whitney U. $p < .05$

restaurant would you a) say nothing, b) don't know, c) send it back?' In earlier times this question discriminated between dominant and non-dominant women. But after the rise in assertiveness training, no one said she would 'say nothing'. Everyone said they would send the food back, even if privately they would much prefer not to. Of course this did not mean that women had become more biologically dominant. It simply meant that in that culture, at that time, there was a shift in the range of dominant behaviours which were socially acceptable in women.

A new test was required, preferably one that was relatively culture-free. It needed to be based on a theoretically sound definition of dominance. It needed to be professionally constructed and tested for validity and reliability. In order to accommodate the full range of potential subjects, it had to be simple to understand and quick to complete. But no such questionnaire appeared to exist. Even questionnaires claiming to measure dominance as a single trait seemed to be based on definitions of dominance which did not coincide with mine. A further difficulty was that most of the tests assumed that the subjects would be men. This meant that, even though the definition of dominance used by the test constructor may have been close to the one used for maternal dominance, the items themselves were not suitable. For example, test designers devised items which asked subjects about their willingness or otherwise to take positions of military command or an active role in law enforcement.

In 1986 I came across a theoretical paper by James A. Russell of the University of British Columbia, and Albert Mehrabian, of the University of California at Los Angeles, entitled 'Evidence for a three-factor theory of emotions' (1977). It described two studies which 'provided evidence that three independent and bipolar dimensions, pleasure–displeasure, degree of arousal and dominance–submissiveness, are both necessary and sufficient to adequately define emotional states'. In presenting their evidence for this claim, the authors listed 151 adjectives describing emotions, and at the same time gave their comparative loadings on pleasure, arousal and dominance.

Here was a paper that not only described dominance in a way I could agree with, but also provided both a strong theoretical base and the raw material for constructing a new test for dominance. In addition it offered a way of bypassing the problem of describing specific behaviours. I could construct the test in such a way that subjects could make full use of their own experience by associating the adjectives with whatever situations were uppermost in their minds. It would solve the problem of having items that went quickly out of date.

I made a list of all those adjectives that had either significantly high or significantly low dominance loadings. I used nearly all of them in my new test, leaving out only a few which I thought too unusual – for example, 'activated', 'egotistical' and 'wonder'. I mixed them in with some neutral adjectives to make a list of 64 altogether, and arranged them in two columns down a single page. At the top of the page I put the words 'I quite often feel . . . ' (see Grant 1992 for further details on construction and administration).

The simplicity of this test belies the sophisticated material which underpins it. Even the instructions, consisting of four short words, constitute an end point in a theoretical argument. The issue concerns the definitions of 'trait' and 'state' in personality theory. After years of debate, most psychologists now agree that all that differentiates between these two is the amount of time each lasts. In contrast to the more transient 'state', a 'trait' is said to have temporal stability. Test instructions ('describe yourself today' or 'describe yourself in general') are probably all that discriminate between the two (Allen and Potkay 1981). The problem was to convey the idea of semi-permanence in an instruction which, though easily understood and simple to carry out, would nevertheless stand up to the scrutiny of theorists.

When using the test, two additional pieces of information are always required: the date and a contact number for follow-up. Questionnaires are scored by a technician, blind to the sex of the infant. When the mother is contacted, a year after filling in the questionnaire, she is asked what sex the infant was, and also the birthdate. From this it can be calculated how far into the pregnancy she was, or how long it was before she conceived, when she completed the questionnaire.

The question of timing has always been difficult and remains only partially solved. The ideal time to fill in the questionnaire would be the day before conception. Since this is virtually never possible, somewhat arbitrary parameters had to be set. The first scientific time constraints were set by the embryologists, as already mentioned, because the male foetus begins secreting testosterone by the beginning of the eighth week of pregnancy. But it was hard to find any account of experimental work which would help decide about a minimum period for psychological stability. Schuerger *et al.* (1989) found that stability of personality as measured by questionnaire declined steeply over a period of 18 months, but biologically based traits (for example, extraversion) appeared less vulnerable to decline than those influenced by environmental factors (for example, anxiety). Forced to make a decision for which there appeared to be no scientific backup, I decided to use the eight weeks post-conception as a guide, and limited later trials to testing eight weeks either side of conception.

Arbitrary though this decision was, it continues to fit what is known. Variations in status-related dominance behaviours in both animals and humans appear to be related to variations in testosterone levels (see Chapter 3). Both may vary in a matter of days in response to changes in the environment. They may also remain stable over months or years. If a postulated threshold amount of testosterone in women provides the physiological context in which a male infant is conceived, it is likely that the time-scale applying to the ratification of the sex of the infant would also apply to the psychological trait. It is possible that both physical and psychological stability over time are necessary to maintain a pregnancy.

Recently it has been suggested that follicular, rather than serum, testosterone might be providing the quantitative differences at the physiological level (see Chapter 5). If follicular testosterone is implicated in the selection and development of a particular ovum each cycle, then the timing of these events may also need to be considered. In that case, eight weeks might appear to be too far from the critical event (hypothesized to take place four to two weeks before conception). On the other hand it might be an appropriately conservative estimate.

There is one further question about the stability of the trait over time. If the personality of the mother is appropriate to the sex of the infant to the extent that mothers differ in their interactions with their newborn infants (as described in Chapter 9), then the temporal stability of the psychological trait must usually be maintained for at least ten months. And if testosterone underpins dominance, then it too must remain relatively stable during that time. This is much longer than the time boundaries selected for testing, and could give rise to questions about the relationship and relevance of the longer-term dominance seen in mother–infant interaction.

Two observations are relevant to this question. First, there appears to be a universally held view that pregnant and breast-feeding women are special and should be treated with care, consideration, calmness and respect. Such regimes, backed by increased levels of hormones in the mothers themselves, promote stability, and may help ensure that, so far as dominance is concerned, most women do not change very much during pregnancy and the first few months of the child's life.

On the other hand, pregnancy does not confer immunity to influences from the environment, and some women's dominance will fluctuate within the nine-month period. This would result in some male infants being exposed to less dominant mothers and some female infants being exposed to more dominant mothers. This phenomenon might be especially noticeable when mothers have a girl and a boy within a year of each other. A girl whose mother conceived a male infant within three months of her birth might grow up to be more dominant because of the early influences from her now dominant mother. Conversely, a boy whose mother conceived a daughter within three months of his birth might equally well be less dominant than other men – 'might' being the operative word. Although some research has been done on this point, and early results appear to support the notion, there is still room for doubt.

When reliability studies had been conducted on the Simple Adjective Test, the Family Planning Association agreed to another trial (1987–8). Results were of the same order as previously – that is, they did not predict for individuals at a statistically significant level, but they showed an overall dominance effect. This could have been another disappointment. In fact it was not, because during the year in which the trial was being run, I saw a paper in *Nature* which completely altered my thinking on what was a worthwhile finding. Entitled 'Maternal dominance, breeding success and birth sex ratios in red deer', the paper described how dominant female deer give birth to more male infants, and submissive female deer give birth to more female infants (Clutton-Brock *et al.* 1984; see Chapter 7). It showed not only that others were working on a similar topic, but that aiming for near-perfect prediction was unnecessary. Simply being able to show a dominance effect was of interest. This work by evolutionary biologists was to provide the pathway whereby my results could be published (Grant 1990).

In the meantime, I tried to think of a way to test mothers before they became pregnant. In 1989 I approached the Plunket Society, an organization dedicated to the care of mother and baby. As part of a new strategy to encourage mutual support among mothers of toddlers, they were arranging coffee mornings in private homes. Mothers and their 1- and 2-year-olds came to meet new potential friends and share experiences. I was given permission to attend these small social occasions and to ask mothers to fill in the questionnaire. To prevent the recurrence of an earlier problem concerning confidentiality, I asked all the mothers to fill in the questionnaire regardless of future plans. By asking everyone, I hoped to get questionnaires from at least some women who would conceive within eight weeks. That is, I judged that within any group of 200 young women with a single infant between 1 and 2 years old, there would be a small subgroup who would conceive a second child within eight weeks. In fact this is what happened. All the women were phoned a year later and asked how many children they had. If they had had a second child, they were asked for the sex and date of birth. By calculating back from the date the questionnaire was filled in, I could ascertain how far either side of conception the woman had been at the time. Theoretically some of the women had been only a week or two pregnant at the time of completing the questionnaire and some a little further into the pregnancy. In the opposite direction, some had conceived very soon after filling in the questionnaire, and others up to eight weeks later. Those that had conceived more than eight weeks after completing the questionnaire were not counted in the study.

The results were no better and no worse than they had been on all the other occasions (see Figure 2). This time I was disappointed because I thought I had solved most of the theoretical problems. Nevertheless, I presented my results at the 1991 London Conference of the British Psychological Society. This conference was special in that every presentation was attended by a critic (or assessor). When I had finished speaking, the man who was appointed to comment on my paper asked me how many subjects I had assessed 'altogether'. I scarcely understood his question, and bumbled my reply. Justifiably impatient, he asked why I had not done a meta-analysis of my data. I had never heard of such a procedure. To this day I do not know who this man was, but he was one of only two or three academics up to that time to take the findings seriously, think about the problems and make a constructive comment. I owe him much. I read all I could about meta-analysis and, with the help of a colleague, did what he suggested (Grant 1994a). By combining the results of all the studies, I was able to show a strong dominance effect (see Table 1).

Notwithstanding the acknowledged clumsiness and many limitations of personality tests, these results provided evidence for a maternal factor in the predetermination of the sex of her infant. One could

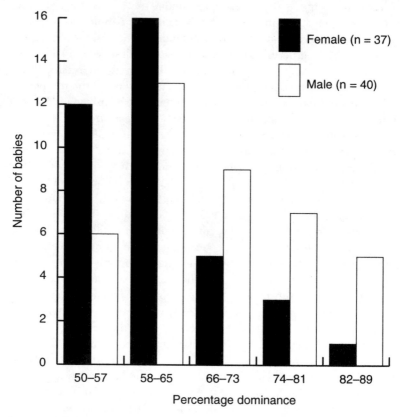

Figure 2 Relationship between percentage dominance scores as measured by the Simple Adjective Test on pre-pregnant and just-pregnant women (n = 77), and sex of infant

Notes: Mean % dominance scores – m = 67.9%, f = 62.0%

Significance Mann-Whitney U. $p < .05$

Table 1 Mean dominance scores of women later bearing male or female infants

Study code and date	Name of test	Pregnancy status	No. of subjects	N (m)	Mean (m)	SD (m)	N (f)	Mean (f)	SD (f)	p value (t test)
NWX 1969	MPQ	3rd trimester	32	14	1.57	1.02	18	1.11	1.18	0.2552
FAA 1969–70	MPQ	1st to 3rd trimester	17	9	2.11	1.45	8	0.63	1.06	0.0310
FPA 1982–3	MPQ	8 weeks or less	36	19	2.84	1.42	17	1.94	1.14	0.0456
KOH 1983–4	MPQ	Not pregnant	16	10	2.20	0.63	6	1.50	0.54	0.0414
FP2 1987–8	SAT	8 weeks or less	39	22	4.50	3.07	17	2.35	1.84	0.0102
PRE 1989–91	SAT	5 weeks or less Not pregnant	15 23	18	4.67	2.95	20	2.95	2.35	0.0538

Notes: N(m) = number of women who later gave birth to male infants

N(f) = number of women who later gave birth to female infants

MPQ = dominance measured by means of the Maternal Personality Questionnaire

SAT = dominance measured by means of the Simple Adjective Test

Mean(m) and SD(m) = mean score and standard deviation for women later bearing male infants

Mean(f) and SD(f) = mean score and standard deviation for women later bearing female infants

The results of all six studies were combined by the method of adding logs (see Rosenthal 1991, 90, 92). The combined probability is $p < .0001$ ($\chi^2(12)$ = 89.5715). When the two earliest studies (NWX 1969 and FAA 1969–70), included here for the sake of completeness, are excluded because their pregnancies were advanced beyond the eighth week, the level of probablity stays the same ($\chi^2(8)$ = 64.6684, $p < .0001$).

Source: First published in the *British Journal of Medical Psychology* (1994) **67**, 343–51.

argue that the very 'softness' of personality testing would make consistency of results hard to achieve. The fact that they are not only consistent, but (taken altogether) statistically significant, is an indicator (I would argue) for an even stronger effect. But because of the limitations of personality testing in general and self-report personality inventories in particular, it will probably never be possible to predict for the individual by this means.

HAVING CHILDREN OF BOTH SEXES

If biological dominance is strongly implicated in the predetermination of the sex of the infant, there needs to be some explanation for the fact that most women have infants of both sexes. Two different factors need to be considered.

The first is the distribution of the psychological trait. It is most likely that dominance, like other human characteristics that vary between one individual and another, will be normally distributed. There will be some people who are high in dominance, some low, and a majority of average dominance. There is no reason to think that any physical human attribute, from height to haemoglobin, would be other than normally distributed. It is most likely that under normal circumstances, psychological traits (including dominance) are also normally distributed.

The second factor is the physiological one. The working hypothesis is that biological dominance is underpinned by a hormone which is also normally distributed. Logically this would be one of the hormones of reproduction, most likely testosterone or a hormone closely related to it. Although women have much smaller amounts of testosterone than men, there is considerable variation in the amounts (see Chapter 3).

To envisage a mechanism whereby most women conceive infants of both sexes, one needs to postulate a critical amount of the hormone underlying dominance in the mother. Just under the threshold, a girl is conceived; just over, a boy. (This point is discussed further in Chapter 5.)

The hypothesis is that a woman's level of dominance at any one time is influenced by both physiological and psychological factors. It may be that the physiological factor with its genetic component, provides the context, or even sets the limits or potential for dominant behaviour. But over and above this, environmental influences will play an important part in her overall level of dominance at any particular time. There is good evidence of the way hormone levels change in response to events and circumstances in the environment (see Chapter 3). It is likely that the large majority of women fluctuate a small amount over time, in both levels of hormone and dominance. These fluctuations occur in response to life events and other changes. Such fluctuations would take most women either side of a critical threshold of hormonally based dominance that leads them to conceive a male or a female infant.

Those women who were more than one standard deviation out from the mean (to refer back to the normal curve) would be more likely to continue to conceive infants of the same sex, in spite of normal fluctuations. That is to say, women who were much less or much more dominant than other women would be inclined to vary within the range for female or male infants, rather than to swing outside it.

Such a theory makes sense of research findings in a number of different disciplines, including the distribution of single-sex sibships (families that have all girls or all boys) and other facts found in population statistics (see Chapter 8). It would explain why, even though there may be a biological and thus heritable part of a mechanism to pre-determine the sex of the infant, there is no clear evidence of it. That is, there is no evidence that a tendency to produce either one sex or the other runs in families, although this may be in part because intergenerational effects are usually traced through the male rather than the female line. In addition there is a strong environmental effect on dominance. Most women are moderately dominant, but life events and other environmental influences will change the level of dominance from time to time and result in their conceiving infants of both sexes.

3

THE BIOLOGICAL BASIS OF DOMINANCE

In arguing that dominant personality in the mother is related to her potential for conceiving sons, one has to show how a psychological attribute can relate to the body. The theory requires that the potential to behave in a dominant manner must be underpinned by a physiological variable. A review of the research literature suggests that the personality trait dominance is most likely to be related to individual differences in amounts of testosterone, and since testosterone is one of the hormones of reproduction it is possible it could be involved in the predetermination of the sex of the infant at the physiological level (see Chapter 5). This chapter explores the research findings relating dominant behaviour to testosterone levels.

Most of the research relevant to this topic has been done in either comparative psychology or physiological psychology, much of it with animals. This was partly because when zoologists look for explanations of behavioural differences they look to physiology (in contrast to psychologists, who for a long time looked predominantly to environmental influences).

The work with animals showed that the hormones of reproduction in general, and testosterone in particular, are related to behavioural differences in dominance. Contemporary work with humans is built on this foundation, and may not have been possible without it. Furthermore, psychologists' reluctance to look for biological explanations for individual differences in humans has meant that age-old questions about the relationship between physiological differences on the one hand, and personality differences on the other, have yet to benefit from late twentieth-century scientific expertise. In returning to biology for clues scientists are following in a long tradition, because the relationship between a person's physical attributes and his or her personality is one that has fascinated human observers for at least 2000 years.

Most attempts to make this link have been on a rather grand scale. For example Galen's (second-century) theory of the humours tried to explain how physiological processes could influence personality. There is something intuitively plausible about the idea that people's bodies would in some way reflect their personalities, and some theories became so influential that the vocabulary they generated is still used today.

In more recent times Kretschmer's theory of 'physiognomy' formed the basis for a study by Sheldon and Stevens (1942). By examining 4000 photographs of men standing naked in a standard position, doing detailed measurements and then arranging the photographs in a series, they were able to describe three basic morphological types, very similar to Kretschmer's. They named their body types endomorph (Kretschmer's pyknic), mesomorph (athletic), and ectomorph (asthenic), these names indicating a preponderance of the corresponding types of tissue in the body. The *Shorter Oxford Dictionary* defines endomorph as 'a person whose build is soft and round', a mesomorph as 'a person whose build is powerful, compact and muscular' and an ectomorph as 'a person of lean build'.

These three physiological types formed the basis for three corresponding types of temperament: the viscerotonic, the somatotonic and the cerebrotonic. In the same way as Galen's vocabulary changed from describing physiology to describing personality (sanguine, phlegmatic), Sheldon and Stevens' physical descriptors are now more frequently used to describe styles of behaviour. According to the *Shorter Oxford Dictionary* viscerotonic means 'temperamentally resembling or characteristic of an endomorph, with a comfort-loving, sociable and easy-going personality'; somatotonic means 'designating or characteristic of an extraverted and aggressive personality type, thought to be associated especially with a mesomorph physique; a person having this type of personality'; and cerebrotonic means 'temperamentally resembling or characteristic of an ectomorph, with predominantly intellectual interest'.

Sheldon's work has been heavily criticized in some quarters. The criticism arose when the photographs were found to include a number of people who later became famous – hardly surprising, since Sheldon's subjects were students at some of America's most prestigious universities. When it was discovered that Sheldon had begun a similar project with women the reaction was hysterical. (Apparently it is perfectly acceptable to photograph naked women for sex magazines, but not at all acceptable to do it for science.) But Sheldon's approach appears to have been scientific – he might be compared to a biologist measuring a number of individuals for the purpose of describing norms. He found that human beings differ according to both temperament and body type, and that there is evidence for a correspondence between the two.

The surprise is that some years later researchers found statistically significant differences in the sex ratio of the offspring according to Sheldon's body types. (This work is described in the section on assortative mating in Chapter 8.)

Very few late twentieth-century psychologists have worked on the biological basis of personality. Among those who have, British-based Hans Eysenck is predominant. One of his most influential books was *The Biological Basis of Personality* (1967) in which he described his research in this area. He is best known for showing how extraversion and introversion could be related to the functioning of the reticulo-cortical loop, the neurophysiological mechanism which underlies individual differences in arousability. His later work showed how personality differences not only have their origins in the body, but lead to different diseases when people are psychologically stressed beyond their body's level of tolerance. Prolific and outspoken, Eysenck and his work have yet to assume their final place in the history of psychology.

Dominance as a characteristic was not one of Eysenck's core personality constructs. He considered it merely as a component of extraversion. In this he may have been mistaken, since in most major studies of humans (and animals) dominance has been shown to be a completely independent personality factor. Indeed, at a more practical level, most people can probably think of a person they know who is both introverted and dominant. It is regrettable that dominance was thus missing from Eysenck's work. It will need someone like him, with knowledge of both physiology and psychology, to explore further the physiological basis of this personality dimension.

DOMINANCE, AGGRESSION AND TESTOSTERONE

While Eysenck's focus was almost entirely on the relationship between personality and aspects of the central nervous system, other researchers had been investigating the possible influences of the hormones of reproduction. By the early 1970s they had begun to find consistent relationships between dominance, aggression and testosterone in male monkeys. Physiological psychologists wondered, therefore, if the same applied to humans.

In 1974 a key study was published in *Psychosomatic Medicine*, showing how both dominance and aggression are related to testosterone levels in humans. This study was carried out by Joel Ehrenkranz and his colleagues at the Yale University School of Medicine. Their subjects were 36 male prisoners at the Connecticut Correctional Institution at Somers.

Before measuring testosterone levels the researchers did everything they could to ensure they had categorized the inmates accurately. Besides administering a large number of personality tests, they sought a variety of views on who was or was not aggressive or dominant. First, one of the authors of the study, possibly the prison doctor, categorized inmates on 'the basis of personal observations and interviews performed over a number of years'. Independently, the prison psychologist and a senior prison administrator did the same. Their views were highly correlated, both with one another and with the offences. As a final check, subjects were asked to rate one another for dominance and aggressiveness. The experimenters found 'substantial agreement' between staff judgements and inmate judgements in both areas. This early study is one of the few to be so particular about the categorization of subjects, one of the critical factors in evaluating the research.

In the first group were men who showed 'evidence of overt physical aggressiveness of a violent nature and of chronic duration'. These 12 men were in prison for violent crimes such as aggravated assault or murder, and continued to show repetitive violent physical aggressiveness while in prison. The second group was termed 'socially dominant'. They were in prison for 'a variety of non-violent crimes such as theft, cheque passing and drug-related felonies. They were recognised by prison staff and other inmates as socially dominant and had asserted themselves into prestigious jobs and positions in inmate hierarchies' (Ehrenkranz et al. 1974). In the third group of 12 were subjects who were considered neither aggressive nor socially dominant.

This experimental strategy, discriminating between dominance and aggression on a number of different measures, invites respect for the results. The researchers found highly significant differences in testosterone levels between the three groups, the non-aggressive men having levels only half that of the aggressive. More interesting still from the point of view of the maternal dominance theory, the researchers were able to demonstrate that the socially dominant men also had high levels of testosterone.

In reviewing their work it occurred to the authors that the relationship between aggressiveness and testosterone might simply be a consequence of testosterone leading to 'strong build and masculine appearance that might facilitate the learning of physical domination'. But upon investigation the researchers found no differences in the heights or weights of the three groups of men, 'nor did their outward appearance suggest obvious differences in masculinity'. 'Rather', they wrote, 'the quality of toughness is apprehended by more subtle clues stemming in large part from intensity and/or malignity of gaze and general posture' (Ehrenkranz *et al.* 1974).

In the same issue of the journal, Robert Rose wrote in an editorial that the authors had demonstrated an association between testosterone and dominance, and that it was possible that 'testosterone is correlated more with assertiveness or an action orientation than with aggression in the usual context of attacking others' (Rose 1974).

Altogether this was a landmark study: it showed that dominance is associated with testosterone in human males, as clearly as other studies had shown the same relationship in non-human male primates. Because of the concern of people everywhere to find out more about violent behaviour, most studies following this one have continued to focus on aggression rather than dominance. But, even though measurement techniques have been refined for both testosterone and aggression, results have not lived up to expectations. The reason for this is that dominance is likely to have more nature in it than nurture; that is, dominance is a biologically based characteristic. But aggression is more likely to be a response to the environment and hence is likely to be less closely related to testosterone.

Although Ehrenkranz *et al.*'s (1974) study continues to be widely cited, many researchers appear to have taken no notice of the findings, since they have continued to measure dominance and aggression as though they were the same thing. In a study conducted at the New England Research Institute and published in *Psychosomatic Medicine*, the authors wrote all the way through of 'aggressive dominance' (even though, in fact, they measured them separately), and concluded that, in future, 'dominance and aggression should be distinguished and assessed independently in studies of humans' (Gray *et al.* 1991).

From the point of view of the maternal dominance hypothesis their most interesting results were that in a random sample of 1709 men aged between 39 and 70 years (mean age 54.7 years) the distribution of testosterone and related hormones was 'reasonably normal'. Furthermore, when the personality measure of dominance was taken on its own, 'dominance was found to relate positively to albumin-bound testosterone ($p < 0.0005$), free testosterone ($p < 0.0005$), and dehydroepiandrosterone ($p < 0.01$)' (Gray *et al.* 1991).

Although the authors were clearly disappointed that testosterone levels did not show the expected relationship to 'aggressive dominance', from the point of view of the present theory they showed exactly what one would expect: that dominance is a biologically based personality trait and aggression is not.

AN INDIVIDUAL'S TESTOSTERONE LEVELS CAN CHANGE

After the link was made between hormones and behaviour, researchers went on to explore it further. Since testosterone levels appear to vary over time, researchers wondered whether they would do so in a predictable way. And if testosterone showed differences between individuals according to personality, would changes in personality within the individual be reflected in changed testosterone levels? These questions are particularly important for the maternal dominance hypothesis, which says that most women have infants of both sexes because their hormone levels change over time in response to events in the environment.

One of the key researchers in this area is Allan Mazur of Syracuse University, New York. Over many years he and his colleagues have done some ingenious experiments trying to discover whether or not a man's testosterone levels change in response to social and other events. As others had done before, Mazur built on the non-human primate research already published in the journal *Hormones and Behavior*. This had shown that 'a male's testosterone level changes when his status changes, rising when he achieves or defends a dominant position, and falling when he is dominated' (Mazur and Lamb 1980).

Mazur and his colleagues set up three different experimental situations to test this finding on human males. The subjects were healthy men aged between 22 and 35 years. All were graduate students. Although the research required 'multiple blood samples', the level of interest and cooperation was uniformly high, possibly because the impecunious students were well paid for their cooperation. In the first experiment, men took part in doubles tennis matches; in the next a lottery; and finally medical students were tested after graduating. The results of all these studies showed that testosterone rose when the men had put effort into succeeding and felt good about the results. Merely succeeding without effort, as in the lottery, produced no changes in testosterone levels.

Almost all studies in this area have shown a positive relationship between testosterone and dominance behaviour (Booth *et al.* 1989). At one time the researchers considered an alternative interpretation. Since most of the studies involved men competing or being challenged physically, the results might simply have been showing a correlation with physical effort. In an attempt to rule out this interpretation, Allan Mazur's team ran a similar study, but this time in a setting which required mental rather than physical effort (Mazur *et al.* 1992). For this they chose a chess tournament. Once again, the subjects were all men, and all were volunteers aged between 18 and 64. To an outside observer a chess tournament is an unexpectedly complex affair and the researchers had to be more than usually careful to eliminate influences which might confound their results. But once again results showed that the men who won, especially in the setting of a hard challenge, had demonstrable rises in testosterone levels, whilst losers experienced falls.

This was the expected result, but there was another, completely unexpected, result. The researchers found that the eventual winners had lower testosterone levels the day *before* the tournament, while the eventual losers had high testosterone the day before. This is particularly puzzling since, of course, no one had any idea who was going to win or lose the next day. It could have been a chance finding, but it is so striking that it invites speculation. What could have caused it? Did anticipatory stress damp down testosterone in those who were highly motivated to win? Could this dampening effect the day before make possible a compensatory surge on the day of the match? What is meant exactly by 'psyching oneself up' for something? Could the psychological process have a physiological counterpart? For these sorts of questions there are currently no answers, yet sportspeople and their coaches everywhere would doubtless be interested. There is still so much to be discovered about the relationship between environmental and biological influences on behaviour.

TESTOSTERONE LEVELS AND SOCIAL INTERACTION

By the mid-1980s primatologists had shown, in several different animal groups, that hormone levels could change simply as a result of everyday social interaction (see Chapter 7). One study had shown this effect in a small group of confined male talapoin monkeys: intrigued by this and other findings relating to stress and hormones, W. J. Jeffcoate and his colleagues tried to replicate the study in a small group of 'confined' men (Jeffcoate *et al.* 1986). Methodologically this study is not particularly good. The experimenters perhaps tried to do too many other things at the same time. This is understandable given the nature of the research, the opportunity for which would occur at best rarely.

Five healthy males aged between 28 and 38 years were to spend their two-week holiday sailing around the north coast of Scotland in a small boat. They were all doctors, and thus not fazed by having to take blood samples. These were done on alternate days after a night at anchor and a leisurely breakfast. They were accompanied by three women, willing to make daily observations of the dominance behaviours of the men. For example, they noted which men insisted on undertaking the 'important' tasks, such as holding the wheel. Only one person on the boat, a man, knew the purpose of the research.

Although all the men had had similar testosterone levels at the beginning of the holiday, and even at the end of the first week, by the end of the second week there were significant differences. The two men who had been given high ratings for dominance by the women observers had testosterone levels of 18 and 25 nanograms (ng) per millilitre (ml) of blood; while the two men rated lower scored 16 and 12 respectively.

One of the most interesting findings of this study was the confirmation of the time-scale: researchers had been wondering how long it would take for changes in testosterone level to become apparent. When new animals are introduced into an existing hierarchy, there can be intense dominance interchanges while new orders are established. When this happens, testosterone levels can change in a matter of hours (Rose *et al.* 1975). In less dramatic situations, the social interactions are more relaxed and the changes come about more slowly.

The rate at which changes in testosterone levels can occur as a result of social interaction may be of particular relevance to the maternal dominance hypothesis. This is because both timing and hormone levels seem to be important in providing the optimum environment for the development of the conceptus. Some researchers (Krackow 1995) have suggested that the hormonal levels at the time of conception might need to stay stable in order to ratify the developmental pathway post conception. If this is so, women's testosterone levels would need to be stable for a period of time. Yet, if Jeffcoate's work is reliable, it appears that social interactions related to dominance may alter hormone levels in a matter of days. If a woman's testosterone levels were very close to the threshold for conceiving a male infant, even comparatively small changes in social relationships might mean that she apparently failed to conceive during unsettled times – 'apparently', because she may have had the right amount of the relevant hormone to conceive a male or female at the time of intercourse, but not enough to ensure its development in the following weeks.

As mentioned above, Jeffcoate and his colleagues used the unusual opportunity provided by the boat trip to do research on a number of different topics (1986). The title of their paper ('Correlation between anxiety and serum prolactin in humans'), the journal in which it was published (*Journal of Psychosomatic Research*) and the fact that they were medical practitioners give an indication of their concerns. But, as so often happens, their most important finding may well be the one in which they were originally least interested.

In another unusual study, Richard Rahe and his colleagues of the Nevada Stress Centre reported on their investigations of the American hostages freed from captivity in Iran. The 52 men had been held captive for 444 days. When they were freed they consented to extensive physical and psychological testing, the results of which were later published in *Psychosomatic Medicine* (Rahe *et al.* 1990). An unexpected finding was the extreme rise in testosterone, 400 per cent higher than men recruited as control subjects who were not therefore experiencing the euphoria of release. The authors suggested that it may have been the contrast between their low status as captives and high status as heroes that brought about such an extreme change in testosterone levels.

In 1994, Allan Mazur wrote a summary of the work done in this area. He said:

> In sum there appears to be a reciprocal relationship between circulating testosterone and dominance behaviour. Heightened testosterone facilitates assertive or challenging behaviour; lowered testosterone inhibits dominant action. Conversely, successfully defending or enhancing one's status raises testosterone, possibly in anticipation of new challenges, while suffering defeat lowers testosterone. This positive feedback between dominance behaviour and testosterone helps to explain the stability of small-group status hierarchies as well as the 'momentum' often associated with strings of triumphs or defeats.
>
> (Mazur 1994, 39)

DIFFERENCES IN TESTOSTERONE BETWEEN MEN AND WOMEN

Given all the above, one might think the case was almost made – that is, that testosterone, already linked with reproductive processes, also provides the biological basis for dominant personality. But all the research cited so far has been done on men. Is it reasonable to assume that similar processes apply to women? Unfortunately, no.

So far as testosterone is concerned, there are two major differences between men and women. The first and better-known difference is in the overall amount, men having ten times more than women. On most physiological measures, the ranges for men and women have considerable overlap. For example, although it is agreed that men are generally taller than women, the area of overlap is much larger than the area of difference. But in the amount of testosterone there is no such overlap: normally men have so much more than women that one would never mistake a man's score for a woman's. On the other hand, as if to make up for this, some researchers think females may be more sensitive to testosterone than males are, with the result that a very small amount of testosterone at a critical time might produce a large effect (Udry and Talbert 1988).

In addition to the amount of testosterone, a second important difference between men and women is where it comes from in the body. In men, most of the testosterone is manufactured in the testes; in women, a small amount comes from the ovaries, but most is converted from androstenedione in peripheral tissues, a process which involves the adrenal glands. An illustration of the consequences of this difference was provided by Finnish scientist Eriksson and his colleagues (1994). Controlling for time of day, age and weight in both sexes, as well as contraceptive use and stage of the menstrual cycle in the women, they gave healthy subjects either alcohol or placebo juice and showed that 'alcohol, even at a very low dose, increases blood plasma total testosterone concentrations very quickly in women but not at all in men'.

Further, because of the way the production of testosterone is associated with the adrenal glands in women but not in men, stress may have diametrically opposite effects on the level of testosterone in women as opposed to men. In men, it is likely that severe or prolonged stress dampens down the production of testosterone (Rivier and Rivest 1991), although the men's attitude to the stress may influence their body's response. This is obviously not something that can easily be researched. The only way is to take advantage of an existing situation, such as that with the released hostages.

In women it seems that testosterone may be very sensitively geared to conditions in the environment. Because its production is associated with the adrenal glands (Gray and Gorzalka 1980), which in turn are responsible for the body's response to stress, an increase in stress may lead to an increase in testosterone in women. Even though the amounts are so tiny, this increase may be critically important, especially given women's extra sensitivity. Such an arrangement – where the secretion of testosterone is closely related to, or influenced by, the stress response – would make evolutionary sense, since women may need to become a little tougher to survive in hard times.

As a working hypothesis one might postulate that 'tough times mean more males'. This would make sense at both the physiological and psychological level. If women respond to stress by producing more testosterone, and if the hypothesis about the relation of the conception of sons to the amount of testosterone were to be confirmed, this would explain why more boys are conceived during wars, epidemics and other times of human stress. It may also be the key to the mystery of conflicting results in the animal literature on sex ratios and maternal dominance (see Chapters 7 and 8).

DOMINANCE AND TESTOSTERONE IN WOMEN

The number of studies which have been done on the relationship between behaviour and testosterone in women can be counted on the fingers of one hand. Since there are so few, and the topic is central to the maternal dominance hypothesis, a higher proportion of them is cited. Unlike other topics in this book, where only a handful of studies have been selected to illustrate the research, the supporting evidence for this topic is virtually all there is.

In 1979 an anthropologist and a statistician from the University of New Mexico at Albuquerque published a paper in *Social Biology* in which they described how a group of women in occupations associated with 'things' rather than 'people' tended to have higher serum testosterone. Their starting point was one of simple curiosity: 'Because androgens have been studied primarily for their effects on males, their role in normal female behaviour is not well established' (Purifoy and Koopmans 1979). Their subjects were 55 healthy women whose ages ranged from 20 to 87 years, which suggests a family-and-friends approach. Apart from controlling for obvious possible confounding factors, such as time in the menstrual cycle, all they did was take one blood sample from each woman and look to see if the testosterone levels corresponded with her occupation (or previous occupation). The serendipitous nature of the project was frankly admitted – the hormone assays were done as part of a 'research project to establish normal laboratory control values'.

The authors analysed their data by age, occupation and testosterone levels, and found a significant effect for occupation. Testosterone was higher in students and professional, managerial and technical workers than it was in housewives and clerical workers. So far as can be seen, it was this difference the authors described as 'degree of job complexity in relation to things' or 'degree of job complexity related to people'. It seems a rather tortuous categorization to make.

However, their thinking on the nature–nurture question has stood the test of time. The authors wondered if there might be a 'feedback relationship between the endocrine system and behaviour, wherein hormones affect behaviour, which in turn, may influence hormone levels'. Not only, they said, do 'these data most likely reflect biological and environmental causes in a hormone–behavior feedback relationship', but

> the genetic potential for increased androgen secretion may affect certain personality characteristics related to career-orientation in females, i.e. those labelled 'masculine' by this culture, such as assertiveness and independence. Moreover, the positive or negative stress associated with an occupation could stimulate or inhibit androgen secretion.
>
> (Purifoy and Koopmans 1979)

So far as the maternal dominance hypothesis is concerned, there were two important findings from this study. First, the description of the effect of testosterone on personality (more 'assertive and independent') could hardly have been more accurate. Although labelled 'masculine' by the authors, the core of it is that part of dominance shared by men and women, albeit in different amounts. Second, virtually every scientist who has done research in the area of hormones and behaviour, whether in animals or in humans, has postulated a feedback loop. At its simplest it appears as though environmental events or stimuli, received and mediated by the central nervous system, elicit a hormonal response. Almost every bit of evidence there is supports such a mechanism.

Since that time, researchers studying the relationship between stages in the menstrual cycle and psychological factors have also found links between occupation and testosterone, usually between those women at home and those in full-time employment, with the latter having more testosterone – but the link is not strong.

MEASURING TESTOSTERONE

Testing for testosterone is not a simple matter, but the collection of suitable samples was greatly facilitated by the discovery of radio-immunoassay techniques which could be used with saliva samples. Provided reliability and accuracy can be maintained, researchers and ethics committees alike favour non-invasive techniques, and naturally subjects would rather spit into little plastic bottles than have needles pushed into their veins.

Confirmation of the range and amounts of testosterone circulating in normal women was provided by Donald Baucom and his colleagues at the University of North Carolina in 1985. In a study which demon-strated a relationship between personality characteristics and testosterone measured from saliva samples, the mean amounts for the various groups of normal young women ranged from 1.75 ng/ml for the most 'feminine' to 2.59 for the more 'masculine'. Personality char-acteristics were measured by using a variety of different scales. Among others, adjectives which correlated with high testosterone scores were 'robust', 'enterprising', 'unconventional' and 'resourceful' – all indica-tors of dominance in women (Baucom et al. 1985).

Another researcher who made full use of this technique was James Dabbs Jr, a psychologist from Georgia State University in Atlanta. He and his colleagues (Dabbs et al. 1987) did the same kind of study on male prison inmates as Ehrenkranz had done earlier (and with the same results; see page 43), but then went on to repeat the work with women prisoners (Dabbs et al. 1988). Unfortunately, so far as the present work is concerned, the researchers' aim was to find a biological basis for crim-inal violence rather than for dominance. And again it seems important to make the point that this is probably misguided, since aggression and criminal violence are much more likely to be the result of environ-mental influences than an excess of testosterone.

In fact, that is just what the study shows. In addition to their 84 recently admitted female prison inmates, the researchers asked 15 healthy women students to act as controls: their testosterone levels were indistinguishable from those of the prison inmates. The study is particu-larly commendable for its design, clàrity and accuracy: the authors give every detail of the complex testing procedure; in addition they give the exact amounts and how these compare with the only other studies that have measured testosterone in women by this method. The upshot was that researchers everywhere had benchmark figures for interstudy comparison.

The testosterone score for each subject was reported in units of nanograms per 100 millilitres. The overall mean testosterone concentration for everybody tested in this study was 2.18 ng/100 ml. For the prison inmates the average was 2.17; for the college students, 2.21. The authors cite other studies in which the values were 2.45 for women with regular menstrual cycles, and 2.50 for post-menopausal women. The lowest scores (a mean of 1.48) were those for the five women in the 'defensive violent' group. These were women who had committed crimes only after being physically abused themselves, usually over a long period of time. It would not be surprising if these women were among the lowest rating on dominance, but the authors did not measure it.

All this work, reported in *Personality and Individual Differences* in 1988, was particularly helpful in enabling interested people to understand the minute physiological differences that might be relevant to the predetermination of the sex of the infant. Not only do 'window of opportunity' theories postulate very short periods of time (see Chapter 6), it now appears that these may be associated with tiny variations in amounts as well.

Up till now the word 'testosterone' has been used as though it were a single uncomplicated substance circulating in the human body. But this is a gross oversimplification. Androgens, of which testosterone is one, exist in the body in a variety of different forms. In the Dabbs study mentioned above, the researchers measured only what is known as 'free testosterone', because this is the only form of testosterone that can pass through the saliva glands. Since that time, researchers have returned to using blood samples to measure testosterone so they can include other related hormones.

Using these more sophisticated techniques, anthropologist Elizabeth Cashdan of the University of Utah in Salt Lake City looked for a relationship between dominance and testosterone in a group of young women living in an on-campus residential facility. Because much of the primate literature on dominance and testosterone is concerned with the relationship to rank or status, Cashdan was looking for a similar relationship in women. This she did not find. What she did find, however, was a strong relationship between testosterone and high 'self-regard'.

In a neat little 'action' measure of personality, devised by Cashdan specifically for this piece of research, subjects rated themselves on a number of different criteria.

> Each woman, interviewed in private, was shown ten cards, each containing the name of one of her [college] mates. She was then asked to place the cards (including the one representing herself), along a yardstick, to indicate their relative positions on some attribute . . . Subjects ranked their peers on

the following: leadership, popularity with men, toughness, caring, popularity with women, athleticism and general status within the group.

(Cashdan 1995)

The results of this study showed that testosterone (as well as other hormones) were associated with

enhanced perception of one's own status, although not with higher status as judged by others. While virtually all subjects ranked themselves higher than their peers did, a tendency to over-rank by a large margin was positively associated with all hormones.

These findings are entirely consistent with that less attractive side of dominance: the tendency to overconfidence and high self-regard.

Finally, and surprisingly, there is a study of testosterone and personality in babies (Jacklin *et al.* 1983). The blood samples were taken from the umbilical cord at birth, thus circumventing the difficulties of taking blood or saliva from very little people. Researcher Carol Jacklin and her colleagues tested for five different sex-steroid hormones. The only one to show significant differences was testosterone. The baby boys had 0.2813 ng/ml and the baby girls 0.2125 ng/ml. This was a highly significant ($p<.0001$) difference, indicating that at birth baby boys have, on average, more testosterone than baby girls.

These results were then compared with the babies' behaviours. The authors tested 162 babies at either 6, 9, 12 or 18 months of age. To test for timidity, the authors collected several toys of different 'fear-provoking potential'. They ranged from 'a soft fuzzy dog which would jump slightly when a bulb was pressed to activate it pneumatically', to 'a wind-up monkey about 10 inches high, which, when activated clapped a pair of cymbals together (producing a crashing noise), bared its teeth and emitted a high-pitched shriek' (Jacklin *et al.* 1983). The babies were sat on the floor with their mothers behind them, and the toys were presented three feet away. The babies' behaviours were recorded in six categories – move toward and/or touch toy (1 point), smile (2), no response (3), look at mother (4), move back (5) and touch mother or cry (6). Thus, the authors wrote, 'the higher the timidity score the more timid the child, the lower the score, the more bold'.

Sex differences proved marginal. But, at every age except the youngest (6 months), the boys were less fearful than the girls. Detailed analysis of the overall results led the authors to agree with other researchers that 'testosterone increased boldness'. They also noted, with other authors, that 'low timidity may be included in the concepts of "independent", "self-assured", and "self-sufficient"', all of which have been shown to be related to dominance. Further, they found consistency over time, which they said lent further support to the idea that there is a biological basis for the personality trait. But here caution is needed, because differing styles of parental management will also contribute to differences in responses to fearful objects. It is the link between increased testosterone and boldness which is important.

WHAT TO MAKE OF IT ALL?

What can be concluded from these studies? Is it reasonable to say that the personality attribute 'dominance', as defined in Chapter 2, is a biologically based personality trait? And that testosterone is its biological basis? In support of the idea, it might be said that every study that could show a relationship between testosterone and dominance, or factors relating to dominance, has done so. But appearances can be deceptive, especially when it comes to published research. Some might argue that, while a number of studies have shown that testosterone is related to dominance in men, women and children, it is also possible that studies showing no relationship have not been accepted for publication. In most circumstances this would be a legitimate reason for caution. But in this case, and contrary to first impressions, one could argue that because so many of the researchers were not looking for the effect, the findings are more, rather than less, persuasive.

An important criticism of the reasoning here would be that so few personality theorists are working in the area. If it were a fruitful topic, or if it held the promise of further discoveries about personality in general, surely hundreds of psychologists would be working in it. There are two responses to this objection. The first has to do with the problems of this kind of research. It is a difficult area of study because it demands expertise in endocrinology as well as psychology. The second has to do with obtaining permission. In some countries, especially during the 1980s, ethics committees discouraged pure research involving invasive procedures on human subjects. This is changing as people realize that, in the social sciences as well as in the physical sciences, pure research provides the basis for applied research.

The other reason is that for decades psychologists have rejected biological explanations of behaviour and have concentrated almost entirely on the environmental causes of individual differences. But, as is so often the case, no 'all or nothing' explanation is going to fit the data. Of course it is not true to say that all or even most psychological differences are biologically based. But neither is it true to claim that psychological differences between individuals are solely the result of different environments or styles in upbringing. Of all the various categories of individual differences, both physical and psychological, personality traits are the most likely to be a mixture of both biology and upbringing. And, as has already been demonstrated (Loehlin 1992), personality traits themselves may be further categorized according to the relative importance of nature and nurture in their development and manifestation.

One of the clearest examples of this is the difference between aggression and dominance. Testosterone appears to provide the biological underlay for dominance, and perhaps to set the potential for dominance behaviours. A person's dominance level at any particular time might be partly a result of his or her genetic potential to produce testosterone and partly a result of how each had been brought up to respond to events in everyday life. Being markedly stronger, tougher or more dominant than average almost certainly means higher than average testosterone levels, but differences in dominance behaviours will also depend on environmental influences and early learning.

It is as though the biological basis, in this case testosterone, provides the physiological setting, or context for learning, so that if a person who is born with higher than average levels of testosterone experiences events early in life that lead him or her towards aggressive or violent behaviour, there will be a physiological backup for those behaviours. If, on the other hand, the person's early experience leads him or her towards more highly socialized forms of toughness (as some occupations require), then the higher levels of testosterone will help provide the necessary physical context for those attributes.

None of this is static. It is known that testosterone levels vary in response to environmental influences. Complex feedback loops appear to be involved in two-way processes in both directions: that is, testosterone increases or decreases according to how the individual interprets and reacts to signals from the physical, social or psychological environment. But how does it all work? How do feelings and perceptions influence the production of hormones? The answers to these questions are being explored in the field of psychoneuroendocrinology, and much remains to be discovered.

Given the physiological differences between males and females in the production and amount of testosterone, it is likely that the mechanisms involved will also be different according to sex. Until the 1990s, few attempted to discriminate between biologically based psychological sex differences on the one hand and environmentally induced differences on the other. David Buss of the University of Michigan is one who did. Noting that psychological sex differences are 'neither artifactual nor unstable' – a masterly academic understatement – he urged psychologists to search for 'a cogent explanatory framework for understanding why the sexes differ in some psychological domains and not in others'. In this he has led the way, pointing out how men and women have faced 'substantially different adaptive problems throughout human evolutionary history' (Buss 1995). He expects the sexes to differ psychologically in exactly those domains where they have faced different sorts of adaptive problems.

Thus evolutionary psychology provides the theoretical context for the maternal dominance hypothesis. The ways in which it could work to provide evolutionary advantage are discussed in Chapter 9. In the meantime it can be stated that men and women differ markedly in levels of testosterone, and this pronounced physiological difference underlies a somewhat smaller difference in dominance and dominance behaviours. Although men on average score higher on measures of dominance behaviours than women, there is a moderate overlap between the two ranges of scores, rather like the overlap between the sexes on characteristics like strength and spatial rotation ability.

So far as the maternal dominance hypothesis is concerned, however, it is the within-sex differences that are of most interest. There are wide individual differences in dominance between women: some are so dominant that their scores on psychological measures of dominance behaviours are indistinguishable from men's. Others are completely non-dominant, scoring zero on the tests. It is highly likely that dominance is underpinned at the biological level by individual differences in testosterone. Dominance behaviour and testosterone levels are known to co-vary over time in response to changes in the environment. Scores on both measures of dominance and testosterone levels appear to be normally distributed. Although women's testosterone is approximately one-tenth that of men, behavioural measures of dominance vary less widely between the sexes, suggesting that testosterone may have a stronger effect in women. Whether it actually does is a topic for future research.

4

EVIDENCE FROM BIOSTATISTICS

The links between dominant personality, an underlying hormonal basis and the conception of sons are based largely on positive correlations, since the mechanisms underlying the determination of the sex of the infant are unknown. Partly because of this elusiveness, researchers have sought clues from a number of topics in psychology and medicine which document peripheral processes. If it can be shown that more girls than boys are conceived under a particular set of biological conditions, this might provide a helpful lead on what does or does not influence the sex of the infant.

The largest number of studies in this area are those concerned with the timing of intercourse relative to the menstrual cycle. Additional topics of interest are the possible effects of coital rate, sex ratio differences between monozygotic and dizygotic twins, the numbers of single-sex sibships (all-girl or all-boy families), and findings related to abnormality or illness in the mother. Almost all the studies rely primarily on statistical analysis for their impact. They report associations between a variety of factors and the sex ratio, without necessarily suggesting how these might arise. With the exception of the timing studies, the evidence they report provides clues – not theory, and certainly not answers. On the other hand, when a well-designed study shows a strong sex ratio effect it is interesting to speculate on how it might fit with current theories. When the findings support one theory but not another they are of particular interest.

Because the effects are statistical, it is particularly important to be sure that the methodology is adequate. A major part of the review process is to ask what else could explain the findings. If an alternative explanation of the data cannot be ruled out, the findings carry less weight; if several alternative explanations are possible, the results are hardly worth considering.

TIMING THEORIES

The key question in this area is: Could the sex of the infant be related to the time in the menstrual cycle at which it was conceived? Like so many other ideas, this goes back to Aristotle, who according to later authors dismissed it because it could not account for the birth of unlike-sex twins. In spite of this unresolved difficulty many scientists since have tried to find a timing effect on the sex ratio. The earliest academic reference to this theory appears to be a paper by J. T. Swift published in the *Boston Medical and Surgical Journal* in 1878, entitled 'Determination of sex by the date of conception'.

Reproductive endocrinologists and endometriologists have built up an impressive body of information about the way the female reproductive tract changes during the 28 days of the cycle. The stages are regulated by complex interactions between pituitary and ovarian hormones resulting in the selection and development of an ovum, its presentation for possible fertilization and the preparation of the uterus by means of histological changes to the endometrium.

If variations in hormone levels or other physiological changes could be shown to relate to the sex of the infant, this would provide clues about what to investigate further. It could even provide a short cut to shifting the sex ratio in a variety of settings, including that of animal husbandry. Simply increasing the chances of conceiving a male or a female offspring would be seen as a welcome advance by many.

Although most of this chapter is about research involving humans, some studies with animals are particularly relevant. Veterinary scientists have long sought a method which would allow farmers to maximize the production of whichever sex they wished, usually females, especially in the dairy industry. Much of the work in this area is done at the practical level: if something works, farmers use it; if it does not, they soon know and drop it. If there were an effective, economically feasible technique for dealing with the problem of excess male calves, farmers would be making use of it. The fact that in some parts of the world there is a highly visible problem with male calves is convincing evidence of the unreliability of all claims to be able to predetermine the sex of offspring.

When the techniques of artificial insemination came into wide use in the dairy industry, there were new hopes that by timing the inseminations carefully, farmers might be able at least to skew the sex ratio in the desired direction. At first there were reports that this was succeeding, but, as so often happens, people were simply reporting chance occurrences. A definitive study was done by R. H. Foote of the New York

State College of Agriculture and Life Sciences at Cornell University. He published his results in a little-known journal called *Theriogenology*. In it he described how he collected information on 35,102 single births of calves in 2254 different dairy herds.

This mammoth task was conducted rigorously. For both virgin heifers and lactating cows, records were kept of whether they were first seen in oestrus in the morning or in the evening; 'Furthermore, the hour of breeding was recorded' (Foote 1977). Not only was there no difference in the sex ratio according to the timing of insemination, there was no difference in the sex ratio for any dimension that Foote could think of, including sire, breed (five in all), or whether the animal was a first-time or repeat breeder. An example of Foote's careful scientific interpretation of his data can be seen in the following.

> Progeny were grouped by the sire producing the semen for the last insemination and which resulted in parturition at approximately the expected time. Among the 111 sires included, six had sex ratios of their progeny which deviated significantly (p<.05) from breed average. The proportion of 6/111 is 5.4 per cent. This is the proportion one would expect to deviate significantly when choosing a probability of p<.05.
>
> (Foote 1977)

Foote was aware that in conducting a large number of studies a few results will deviate from the norm just by chance, and this does not mean that something important has been found.

Another of Foote's results appeared significant. He noticed that a small group of cows that had needed six or more services before they finally became pregnant gave birth to 20 males and 53 females. This is a statistically significant result. But instead of immediately concluding that lowered fertility implies more female births Foote tried to replicate this result with a larger group of animals. He did a second analysis of 'repeat breeder cows grouped by number of services' and found there was no effect on the sex ratio. This work highlights the importance of replication. Nothing can be considered definite until it has been demonstrated more than once and preferably in a variety of settings by different teams of researchers. Overall, Foote's results showed a sex ratio of 50.8 per cent males no matter what the conditions, including the timing of inseminations.

Although it appears that timing of insemination does not influence the sex ratio in ungulates, there is equally good evidence to suggest that it does in other animals. In 1990 two psychologists from the University of Chicago reported a timing effect in Norway rats. In earlier work they had found that 'whether a female rat is mating during a cycling or post-partum oestrus has a profound influence on the timing of inseminations by female/male pairs mating spontaneously in a seminatural environment' (Hedricks and McClintock 1990).

Controlling for this and other variables, they designed the study environment so that it 'would be viewed by a video camera on the ceiling with a wide-angle lens'. The rats were filmed continuously, and later 'all female and male mating behaviours were transcribed from tapes played back at real time or single frame mode' so that every detail of the rats' behaviours could be accurately recorded and checked.

The results of this study showed that the timing of insemination had a significant, curvilinear relationship with the secondary sex ratio of litters conceived during cycling oestrus, and linear decline in sex ratio following postpartum oestrus. These findings added support for earlier work with humans and provided the possibility of a useful animal model.

TIMING STUDIES WITH HUMAN SUBJECTS

Scientists and veterinarians are not the only ones interested in timing theories. Prospective parents also want to know whether they can pre-determine the sex of their infant by timing intercourse. There have been both advantages and disadvantages in working with humans: since mammalian mechanisms differ, it has been advantageous to work directly with people, but one cannot watch humans day and night in order to monitor what they do and, even when they want to, people do not always report their behaviour accurately (see Chapter 2).

In addition to the problem of who or what to use as subjects, there is a problem concerning who should do the research. It is both risky and conceited for people who are not trained in reproductive physiology to make pronouncements about how the hormones of reproduction could be influencing sex ratios. This can lead to false attributions, and perhaps has contributed to a situation in which many reproductive physiologists no longer want to read about findings in the social sciences. Nor is this a one-way problem: obstetricians, gynaecologists and reproductive endocrinologists have been known to make errors of a similar magnitude in analysing their data.

On the other hand, some of the most exciting discoveries in science come when people reach out to others across disciplinary boundaries. For this to occur there has to be both mutual respect and a willingness to read, as much as one's limited scientific vocabulary will permit, in others' disciplines. It is also important to allow for the possibility of misunderstandings, and to check one's impressions with colleagues from the unfamiliar discipline.

Such is the situation here. In order to understand biological influences on the sex ratio, the researcher needs to develop some knowledge of the basic processes involved in conception. The skills of statisticians or demographers are also needed to collect and interpret the relevant data. Fortunately there are a few studies which fulfil the criteria for good scientific methodology and straddle the two disciplines – the reproductive physiology of the timing of intercourse and the mathematical analysis of sex ratio data.

Some of the best work in this area was done in the late 1960s and early 1970s by a researcher at the Harvard School of Public Health, Rodrigo Guerrero. He wrote a thesis entitled 'Time of insemination in the menstrual cycle and its effects on the sex ratio', later publishing his results in the *New England Journal of Medicine*.

From the beginning, one of the problems associated with this research was how to pinpoint the time of ovulation. Earlier studies had simply used the 14th day after onset of menstruation. But Guerrero's subjects took their temperatures every morning before rising. When the ovum is released from the ovary, 'the corpus luteum starts functioning, and the resulting progesterone levels cause a rise of a few tenths of a degree in the basal body temperature' (Guerrero 1974). This was the information commonly used by couples who wished to plan their families without recourse to artificial means of contraception. It was often referred to as the 'rhythm method'. The same temperature-taking regime was used by those wanting to maximize their chances of pregnancy. Instead of avoiding intercourse at the time of ovulation, they made a point of it.

Guerrero collected his basic data from two different sources – natural family planning programmes and infertility clinics. In both settings the women were keeping daily diaries and 'were motivated to record accurately both temperature and the time of insemination because they were trying either to avoid or achieve conception'. Guerrero collected as much data as he could, working with women from many different clinics in several different countries. In all he was able to acquire complete records for 1318 women who later became pregnant.

A number of rules were formulated for coding the information on 'thermal shift', the 'fertile period' and the 'responsible insemination'. Not the least of these was the one that stated: 'The days of the shift and responsible insemination were coded without knowledge of the outcome of the pregnancy.' In addition, the sex of the child was ascertained independently from each clinic's records. Such details help decide how much weight to give the findings. In this case, there are scarcely any methodological doubts about the quality of the research, and the results are therefore correspondingly reliable.

After abortions, tubal pregnancies and multiple births were all excluded (along with inconsistent or defective records), Guerrero was left with 875 pregnancies resulting from natural insemination. His data showed clearly that the greater the time before ovulation, the more likely it was for male infants to be conceived. Counting back from day zero ('the day the temperature rose to stay') he found a sex ratio of 0.683 for babies conceived on days −9 to −6 and a ratio of 0.605 for babies conceived on days −5 to −4. Sex ratios began to approach equality on subsequent days, but dipped below equality on days −1, (0.464) zero (0.435) and +1 (0.480). These ratios can be directly translated to percentages of male births. For example, 68.3 per cent of babies conceived on days −9 to −6, and 43.5 per cent on day zero, were male.

These results suggested that there would be a slightly higher chance of conceiving a female infant if the couple had intercourse as near as possible to ovulation, and a slightly higher chance of conceiving a male infant if the couple had intercourse a few days before ovulation. But the effect was a small one and offered only a clue about what might be going on at the physiological level. There was so much variability in the data that couples could not make reliable use of it. It appeared most likely that timing would provide an indicator of other factors which were closer or more relevant to the predetermination of the sex of the infant.

So far as the maternal dominance hypothesis was concerned, however, it presented a valuable piece of supportive evidence, namely the possibility that the sex of the infant might, at least in part, be determined by a factor or factors within the mother. This was the first piece of solid evidence for a theory based on differential access for X- and Y-chromosome-bearing spermatozoa under the control of the mother. Back in the 1970s this was particularly important, since till then few had considered this a realistic proposition.

These results of Guerrero's, though published in a journal of high reputation, were not taken seriously at the time, the main reason being that they were contradictory to others. In particular, they showed the opposite effect to the one being promoted by well-known American obstetrician, Landrum B. Shettles (1960, 1970). He, too, wondered if the sex of the infant might be in part under the control of the mother.

He speculated about how this could work, suggesting – without any scientific grounds for doing so – that the acidity or alkalinity of the uterine environment might be relevant. Next he claimed to have seen differences in X and Y sperm while looking at some live specimens under a microscope one night alone in his laboratory. Putting these and a number of other ideas all together he issued a complex set of instructions to prospective parents trying to predetermine the sex of their infant. These included: timing intercourse (in the opposite direction to that found to be relevant by Guerrero), douching with either a mild acid (white vinegar) or a mild alkali (baking soda) immediately beforehand, assuming different positions during intercourse and timing orgasms.

This was one of those occasions when poor science masqueraded as good science, and was given a prominence it in no way deserved. Shettles' work was based almost entirely on speculation, but was written up as fact. In addition it was picked up by women's magazines all over the world and thus became very well-known. Couples everywhere read Shettles' burdensome instructions and tried to follow them – all for nothing. It is reprehensible that Shettles' results are still sometimes cited by social scientists who have not read the original papers.

Because of the high reputation of the journals that published Shettles' work, this dismal situation pertained for many years. It changed only slowly after some small, brave research teams offered results which showed that Shettles' methods did not influence the sex ratio at all. One of these was published in the *Journal of Biosocial Science* in 1978. Nancy Williamson and her colleagues worked in a sex preselection clinic in Singapore. They set out to test Shettles' method as carefully as they could, 'in the hope that if couples could have the son they desired, they would keep their families small in accordance with the government's strong commitment to population control' (Williamson *et al.* 1978).

From March 1975 to July 1977, letters were sent to newly wed women inviting them to attend the clinic. One in ten women opted to join the programme and start keeping records. Although some dropped out, the clinic held completed records for 1026 women. The real attrition rate began when women failed to return to the clinic for their one-, three- and six-month appointments. Finally there were 31 women, all wanting boys, who attempted to follow the method and who finally gave birth. In a sad little summary, Williamson reported: 'By chance alone, one would expect about 16 to have boys. In fact, 14 had boys.'

There is no doubt that work in the area of the predetermination of the sex of the infant can be discouraging. If there were to be a prize for those who do a scientifically rigorous study which demonstrates that a popular idea does not stand up when put to the test, then a proper candidate to receive it would be Dr John France, a researcher in New Zealand.

In 1980, France and Freddie Graham were academics working at the National Women's Hospital in Auckland. They began their study because they were getting frequent enquiries from couples who had read the magazine articles on sex preselection and wanted to know if the methods were worth trying. Knowing that the published data were unreliable, France and Graham were scrupulous in designing their own study. By this time most of Shettles' recommendations had been found to be nonsense, but there was still a question-mark over timing, so they concentrated on that.

One of the most important problems was how to ascertain the time of ovulation. After carefully screened volunteer couples had been fully briefed and admitted to the programme, the women were passed on to a specialist nurse. Over a number of cycles she taught each woman individually how to observe her cervical mucus symptoms and record them on a chart. In addition, women recorded their basal body temperature each morning before rising (as Guerrero's subjects had done) and, finally, after the trials began, they collected their first morning urine, storing it in the refrigerator so it would be available for later analysis should they conceive in that particular cycle.

When all these instructions had been thoroughly understood and practised through several cycles, couples were given the following instructions.

> Abstain from the onset of fertile mucus symptoms or from day seven of the cycle whichever comes first. If a female infant is desired, have intercourse two to three days before the mucus 'peak' symptom, using the pattern and duration of symptoms observed in previous cycles as a reference guide. If a male child is desired, have intercourse on the day after the mucus 'peak' symptom.
>
> (France *et al.* 1984)

Because the research was a trial of Shettles' recommendations, the instructions were in accordance with his findings, not Guerrero's.

France and Graham published a table which showed what happened to *all* their subjects. This is rare: most researchers who have published results in this area show only what happened to those who delivered live babies. They do not give the numbers of women who either failed to become pregnant or who miscarried early in the pregnancy. This serious omission in reporting lies at the base of many misleading conclusions.

Even though France and Graham had briefed couples fully about what would be expected of them, 100 of the original 185 dropped out. Others failed to become pregnant by the sixth try, and some had miscarriages. Of the 52 couples whose pregnancies resulted in a live birth, only 33 had followed the instructions on the timing of intercourse precisely enough to be sure about which was the actual occasion of fertilization. Of these 33, 19 had entered the study hoping to conceive girls, and 14 wanted boys. The infants born were 22 boys and 11 girls, but only 13 (39 per cent) of the couples got an infant of the sex they had hoped for. Not only did this research not confirm Shettles' findings, the results were significant in the opposite direction, thus providing confirmation for Guerrero's long-ignored work.

These findings have stood for many years and are still important for the maternal dominance hypothesis. This is because the timing effect provides a way of thinking about the predetermination of the sex of the infant which allows for a role for the mother. In the past the idea was that the presence of more or less maternal testosterone (or a related hormone) could provide a means for differential access of spermatozoa under control of the female. Individual differences in levels of maternal hormones could underlie the potential to conceive a male infant by providing a slightly different uterine environment. If the presence of the relevant hormone was also related to the menstrual cycle, this could mean it was easier to conceive a child of one sex during one part of the cycle and a child of the other sex during another part. If intercourse took place only when conditions were not right for that particular woman, she would not conceive at all.

Ideas about what aspects of timing might be relevant to the conception of one sex or the other have changed as reproductive physiologists discover more about the processes involved. More than a decade after John France and his colleagues published their study, Clarice R. Weinberg and her colleagues reported another, which suggested that the key element might be the length of the follicular phase of the cycle.

These researchers had access to data from 221 couples in North Carolina, all of whom had discontinued contraception in order to conceive. The women, most of whom were in their mid- to late twenties, collected the first urine specimen every morning and kept a daily record of whether they had had intercourse and whether menstrual bleeding had commenced. The day of ovulation was estimated from the ratio of oestrogen to progesterone metabolites in the urine and the length of the follicular phase was defined as the number of days from the onset of menstrual bleeding to the estimated day of ovulation. Thus, if day one denotes the first day of reported menstrual bleeding, and ovulation occurred on day 16, the follicular phase length would be recorded as 15.

(Weinberg *et al.* 1995)

The results were statistically significant at a high level: conception cycles resulted in girls having a mean follicular phase length of 17.6 days, compared with 15.4 days for conception cycles resulting in boys. When the authors grouped the cycles by length of days, they found that 'three-quarters of the cycles with short follicular phases (the lowest group) resulted in boys, while more than two-thirds of the cycles with long follicular phases (the highest group) resulted in girls'. In the discussion section of their report the authors suggested three possible mechanisms whereby this phenomenon might be explained. One of these was that 'the ovum produced in a cycle with a short follicular phase might be more receptive to Y-bearing than to X-bearing spermatozoa, with the reverse being true in cycles with long follicular phases' (Weinberg *et al.* 1995).

Even though it was cited as only one of three possibilities, from the point of view of the maternal dominance hypothesis this was a particularly welcome suggestion; especially as it came from an independent group of researchers who had never heard of the maternal dominance hypothesis.

As the evolutionary biologists have pointed out, it would make biological sense for whatever mechanism was involved in the facultative adjustment of the sex ratio to operate as early as possible in the reproductive process. Since it was beginning to look more likely that the predetermination of the sex of the infant might be influenced by the mother, this very early event in the reproductive process would be the most appropriate. If, each month, the ovum itself was specially adapted, according to environmental conditions, to be more receptive to a Y-rather than an X-chromosome-bearing spermatozoon, this would be among the most efficient processes imaginable.

These and other related findings (see Chapter 5) continued to point researchers towards a possible maternal role, thus providing further support for the maternal dominance hypothesis. It began to look as though the hormonally based personality differences between dominant and non-dominant women might translate not just into chemical differences in the uterine environment, but go even deeper into the reproductive system, right to the selection of the ovum itself.

EARLY CONTRIBUTIONS FROM WILLIAM H. JAMES

No contemporary demographer has studied the human sex ratio more assiduously than William H. James of the Galton Laboratory, University College London. For more than 25 years Dr James has been collecting data on both human and animal sex ratios, analysing them and trying to make sense of them. James has described himself as 'an amateur armchair epidemiologist trying to identify the determinants of the sex ratio'. He says that he patrols the libraries' latest journals accessions every day, 'and mulls over the relevance of the day's scientific offerings to the ad hoc construction of truth . . . ' (James 1987b).

Over the years James has made a number of suggestions about what might influence the sex ratio. One of his earliest papers was published in the *Lancet* in 1971. As an epidemiologist he had always taken an interest in the statistical analysis of data sets: in this case the data had been collected between 1924 and 1927 by German researchers and James's analysis of it was in part prompted by a controversy. Although some had suggested that the data showed an effect on the sex ratio of the 'cycle day of insemination', others claimed that people do not report such dates accurately enough to draw any reliable conclusions. James joined the argument:

> In general women report more accurately the date of the last menstrual period than may be supposed. But they report (as opposed to record) inaccurately on coital dates. This latter point illustrates one of the weaknesses of earlier German data . . . [but, in this case the authors] took the precaution of determining coital dates by ascertaining (from the German War Office) the dates on which their subjects' soldier husbands were home on leave.
>
> (James 1971a)

Thus, well before Guerrero and others, James had demonstrated (albeit indirectly) the possibility of a timing effect on the sex ratio. In addition, he acknowledged that 'a large quantity of empirical data supporting this hypothesis was published in the Continental literature about half a century ago'. It thus appears that Europeans were for a long time better informed on this point than English-speakers.

In the same paper James looked at the topic of coital rate. He raised the idea that frequent intercourse might lead to more male births, arguing that if male infants were conceived earlier in the cycle than female infants, then one would expect high coital rates to lead to more males. In support of this suggestion he referred to the higher sex ratios among infants conceived early in marriage and to the higher wartime and postwar sex ratios.

This last suggestion was later taken up by others, especially anthropologists, who used it to explain high sex ratios. James responded that the association, if there was one, between coital rate and the sex ratio was very weak, and that he was mentioning this because 'recently four anthropologists have used my work (invalidly in my opinion) to derive inferences about coital rates from sex ratios' (James 1995b).

Both reproductive endocrinologists (Greenstein 1994, 62) and psychologists have reported a positive association between female testosterone and libido. In a review beginning with the observation that 'removal of the ovaries alone appears to have little or no effect on sexual interest or performance in the human female', Gray and Gorzalka (1980) concluded that 'adrenal androgens, particularly testosterone are significantly and positively correlated with both behavioural and psychological measures of sexual behaviour in women'.

If female testosterone does increase libido, it could be argued that a higher frequency of intercourse would mean an increased chance of fertilization earlier in the menstrual cycle and hence, theoretically, an increased chance of conceiving a male offspring. But, equally, this reasoning could be quite wrong. It does not follow, just because female testosterone is said to be related to both libido and the conception of male infants, that libido is necessarily associated with the conception of males.

This is an ancient trap in logic. It is nicely illustrated by the story from Denmark where it is known that the number of industrial chimneys in a particular province is closely related to the number of stork nests. It is also known that the number of chimneys is closely associated, in the same direction, with the birth rate. Furthermore, when the number of chimneys decreased, so did the birth rate. These associations 'prove' that storks bring babies.

It would be the same kind of *non sequitur* to argue that because female testosterone was associated with both libido and the conception of male infants, there was therefore a connection between the two. It is not logical and probably not true. The theory behind the maternal dominance hypothesis is that the conception of a male offspring may be related to the production of a specially adapted ovum, which because of the way testosterone is implicated in its original production is set to be fertilized by a Y sperm or nothing. If this is so, then coital frequency would be irrelevant to the determination of the sex of the offspring, even if testosterone were positively associated with both libido and the conception of males.

There might be an association, however, if timing is important. If male infants are conceived earlier in the cycle, and if the fertile period extends over a longer time, more frequent intercourse could enhance the possibility of conception in a woman predisposed to conceive a male. Conversely, if the time during the menstrual cycle in which a female may be conceived is shorter (three days, say, rather than six days), then a woman might take a longer or a shorter time to become pregnant depending on how frequently she had intercourse. This kind of reasoning would support those who believe that lowered fertility is associated with the conception of females, and would suggest that Foote's (1977) original finding in animal husbandry of a relationship between the number of services required and a low sex ratio might be further investigated.

TWIN RESEARCH

A third suggestion made by James in his paper (1971a) concerned twins. Since monozygotic (MZ) twins come from one ovum and split into two separate individuals during the first few cell divisions, they are always the same sex, whereas dizygotic (DZ) twins, coming from two separate ova, may be the same or different sexes.

Interest in the sex ratio of twins goes back to the beginning of the twentieth century, when the German researcher Weinberg formulated a rule for calculating the expected proportions of like and unlike sex dizygotic twins. If the sex ratio was 100:100, or 0.5, the same number of opposite-sex (MF or FM) as same-sex (MM or FF) dizygotic twins could be expected.

When it seemed possible that timing of intercourse might affect the sex ratio, James wondered if the two ova that later became DZ twins might be affected in the same way. If they were released from the ovary at the same time, they might also then reach the uterus and be available for fertilization at approximately the same time. If some additional factor related to the mother's menstrual cycle made it more likely that one sex or the other would be conceived, depending on the time in the cycle, then there ought to be more same-sex than opposite-sex DZ twins than mathematics would predict.

At that time James confined his analysis to 842 pairs of twins who had been identified as DZ by blood-typing at birth. In this sample he found that same-sex pairs (453) outnumbered the opposite-sex pairs

(389). He calculated that the difference between the observed ratio and the expected ratio was statistically significant at the $p<.03$ level. Thus he concluded that there were more same-sex DZ twins than there 'should', be and that the finding supported the notion of a maternal timing factor relevant to the sex of the infant (James 1971b).

Since then, however, a number of doubts have been raised, and James himself has published more than a dozen scientific papers in which the sex ratio of twins has been further explored. The earlier techniques for assigning zygosity have been called into question, casting doubt on the original allocation of twin pairs to their correct groupings. By the 1980s it had become clear that this was a serious confounding factor. The correct allocation of twins to either MZ or DZ categories could only be decided after doing a number of difficult and expensive tests. In 1984 Hrubec and Robinette wrote: 'the elusiveness of a reliable method for determining zygosity has continued to bedevil researchers'. Not even the identification of a single placenta was sufficient to establish monozygosity. Researchers said that if a 2–5 per cent error was acceptable, the best way of deciding whether twins were MZ or DZ was simply to ask them if they were mistaken for one another as children.

But in most studies the possibility of a 5 per cent error is not acceptable, and this meant that earlier twin studies were seen as not quite as valuable as they had been before, depending on how the original classification into MZ and DZ twins was done. To solve the problem, contemporary twin studies make use of DNA testing wherever possible. Earlier studies need to be re-evaluated individually.

In 1992 James did another analysis using the higher ratio representing the normal male to female secondary sex ratio (0.514). In a sample of twins 'known to be dizygotic on the basis of autosomal markers alone', he found 1393 same-sex twins compared with 1233 opposite-sex twins, thus suggesting that Weinberg's Rule (for a mathematically predictable distribution) did not hold, and concluding again that same-sex twins might be occurring at a greater than expected rate. But the continuing difficulty in accurately assigning zygosity in a high proportion of total twin samples appears to mean that the question cannot, at present, be settled with any degree of certainty (James 1992).

Regardless of zygosity, it is difficult even to know whether there are more female than male twin pairs overall. Twin researchers think there are (Hrdy 1987, 107). Twin registers tend to hold records for more female twin pairs. For example, in July 1996 the Australian National Twin Register held information on 2462 female MZ pairs, but only 1134 male MZ pairs; 1496 female DZ pairs, but only 700 male DZ pairs. This imbalance was ascribed to a response-rate bias in favour of females, but the research on compliance provides no evidence for a sex effect of this magnitude. It seems at least equally plausible that there is a predominance of female twins.

So far as the maternal dominance hypothesis is concerned, opposite-sex twins present a tricky problem. Whenever I give a paper on my research, someone in the audience asks me to explain unlike-sex twins. Once someone put two questions at once by asking me to account for a well known ex-prime minister's opposite-sex twins.

At present the only way to explain it would be in terms of quantity. It has been shown that biological dominance could be underpinned by one of the hormones of reproduction, probably testosterone. It has also been shown that women vary both in dominance and in the amount of testosterone in a predictable way, probably in accordance with the normal distribution curve. That is to say, some women have small amounts of testosterone, some large amounts, and most an average amount. (The evidence to support this is described in Chapter 3.)

One of the assumptions of the maternal dominance hypothesis is that to conceive, and/or ratify the conception of a male infant, there might need to be a sufficient quantity of the particular relevant hormone. Just over the threshold and a male child is conceived, just under the critical amount and a female is conceived; or, if the ovum itself is specialized to receive a Y-chromosome-bearing spermatozoon, enough follicular testosterone for one such ovum, but not for two. Timing may also be an important factor. The hormone may create the necessary conditions for the conception of the male to be ratified, but may not last long enough for the ratification of a second conception. This reasoning is entirely speculative. It is included only to demonstrate that one can imagine a possible pathway, not that there is one.

SINGLE-SEX SIBSHIPS

It is tempting to think when a woman has her fourth, fifth or sixth consecutive girl (or boy) that there could be a reason for it. Among people who remember their school biology lessons, the question has been: Is her husband or partner capable of siring only one sex? Among those who think that there may be some factor within the woman which predetermines the sex of the infant, the question is: Are there some women who can conceive only male infants, or only female infants?

When thinking about this question, it is important to take into consideration the number of single-sex sibships that would occur by chance. Suppose the process underlying the conception of a boy or girl could be modelled on tossing a coin. In families having three children, how many would have three boys and how many would have three girls? There are eight possible combinations – GGG, GGB, GBG, GBB, BBB, BBG, BGG, BGB – six of which give mixed-sex families and two result in single-sex families. In dealing with very large numbers, one must work with a modified binomial distribution to account for the fact that more boys are born than girls. But the mathematics, although complicated by this fact, follow the same principles.

Although the chances of having a boy or a girl are about 105:100 for the population as a whole, it looked as though for some individual women the chance of the next child being the same sex as her earlier children was greater than 105:100. Intuitively, or perhaps unthinkingly, people sometimes argue that if a woman already has five sons then the chance of her having a daughter must be higher. But, of course, if conceiving a girl or a boy carried the same odds as tossing a coin, the chances would be exactly the same on every occasion, be it the first conception or the 21st. As it happens, there is more evidence to support the opposite idea. If a woman already has five daughters, statistically speaking she has a very slightly higher chance of conceiving another girl.

This is another question that has interested demographers as well as parents. If some women produce children of one sex only, there ought to be some evidence for this in population statistics. In 1955, D. Hewitt and his colleagues in the Social Medicine Unit at Oxford University studied this question after others had found that all-boy families seemed to be occurring at a greater than expected rate.

Hewitt and his colleagues obtained their data from a study of newborn infants in five areas of England. The primary criterion for inclusion in the study was that a child had been born into the family during 1952. The sample comprised 3909 Northamptonshire families ranging in size from 1 to 12 children, containing 9010 children, of whom 4736 were boys (thus giving an overall sex ratio of 0.526). Among the mixed-sex sibships, the authors found no statistically significant variations in the expected numbers, but they did find a tendency for single-sex sibships to occur more frequently than would be expected by chance, at least among the all-male sibships. For example, of the 19 families in which five or more children of the same sex had been born, 16 were families of boys. And in families of six or more of like sex, all were boys. From this, Hewitt and his colleagues concluded that there might be 'matings which can only produce male offspring' (Hewitt *et al.* 1955), but they could think of no reason for this.

Since 1962 it has been clear why it is not possible to be sure exactly what is going on. The mathematics involved in arguing the problem are sophisticated and require a working knowledge of the differences between Lexis, Poisson and Markov variation. A paper describing these differences was published in *Biometrics* (Crouchley *et al.* 1984). In more accessible language, demographers try to make allowances for the possibility that there may be subsets of families, or groups of families in the population, with more likelihood of varying than other families (or, in terms of the present hypothesis, subsets of women who vary). If there were, however, the variation within the group would be unlikely to be visible in the overall analysis because whatever was causing the variation in the distribution was itself normally distributed.

Hence population statisticians find it difficult to isolate any substantial evidence for anything but the expected occurrence of single-sex sibships. This difficulty would apply to the maternal dominance hypothesis as much as to any other theory. If the hormone that underlies the conception of male infants is itself normally distributed, and there is a critical threshold at which it is insufficient to promote the development of a male conceptus, then one would expect to see male and female children normally distributed in the population, even if there are some women who have a tendency to conceive one sex only. The fact that whatever is causing the development of one sex or the other is also normally distributed masks its effect.

James explains this more elegantly.

> Consider a model in which the probability of a male conception *increases* from pregnancy one to pregnancy two in some women, and *decreases* in others: such variation would then go undetected if it were masking Lexis variation of a comparable magnitude. In the present context [a discussion of the maternal dominance hypothesis], such variation would seem entirely possible. One may envisage the individual probability of a male conception varying across time in response to the fluctuating environmental conditions.
>
> (James 1996)

Occasionally studies are published that do show an excess of single-sex sibships. The difficulty is that it is impossible to interpret them. It could be argued that they support the maternal dominance effect, but to do this several other parts of the hypothesis would need to be firmly established. The most important of these would be the distribution of the hormone that was relevant to both dominance and the conception of a male.

In addition to being normally distributed, this hypothesized hormonal effect would need to have two further characteristics. First, it would need to be responsive to environmental changes, thus accounting for the fact that most mothers have infants of both sexes. This responsiveness and consequent variability in the amount of the hormone would probably be similar for all women. (And in fact this seems to be the case, as discussed in Chapter 3.) Second, within the normal distribution individual women must have upper and lower biological limits that vary considerably between individuals, thus explaining why some women, even though they vary the same amount as others, continue to have children of the same sex.

MEDICAL DISORDERS AND THE SEX RATIO

In 1987 William H. James published two papers in which he reviewed every study he could find on the sex ratio – over 240 of them. Among these were some smaller medical studies which showed some unusual and puzzling results, including a group of studies that showed quite a strong tendency for the children of mothers suffering from multiple sclerosis to be male.

These studies are particularly interesting because they give the figures for the sex ratio of infants of male patients suffering from multiple sclerosis as well as for females. Male patients had the same numbers of boys and girls (364 to 359), which is what one would expect. But female patients suffering from the same disease had 858 boys and 713 girls, a significantly larger number of boys. Is this a chance finding or could it mean something? All three studies done on the topic, by different researchers at different times, found the same effect (James 1987a). Why would this be? At present the answer is not known.

Similarly puzzling was the finding that women who suffer toxaemia of pregnancy also have more male infants. In his paper James cited 13 studies on this topic going back to 1903. Two studies reported that the more severe the condition, the more likely a boy would be born. In 1995 James reported again, adding a further eight studies to the total. All except one showed that a significantly larger number of boys was born to women suffering this condition. Combining all the studies, women who had some form of pregnancy-induced hypertension had 14,291 male infants and 12,447 female infants. James summed up these findings: 'The overall sex ratio of these data, 0.534, is highly significantly different from an expected livebirth sex ratio of 0.514 (chi square = 45, P<0.00000001)' (James 1995a). In his comments on these results

James noted that 'a systematic increase of sex ratio with severity' might be influencing the ostensible heterogeneity.

Some of the researchers involved in the original presentation of these data wondered if the differences in the sex ratios might reflect influences such as 'gonadal hormones'. James said he thought this was correct, and furthermore that the gonadal hormone concentrations (high in cases of pre-eclampsia) would predate the pregnancies. In addition, some obstetricians have noticed that their toxaemic patients appear to be the more highly strung women, an attribute associated with dominance in women by no less a psychologist than Cattell himself (Cattell *et al.* 1970, 85). But the direction of the causal arrow is a major problem. A mother might become anxious and highly strung as a consequence of suffering from toxaemia of pregnancy, rather than as a cause.

The same difficulty is relevant to the interpretation of two studies linking low waist-to-hip ratios with higher sex ratios. Do the findings reflect a cause or a consequence of bearing male offspring? In this research, however, the issues are a little clearer.

Its origins go back to 1983, when David Evans and his colleagues at the Medical College of Wisconsin, who had been doing a series of studies on obesity, found a relationship between body fat distribution and hormones. Working with 80 pre-menopausal Caucasian women, they demonstrated that distribution of body fat in women is related to the amount of free testosterone. 'We propose', they wrote, 'that a relative increase in tissue exposure to unbound androgens may be responsible in part for localization of fat in the upper body . . . ' Their work suggested that the women were exposed to androgens over long periods of time rather than simply during pregnancy.

There followed a series of studies which confirmed this finding. Body fat distribution in women appears to fall into two categories, the 'gynoid' and the 'android', the latter being categorized by low waist-to-hip ratios.

Noticing that James had suggested many times that parental hormones may be related to the sex ratio, and also noting the maternal dominance hypothesis, two teams did studies to see whether waist–hip ratios were related to the sex ratio. Taking an evolutionary perspective, and working with 102 women aged between 35 and 55 years, researchers at the University of Liverpool found a positive correlation between several related body measurements and the proportion of sons in the family, and a statistically significant relationship between waist circumference and proportion of sons (Manning *et al.* 1996). Devendra Singh of the University of Texas found the same phenomenon.

Working with 69 nurses aged between 23 and 50 years, he found that 'waist-to-hip ratio significantly predicts the number of male offspring' (Singh and Zambarano 1997).

Since both sets of measurements were taken years after the birth of the children, and since the researchers postulate a slow buildup of fat cells over time, it is likely that the effect is related to lifetime levels of testosterone. There is thus some support for a logical corollary of the maternal dominance hypothesis – namely, that anything that is reliably associated with testosterone in women should itself be associated with the conception of male infants.

POLYGAMY AND THE SEX RATIO

From time to time studies are published on the sex ratios of children born of polygamous marriages. Most of these studies have been done by anthropologists studying records from early Mormon pioneers (Mealey and Mackey 1990) or native tribal groups. Whiting (1993) collected data on 882 women living in seven different cultural groups in Kenya. He found that 'polygynously married mothers' gave birth to more female infants than did monogamous women. On the other hand, Mulder (1994), 'in a larger demographic study of one of Whiting's groups, found no significantly different sex-ratio variation'.

Because the findings were contradictory, some assumed that both must be chance findings. It now appears that an important factor in discriminating between high and low sex ratios in polygamous group-ings may be the way in which the women are housed. Some researchers have found that if the wives all live together sex ratios are likely to be high. If each wife lives alone with her children in a separate dwelling, sex ratios are likely to be low.

If the women living alone felt safe and well provided for, then it is possible that their lives were lacking in the sort of social stimulation required to produce levels of testosterone high enough to conceive the expected number of male infants. Conversely, those women living in groups might experience a certain competitiveness in everyday living which could result in a slightly higher level of stimulation and therefore a slightly higher level of testosterone.

The trouble with this kind of 'reasoning' is that it is perfectly possible to argue a contrary view. One could say that a woman living on her own, independently, would need to develop a certain amount of tough-ness in order to manage the dwelling and protect her child; and that women living in a harem might need to develop non-dominant behaviours in order to adapt comfortably to living in a group. All or none of these interpretations might be justifiable, but certainly none could be used as evidence.

Something much more rigorous is required. The curious thing is that there is an animal study which contributes exactly that rigour. In 1990 Martine Perret of the Laboratoire d'Ecologie Générale at Brunoy in France published a paper in which she described her work with lesser mouse lemurs (tiny monkeys). She was looking to see if social factors influenced the sex ratio. Her experimental animals were 51 females, born in captivity. Although she investigated several social factors, the critical one was the way in which the animals were housed. Over five successive breeding seasons Perret showed that females housed in groups 'produced significantly more sons than daughters (67 per cent males for 189 newborn) while females living alone except during the mating period demonstrated a significant inverse tendency (39.6 per cent males for 96)' (Perret 1990).

Even more interesting in terms of the maternal dominance hypothesis was the way in which Perret interpreted her data. She is one of only a handful of primatologists to have considered what might be happening at the physiological level. She argued that sex ratio bias in the female mouse lemur must occur 'pre-conceptually'. She also said: 'Differences between isolated and grouped females leading to a pre-conceptual bias probably occur before oestrus in relation to hormonal differences.' And (in these animals) 'hormone levels throughout the ovarian cycles can be strongly modified by the presence of other females' (Perret 1990).

Whether or not this effect can be applied to women living in groups or to women living alone remains to be seen. Perret has, however, provided valuable supportive evidence for what might otherwise have seemed a rather far-fetched line of reasoning. Her results not only imply a major role for the mother in the predetermination of the sex of her offspring, but go even further towards concordance with the maternal dominance hypothesis in suggesting that the social environment is relevant and that there must be 'a pre-conceptual bias' towards conceiving a male or a female offspring.

5

THE PHYSIOLOGY OF SEX
DETERMINATION

For the maternal dominance hypothesis to be credible it has to be compatible with what reproductive physiologists know about the determination of the sex of the infant. In the early days of the hypothesis (1960s and 1970s) this compatibility rested on theoretical differences in the uterine environment and on the timing of intercourse, both theories postulating maternal influence in the determination of the sex of the infant. The timing theory continues to provide useful evidence for a maternal role. In addition, since it is known that testosterone varies with dominance status in primates, female testosterone or a related hormone could also play an active role in predetermining the sex of the infant.

After most of the early ideas in this area were discredited, many reproductive physiologists changed the direction of their research. As in many areas of science, a gold-mining metaphor may be apt here. Scientists follow a promising seam until it appears to run out. In this case, many gave up on the problems concerned with the determination of the sex of the infant and began to do more intensive research in the area of infertility. Of those that continued to be interested in the determination of the sex of the offspring, only a very few continued to investigate the possibility of a maternal influence. Instead, a number of researchers began to work on sperm morphology, trying to devise ways of separating X- and Y-chromosome-bearing spermatozoa.

Before beginning any research project, modern scientists and their research teams must satisfy both lay ethics committees and external funding criteria. This means they must be able to convince a large number of people (not just the head of the university department) that one particular idea is more likely to produce interesting or useful results than all the others. In an area like reproductive physiology, laboratory and equipment costs are so high that research scientists have to be very convincing about the potential value of their ideas. Inevitably this leads to a situation in which the funding goes to the researchers whose work most clearly fits current paradigms and promises specific benefits.

In the case of the determination of the infant's sex, two benefits are frequently cited. The first is the possibility of avoiding sex-linked diseases by being able to select the sex of the non-carrying infant – that is, 'for the betterment of humankind'. The second is the likely commercial benefit in animal husbandry. Of course there is nothing intrinsically wrong with either of these goals; but if scientists are rewarded only for staying within the paradigm it should not be a surprise to anyone to find that the *Zeitgeist* is both accentuated and prolonged. For all today's quite proper emphasis on accountability, it does raise the question of whether the balance has swung too far in the other direction. If the less plausible hunches are not explored, will future generations have as rich a pool of ideas to draw from?

Whether or not there is a question to answer here, during the 1980s and 1990s research on the predetermination of the sex of the infant centred on sperm separation. The thinking behind this idea is basically simple. If the sex of the infant is a matter of chance, and if the male produces X and Y spermatozoa in equal numbers (which appears to be the case – see, for example, Lobel *et al.* 1993 and Griffin *et al.* 1996), then the easiest way of ensuring a female conceives an infant of the desired sex is to expose her to either X- or Y-enriched semen, or better still, semen in which there are only X or Y spermatozoa present. Not only is the original supposition suspect but, as described below, this task has proved far from easy.

THE SEARCH FOR DIFFERENCES BETWEEN Xs AND Ys

The origins of this research go back to the 1920s, when W. E. Castle, of Bussey Institution, wrote in a letter to *Science*

> of a case of human inheritance which has very great theoretical interest ... It has the distribution in heredity of a Y-chromosome, a structure found only in the male-determining spermatozoa of certain animals and never in their eggs. The Y-chromosome accordingly is a structure possessed by male individuals only and thus forms an appropriate vehicle for the transmission of characters from father to son, quite independently of the female line of descent ... Schmidt described in a fish the first known case of inheritance of this

type. This has since been confirmed ... [thus furnishing] evidence that the Y-chromosome type of inheritance occurs in man as well as in fishes.

(Castle 1922)

Two years later Professor Theophilus S. Painter of the University of Texas reported as follows:

Recent studies in human spermatogenesis have cleared up the doubt which has so long existed over the number of chromosomes possessed by mankind. The somatic or diploid number for the female is 48, and this must be taken as the basic number for the race ...

(Painter 1924)

From the 1960s onwards a number of reproductive physiologists worked on the problem of identifying and separating X and Y spermatozoa. An American scientist, Barton Gledhill, took a particular interest in this area. After years of research at the Lawrence Livermore National Laboratory, University of California, he wrote a summary of what was known at that time. He said that, in spite of theoretical arguments showing that X spermatozoa should be larger than Y,

no repeatable experimental evidence exists to substantiate this hypothesis ... The claims made by Shettles in 1961 that two morphologically distinct classes of human sperm exist and represent X- and Y-bearing sperm have not been accepted by other workers. No one has been able to detect a bimodal distribution in sperm head dimensions.

(Gledhill 1988)

Gledhill's review covered all the ways that had been tried till then to separate X spermatozoa from Ys, and countless hours and dollars have been poured into this search. Of course the problem is complicated by the fact that whatever is done to the spermatozoa to make them easier to separate must not destroy or damage them in the process. For example, in discussing electrophoresis as a technique Gledhill noted that, while there is 'no a priori reason why X-bearing and Y-bearing sperm should differ in surface charge', in fact 'in an electric field, some sperm do move towards the anode and some towards the cathode'. But, he said, 'Motility of the sperm following electrophoresis is lost.'

Other techniques for separating Xs and Ys which were reviewed by

Gledhill included flow fractionation (thermal convection, counter-streaming sedimentation, galvanization and laminar flow), separation based on density characteristics, Sephadex Gel filtration, and albumin centrifugation; flow cytometry and flow sorting. Up till that time, none had proved either effective or practical.

An important part of Gledhill's review was devoted to discussing ways of verifying the results of separation techniques which were being increasingly claimed as successful in agriculture. In the past, he said, success was 'scored by the laborious procedure of determining the sex ratio among progeny after use of processed semen'. Not only had this limited the volume of data but it was also vulnerable to criticism on a number of other counts. So, he said, 'It would be an immense technical advantage if X and Y sperm could be recognized individually. The progress of experiments to separate them could then be monitored directly.' Gledhill's contribution was to do just that. He and his team devised a technique involving measurement of the DNA content of the sperm. Not only did it prove a very useful research tool but at that time his team could find 'no apparent effectiveness of seven commercially available methods for enrichment of bull sperm', in spite of claims to the contrary.

One important finding from the research done on trying to separate X and Y spermatozoa was the confirmation of equal numbers of each. In all the animals tested, both ungulates and primates, the ratio of Xs to Ys has remained constant at 1:1 (or 50 per cent of each). The same is true for human sperm. Darren Griffin and his colleagues (1996) tested semen samples from 24 healthy volunteer sperm donors, and scored a total of 296,731 sperm. The ratio of Y- to X-bearing sperm was 'almost unity (0.996)'. There is no evidence at all to suggest that the skewed human sex ratio (105:100) could be based on skewed production favouring Y spermatozoa.

SPERM MORPHOLOGY

In 1994, two scientists from the University of Adelaide reported in *Nature* that they had discovered a size difference between X and Y spermatozoa. Their discovery was made possible by the use of 'primers', 'suitable for distinguishing between male and female DNA' (Cui and Matthews 1993).

The same primers were used to determine the sex of 233 non-motile sperm (11 donors) which were individually selected for direct photography before polymerase chain reaction. Two hundred and seventeen sperm (93.1%) showed satisfactory amplification, 106 (48.8%) being Y and 111 (51.2%) being X. Under 'blind' conditions, we magnified photographs of individual sperm a further thirty times and directly measured them. Statistical analysis showed the length, perimeter and areas of the heads and the length of the neck and tail in X sperm are significantly larger than those of Y sperm . . . our direct methods show for the first time that human X sperm are statistically larger and longer than Y sperm.

(Cui and Matthews 1993)

Ironically, these results confirmed what Shettles had said more than 30 years before, but this time the authors described a repeatable procedure which other scientists could use to ratify the results. Furthermore, it is important to note that what they were saying is that X spermatozoa are *statistically* larger than Y spermatozoa. This is the same kind of statement that can be made about a number of measurements in nature, meaning that overall Xs are larger than Ys, not that every X is larger than every Y. It is the same kind of thinking that underlies statements such as 'men are taller than women'. It means that the average is higher, not that an observer could predict from any one measurement whether it was an X or Y sperm.

In the 1990s, computerized technology was brought in to help with the detailed study of spermatozoa. Professor Russell O. Davis, a co-director of the Andrology Laboratory at Davis, University of California, was part of a team which developed automated sperm morphology and computer automated sperm analysis (CASA). Davis has described how the techniques in this area have changed. The first sperm counts were done using time exposures, then by using multiple rapid exposures, then by cine-camera and frame-by-frame analysis, and later still by using video equipment with computer links.

Until the early 1990s one of the major problems in this area had been a totally unacceptable variation in sperm counts between laboratories. Even among prestigious laboratories, the same semen sample could receive widely different counts. The reasons for this variability were difficulties relating to the collection of the semen, sampling error (it was all too likely that the tiny amount of semen on the slide under the microscope would not be representative of the semen sample as a whole), and errors relating to the subjectivity of the assessor. Even two well-trained and experienced technicians could differ in their views of what was on the slide.

One reason for this is that spermatozoa are much more variable than was first thought. To make their study more accurate, a number of scientists set about constructing a descriptive morphology. In 1988, the year that Gledhill had published his review, J. F. Moruzzi and his colleagues, also of the Lawrence Livermore National Laboratory, published a paper in *Fertility and Sterility*, entitled 'Quantification and classification of human sperm morphology by computer-assisted image analysis'. In it they described how they had developed a 'quantitative, semi-automated method for classifying human sperm based on objective measurements of head shapes and sizes'. They used spermatozoa from eight healthy men. In one part of the exercise they selected 283 sperm as prototypic examples of the 10 morphological classes used in their classification system. This in turn was based on sperm-head silhouette described as either normal, small, large, round, pear, narrow, taper, flame, ghost or double. The measurements also included stain content, length, width, perimeter, area, and some arithmetically derived combinations. For example, 'each sperm was optically sectioned at right angles to its major axis to give a measure of lengthwise heterogeneity of shape' (Moruzzi *et al.* 1988). They believed their classification procedure 'distinguished normal from abnormal sperm with 95% accuracy and correctly assigned 86% of the sperm to one of the ten shape classes'. They also came to the view that 'morphology is a more sensitive indicator of damage than is sperm count', a new suggestion which, if supported, would have important implications for the diagnosis of male infertility.

Since then, however, others have questioned the idea. By 1992 Davis and his colleagues were fairly sure of the negative implications, but not so sure of the positive. They wrote:

> Although some research has failed to show a correlation between abnormal morphology and IVF fertilisation rate, or embryo cleavage, numerous studies have reported positive correlations between sperm morphology and disease, infertility, and exposure to reproductive toxins or hazards. Most clinicians believe that knowledge of sperm morphology is important in diagnosing and treating male infertility.
>
> (Davis *et al.* 1992)

Whether this belief is justified is not yet known.

Sperm motility was another area of intense investigation. Having studied sperm numbers and quality, it was an entirely natural step to study how and to what extent these two factors were related to their most famous form of behaviour, namely swimming. This was particularly important to the long-term goals of sex predetermination because of the long-entrenched idea that Ys could move faster than Xs and thus get there first – one of the theories underlying the interpretation of results in the timing studies. Again with the help of sophisticated technology, scientists were able to reconstruct spermatozoan trajectories, to make detailed measurements of them, to calculate pathways and comparative speeds, and thereby derive a measure of 'progressive motility' or 'progressiveness'.

By the mid-1990s, much more was known about spermatozoa than had been even a few years previously. But, in spite of the intensive study and superb technology, nothing has been published about differences between Xs and Ys, except that on average Xs are larger. No differences have been reported in numbers, shape, general motility or progressiveness between X- and Y-chromosome-bearing spermatozoa. Contemporary British scientists who have spent decades studying spermatozoa write little about the determination of the sex of the offspring. They note only that adjustment of the sex ratio is likely to be 'achieved by the female' and cite the various ways in which this could be done. These include 'selective transport or access of X and Y sperm to the egg before fertilization' and 'selective passage of X and Y sperm through the outer egg layers during fertilization' (Baker and Bellis 1995, 78). But so far no one knows for sure whether either of these is relevant or not.

SEX SELECTION CLINICS

Although the most intense effort to describe X and Y spermatozoa had to await the arrival of new technologies in the late 1980s and early 1990s, a group of scientists appeared to have separated them in the early 1970s by the albumin column method (Ericsson et al. 1973). Having discovered a way of doing so without damaging the spermatozoa, they offered the technique to couples who wanted to select the sex of their next infant. Broadly speaking, the process involves washing, dilution and centrifugation of the sperm sample before layering it over albumin columns, leaving it for a period of time, aspirating the lower layer, centrifuging again, re-suspending in solution and then re-layering. Different times, speeds and solutions characterize the different protocols, depending on the sex of the infant desired.

Twenty years later Beernink and Dmowski (two of Ericsson's clinical colleagues) described the cumulative results of using this technique for a total of 1407 births. Refinements to the technique over time resulted in either 71 per cent or 76 per cent of parents getting what they wanted, depending on the technique employed (Beernink *et al.* 1993).

Pyrzak (1994) attempted to explain the seeming success of the albumin column method. He said:

> Recently it was reported (Cui and Matthews 1993) that X-bearing spermatozoa are larger than Y-bearing spermatozoa. This may affect the weight, speed, and the surface area of the spermatozoa. The albumin gradient method is based on the differences in the density and viscosity between the albumin fractions. If there is a difference between X- and Y-bearing spermatozoa, this may explain why the Y-bearing spermatozoa reach the bottom fraction of the high density albumin faster than the X-bearing spermatozoa.
>
> (Pyrzak 1994)

Pyrzak also said that with hindsight it was clear that the smaller the final proportion of the total sample, the more likely a male offspring. When the recovery of total motile spermatozoa was as low as 0.4 per cent to 5 per cent, he said the ratio of offspring was 15:1 male/female. When the recovery increased to between 5 per cent and 10 per cent, the ratio was 8:1 male/female. When it was greater than 10 per cent, the ratio fell to 2:1. Overall the total offspring of those wanting a male and bearing an infant was 81 per cent male and 19 per cent female.

While Pyrzak's results thus supported Ericsson's theory and methods, there were many other scientists whose work did not. As Ericsson himself reported in the same issue of *Human Reproduction*, in the 20 years following their 1973 paper describing the albumin method of separating Xs and Ys, 102 papers using as subjects seven different mammalian species have been published in the scientific literature. Yet the topic continues to be deeply controversial. Ericsson, clearly still a strong believer in his methods, wrote about the inadequacies of others' attempts to prove him wrong:

> Papers that do not duplicate the methods and materials obviously cannot confirm or not confirm work of others. Papers without valid sample sizes, or without adequate controls, or that selectively evaluate spermatozoa or fertilized eggs are to be dismissed summarily.
>
> (Ericsson 1994)

Furthermore, he is not without scientific caution. More than 20 years of research have made him soberly aware that 'sex selection is still capable of springing biological surprises'. On the other hand critics of his methods have found little evidence to support him. According to Martin (1994), 'not a single controlled study on the sex ratio in newborns following the use of the albumin technique in spermatozoa has been published . . . reports on livebirth data have all come from Ericsson. None have been confirmed by independent laboratories.'

Although the scientific controversy continues, Ericsson's methods are applied in 65 clinics across the United States and in Europe. Many thousands of hopeful couples go for advice and help to select the sex of their infant. The clinics are privately owned, and people pay.

For all Ericsson's claims to methodological excellence, there may still be a major fault in the design of his research trials. A fundamental question yet to be addressed is: Even if X and Y spermatozoa are being successfully separated by Ericsson's method, does that mean that an infant of the desired sex will necessarily be conceived? The maternal dominance hypothesis would say no. If some factor within the mother provides for differential access for spermatozoa, then exposing her to any number of spermatozoa of the kind she is not providing access for will make no difference.

Suppose that 100 women come to the clinic, each seeking a male infant. Suppose that all their partners provide sperm samples and every one is reliably and accurately treated by the albumin gradient method (or any other method) so that it is 100 per cent Y-enriched. (This is a hypothetical, best-case scenario and not what Ericsson or anyone else has claimed.) Finally, suppose that every woman who conceives and bears a child has a male infant. What more would one need to know to be sure that the sex of the infant was predetermined solely by the arrival of a Y sperm? The obvious 'answer' is: How many of the women became pregnant? If only half the women conceived and bore males, one could argue that the only women to become pregnant were those who would have conceived males anyway. In terms of the maternal dominance hypothesis, only those women who were physiologically and psychologically suited to conceiving males would have done so. The women who were not receptive to Y chromosome bearing spermatozoa simply would not conceive at all.

To rule out the possibility that the sex of the infant was under the control of the mother, it would be necessary to demonstrate that *all* the women who were impregnated with Y-chromosome-enriched semen conceived and bore sons. If the sex of the infant is under the control of the mother, then none of the data presented so far on the results of separating Xs and Ys is strong enough to dispute it. It would only be so if failure to conceive could be reliably attributed to reasons other than the sex of the infant. But this is currently an impossible stipulation. Reproductive physiologists have already shown, in the context of trying to establish the primary sex ratio, that less than 30 per cent of conceptions go on to the implantation stage, and even fewer progress beyond that. At present it would be very difficult to calculate how many conceptions 'should' be male under the conditions Ericsson offers. So the problems remain. All that can be said is that until scientists report the exact number of women coming in for treatment, and what happened to every one of them in any particular trial, it will be hard to be convinced of the efficacy of any method.

It is rare to find research reports in which these numbers are presented, but there are some. One is the work on natural family planning and timing of intercourse – see, for example, John France's work, already described in Chapter 4. It should also be noted in passing that trials of this method with ungulates, rather than primates, have been better documented, and may be more successful. It is likely that the predetermination of the sex of the offspring is the result of a somewhat different process in these animals. Chance may even play a role. Nevertheless, in a complete review of the research in this field, D. P. Windsor and his colleagues of the departments of Veterinary Physiology and Animal Science at the University of Sydney concluded that 'None of the many separation techniques proposed to date for use in livestock has proved to be consistently reproducible' (Windsor *et al.* 1993). They note that a 'possible exception to this is cell sorting by flow cytometry', but that the technique is not yet sufficiently well developed to be sure.

NARROW WINDOWS OF OPPORTUNITY

Within the group of scientists working with spermatozoa is a small subgroup investigating the movement of sperm within the female reproductive tract. Sperm chemotaxis, they explain, 'is a response of motile cells to the gradient of a chemical stimulus, resulting in modulation of the direction of travel either to approach an attractant or to retreat from a repellant' (Eisenbach and Tur-Kaspa 1994). These scientists from Israel explain how the seemingly conflicting results from previous work on the topic might make sense. They and others have noticed that only a small number of spermatozoa are chemotactic (i.e. responsive to the fluid in the female) at any one time, and they wonder if the fertilizing spermatozoon must be one from this small, continuously changing group. They suggest that, unlike other species in which the role of chemotaxis is to convey as many spermatozoa as possible to the egg, in humans it may have a slightly different function, namely 'to select the fertilising spermatozoa and to ensure their continuous availability for an extended period of time'.

Eisenbach and Tur-Kaspa, like many others, use the concept of the 'narrow window of opportunity'. In this case, they use the phrase to describe the fact that the chemical concentration has to be exactly right for the chemotactic effect to be observed. Other workers in reproductive physiology use the narrow window concept to describe limitations on timing, and still others to describe a combination of factors that may be related to conception. Most of this work has been done in the investigation of infertility, especially in the lower animals. It begins to look as though the process of fertilization depends not only on a large number of different factors, but on these factors themselves all being at just the right stage or state at a critical moment in time. It is this that some biologists call the 'narrow window of opportunity' for conception, and it is possible that it also applies to the predetermination of the sex of the offspring. If it did, then the findings on several different aspects of the sex ratio – including those on the timing of intercourse, and perhaps coital rate – might begin to be seen as contributing helpful pieces of the puzzle.

The subject matter of this book is confined to mammals and, within this order, almost exclusively to ungulates and primates. But in referring to the phrase 'narrow window of opportunity' it seems reasonable to point out that this concept is taken seriously by zoologists working at all levels of the animal hierarchy. For example, just the right temperature, from within a narrow range, determines the sex of the offspring in alligators: 'Alligator eggs incubated at 30 degrees centigrade develop into females, but eggs incubated at 33 degrees centigrade develop into males' (Haig 1991). Apparently this is because temperature 'affects the developmental rate of some tissues more than others'. The 'embryos develop as males if a male-inducing signal is produced before the gonads become insensitive to the signal'. Thus, not only does the timing have to be just right for the development of a male or a female, but so does the temperature.

Zoologists have made what David Haig calls 'a convenient distinction' between 'species with genotypic sex determination, in which females and males have different genotypes, and species with environmental sex determination, in which individuals of the same genotype can develop as males or females depending on environmental conditions' (Haig 1991). Naturally all the mammals are firmly in the category of genotypic sex determination. But if the maternal dominance hypothesis is true it could be said that there is more than a hint of environmental sex determination even in primates. (For further discussion of this idea see Chapter 8, pages 156–63, and later sections in this chapter on stress and female testosterone.)

The conditions at conception clearly need to be perfect. Time, temperature, chemical environment, sperm morphology and motility, and all the complex development of the ovum and its surrounding structures in the female reproductive tract – each must be exactly right, functioning perfectly and in synchrony with all the others. No wonder it is taking so long to unravel the mysteries. The moment when every part of it comes together seems aptly described as the narrow window of opportunity.

EARLY RATIFICATION OF THE SEX OF THE INFANT

Throughout this book the term 'sex determination' is used to describe what happens at the point of conception, and 'sex predetermination' to describe the conditions which prevail immediately before conception which may influence the sex of the infant. This implies that a series of events prior to conception may be important in deciding the sex of the infant. In addition, there are factors which may be relevant to the ratification of the sex of the embryo after conception, especially in the first 40 days of life. This is why many researchers think it is misleading to view the determination of the sex of the offspring as a discrete event.

In recognition of this, and in order to fill out an aspect of the maternal dominance hypothesis which otherwise would go unaccounted for, it is necessary to go back and trace the development of ideas about how the sex of the infant is ratified after conception.

In 1969, *New Scientist* published an article entitled 'Struggling into manhood'. It was written by Graham Chedd, the life science editor at that time. He had attended a Royal Society symposium on 'The Determination of Sex' and was reporting on the collective findings.

The scientists at this symposium had found an entirely new way of viewing the development of the sex of the foetus in the uterus. The main message was that for the foetus to develop successfully as a male, something additional had to happen to it. If this additional something did not happen, it remained a female. Professor A. Jost, of the Laboratoire de Physiologie Comparée, Paris, is quoted as saying:

Even if the Y chromosome is present in a tiny foetus, that foetus is still far from home and dry on the male side of the fence. It has to force its maleness on a body and brain which are only too inclined to choose the path to femininity.

Another scientist, Professor Dorothy Price, of the University of Leiden, said: 'The problem for the foetus is to go in one direction or the other; the problem for the researcher is to find out how it does' (both cited in Chedd 1969).

Thus it began to appear that the determination of the sex of the infant might not be a 'one-off' event. Even if the ovum had been fertilized by a Y-chromosome-bearing sperm, the foetus would not develop as a normal male unless this maleness was somehow ratified before the sixth week of pregnancy. If this did not occur, the offspring would probably abort spontaneously. Since it was not clear what the nature of that ratification might be, there was room for the possibility that it might be under maternal control.

The scientists were saying that this critical point in the development of the sex of the foetus took place in the fourth or fifth week of gestation. It was as though the sex of the infant had to be ratified in some way at this very early stage of life. They said it was 'the first and most crucial decision' and that it was 'akin to a switch being thrown'. It was the nature of the all-important switch which occupied their minds.

At the time this provided an interesting and useful theoretical solution for a problem in the maternal dominance hypothesis. It supported the idea that dominance would need to be stable over time, and corresponded with the theoretical differences between state and trait in the research on personality. Being dominant for a day or so, perhaps in reaction to a specific event, would not necessarily lead to the conception of a male infant. Reproductive physiologists' new theories on the development of sex in the very early stages of pregnancy provided a way of thinking about dominance and its postulated hormonal substrate. Whatever the hormone, it might need to be consistently present in a critical amount for a minimum period of time. If dominance were more transitory than that, then it would be insufficient, not only to conceive a male infant, but also to provide the kind of environment necessary for ratification and early development.

Many years later, Ursula Mittwoch questioned the switch idea. In the human male foetus Sertoli cells begin secreting an important sex-determining substance at about the seventh or eighth week of uterine life. For some time it was thought that this was the first sex-determining event after conception. But Mittwoch noticed that the rate of growth of

XY gonads was faster than that of XX gonads *before* the formation of Sertoli cells. Like other scientists working in this area, much of her work was done with rats: 'Measurement of gonadal volumes in rat embryos aged 13.5 days showed XY larger than XX litter mates, although no histological difference was detectable. The average difference in volume was 40%, rising to 63% and 112% on days 14.5 and 15.5 respectively' (Mittwoch 1989). This, she said, strongly suggested 'different developmental rates initiated at an earlier age'. It explained why the switch idea was not good enough, because the 'presence or absence of Sertoli cells is not the first phenotypic difference' in development.

As a result of this work, Mittwoch proposed a new model 'in which gonad differentiation depends on developmental thresholds. The formation of Sertoli cells needs to occur by a particular stage in time in a sufficiently developed gonad, failing which the gonad will enter the ovarian pathway' (Mittwoch 1989). More recently she has also suggested that this early development of male zygotes could confer an advantage at implantation (Mittwoch 1996).

Thus the 'default pathway' model of the late 1960s retained its currency for several decades. It was reinstated in a refined form in 1990 in a paper in *Nature*. Gubbay and his colleagues from the National Institute for Medical Research in London described their work on the sex-determining region of the mouse Y chromosome. They drew again on the 'switch' idea – 'Whether an animal develops into a male or a female depends on a switch mechanism' – and wondered whether the switch could be genetically controlled in mammals where a gene on the Y chromosome is responsible for male development. This gene is called TDF in humans and Tdy in mice.

> In eutherian mammals, evidence suggests that sex determination is equivalent to testis determination . . . The ovarian pathway can be thought of as the normal or 'default' pathway, and the consequence of expression of Tdy in the male is to switch the fate of the supporting cell precursors in the indifferent gonad (genital ridge) from that of follicle cells to that of Sertoli cells.
>
> (Gubbay *et al.* 1990)

During the 1990s further clues have been discovered, all pointing to the possibility of sex differences at a much earlier stage than had been thought. In a review paper, German scientist Sven Krackow (1995) cites findings from four different research teams, which provide evidence from mice and cattle 'that male blastocysts develop at a higher rate than female ones prior to implantation'. Two Finnish researchers concluded from their work with mouse embryos that variations in embryonal energy metabolism during the pre-implantation stage could be due to sex differences (Peippo and Bredbacka 1995). And a team of reproductive physiologists from Spain noticed that there is evidence to support the same phenomenon in humans. Their data suggest that 'sex selection may be inadvertently performed in IVF-embryo transfer programmes when selecting for high quality embryos at the fresh transfer cycles' – 'high quality' meaning simply having developed a little faster (Tarin *et al.* 1995).

The mystery about what has to happen to set the direction toward the development of one sex or the other, after conception, has yet to be solved. Scientists have found evidence for contributions from the sex-determining gene, as well as from cells in the developing embryo. Indeed, to maintain clarity, scientists must now refer to three separate but related areas of sexual development in the embryo. First there is genetic sex, which is 'determined by its chromosomal constituents, the most important of which is the sex-determining gene'; second is gonadal sex or testis formation, which 'is thought to be determined by this gene and by other secondary pathways'; and third is phenotypic sex, the development of the internal and external genitalia, promoted by hormones produced by the male gonad. A review entitled 'Male sex determination' (Gustafson and Donahoe 1994) describes current thinking.

The studies mentioned above are but a small sample of a vast and complex research area, and in no way representative of it. They are cited here to illustrate the many dimensions of sex determination, which scientists already know include variables in structure, composition, environment and timing, as well as genetics and biochemistry.

THE PRIMARY SEX RATIO AND SPONTANEOUS ABORTIONS

In general it is hard to find explanations for unusual sex ratios. One that is sometimes offered is that the primary sex ratio (numbers of male and female conceptions) might be much higher than the secondary sex ratio (numbers of male and female births). Since this is likely to be true, some have argued that researchers studying altered birth sex ratios ought to focus first on what was happening during pregnancy. Male vulnerability has been well documented at every stage of the lifespan (see, for example, Gualtieri and Hicks 1985), including the antenatal phase. If the primary sex ratio was the same as the secondary sex ratio, one would expect that mothers whose pregnancies coincided with stressful times would be more likely to lose male embryos and therefore the secondary sex ratio would be lower than normal. But in humans the opposite appears to be the case (see Chapter 8, especially pages 156–63).

When problems concerning the determination of the sex of the infant and the sex ratio overall were proving so difficult to solve, some researchers welcomed what seemed like a more straightforward task, namely establishing the primary sex ratio. Presumably it would be necessary only to establish the sex ratio of spontaneous abortions, and then extrapolate to calculate the primary sex ratio from the results. But, as so often happens, the task was much more complicated than originally envisaged. In a notable paper, Hassold and his colleagues at the University of Hawaii Medical School explained why earlier findings may not have been sufficiently accurate. Earlier researchers had assumed that deciding the sex of an aborted embryo would be a simple matter, but it was not. First, 'tissue expelled in association with a spontaneous abortion frequently does not include a recognizable fetus even though other products of conception may be clearly visible'; second, 'among young fetuses the prominence of the clitoris makes it difficult to distinguish macroscopically between male and female abortuses'; and, most important, 'no less than one half of all abortions are chromosomally abnormal' (Hassold et al. 1983).

In addition to these confounding factors, Hassold and his colleagues were the first to notice that conflicting results from other workers might be accounted for by their failure to discriminate between foetal cells and maternal cells. In their own work, they immediately changed tactics to eliminate this possible source of confusion. 'Whenever possible,' they wrote, 'parental blood samples were obtained and the fetal and parental heteromorphisms examined by two independent observers. A sample was considered to represent a conception if the heteromorphisms differed . . . from those of the mother.'

Taking into consideration all the reliable work done up till that time, as well as their own careful studies conducted over a period of years, the authors concluded that the primary sex ratio is indeed higher than the secondary sex ratio. More spontaneous abortions are male, and therefore more males must be conceived in the first place. The authors also cited evidence 'which indicates that at least 40% of all human conceptions spontaneously abort after implantation, with the majority terminating before the time of clinical recognition'. Further, they note, 'It is not yet possible to estimate the incidence of pre-implantation loss in our species or the sex ratio among such conceptions.' Their best estimate of the sex ratio for chromosomally normal foetuses surviving implantation was 115:100, significantly higher than the live-birth sex ratio of 105:100.

A higher primary sex ratio does not present a problem for the maternal dominance hypothesis. The mechanisms involved may be likened to a thermostat, a simile already used by Robert Trivers in a related context (see Chapter 7). Similar reasoning applies: if one assumed that female testosterone was the critical hormone, and that it must rise above a particular threshold for a male infant to be conceived, the position of the actual threshold, and how high or how low it was set, would be simply a question about levels, not a question about whether there is a threshold. If the male is more vulnerable, even from the moment of conception, the threshold for the conception of a male would have to be set a little above the mean so that more male infants were conceived in the first place. This happy arrangement appears to go on into life after birth, where, as many commentators have noted, the more adventurous lives of younger men would otherwise have left an imbalance of the sexes at the optimum time for mating. As it is, the numbers are equal when it matters.

DIET AND 'PRE-CONCEPTUAL SEX SELECTION'

The best-known names associated with this idea are Joseph Stolkowski, of the Université Pierre et Marie Curie in Paris, and his collaborator, Jacques Lorrain, of the Hôpital Sacré Coeur in Montreal. To begin with, Lorrain apparently read a number of papers published in German language journals which

> showed that the phenomenon of sex distribution is linked, in certain aquatic animals, to concentrations in potassium/calcium and magnesium ions, from an outside environment; the greater the potassium/alkaline–ash ratio, the greater the incidence of male offspring; the smaller the ratio, the greater the incidence of female offspring.
>
> (Lorrain 1975)

The 'aquatic animals' may have been toads, although the authors later refer to sea urchins as well. Similar alterations to the sex ratio had been reported by Stolkowski in 1970, in 'bovines' which had been given sodium chloride lumps to lick.

These two authors later collaborated in research involving diet with humans. Although they knew that Shettles' theories about the pH of the uterine environment had been discredited, they wondered, on the basis of the research with animals, whether some other chemical attribute of the female reproductive tract could be relevant, providing differential access for X or Y spermatozoa. In a paper published in the *International Journal of Gynaecology and Obstetrics*, they reasoned thus:

> In superior animals, and more specifically in bovines it has been shown that the more the potassium/calcium and magnesium ratio increases in the diet, the more male births there are; and the more this ratio decreases, the more female births there are. Therefore, food intake prior to fertilization must be considered.
>
> (Stolkowski and Lorrain 1980)

In an addendum to the 1975 paper, Lorrain gave examples of a typical day's food for the two diets. Each consisted of common foods, except that the diet for girls was to be supplemented with 500 milligrams of calcium per day.

There is no doubt about the scientific orientation of these researchers. The mere fact that they published the details of their diets in a scientific journal for all to see puts them into the non-commercial category. But what of their results? Like so many other workers, they claimed a success rate of over 80 per cent. The study was carried out with two groups of subjects, one living in Paris and the other in Montreal. Altogether it 'included 281 couples who volunteered to follow a diet designed for preconceptional sex selection. The women were all healthy and were aged 19–39 years. All of the couples had 1–4 children.' All the women were asked to begin the diet four to six weeks before fertilization, and husbands were asked to follow it too, for 'psychological reasons'. In the results section, the authors report that '21 couples were excluded because they did not want to follow the strict diet, because they discontinued the diet before becoming pregnant or because they had secondary reactions to the diet' (Stolkowski and Lorrain 1980). For example, four women who were on the high salt (boy) diet 'experienced water retention'.

Overall, however, 'of the 36 couples studied by Stolkowski, 31 (86%) conceived a fetus of the anticipated sex, and of the 224 couples studied by Lorrain, 181 (81%) conceived a fetus of the predetermined sex'. According to the authors, 'Success depended largely on the seriousness with which the participants stuck to the prescribed diet.' These results led the authors to the conclusion that selection between spermatozoa must occur somewhere in the genital tract or even by the ovum itself. Without saying so in so many words, their work implied at least some maternal control over the sex ratio.

If their results were indeed as they appear, this could be an important finding. It could mean that whatever the mechanisms at work to predetermine the sex of the infant, they can be disrupted or modified by changing the chemical environment. But a serious question mark hangs over the issue of whether a highly distorted diet would defeat the body's natural mechanisms of homeostasis. As Levin (1987) asked: 'Do the imbalances actually change the plasma levels of the ions, let alone at the level of the ovum'? It is perhaps not beyond the bounds of possibility, if the mechanisms are as finely tuned as they appear to be, that an exaggerated diet could produce small but significant temporary changes in chemical balance. This is a researchable question, for which there is already a suitable animal model, but so far it remains unanswered.

Leaving that aside, is there anything in the methodology of the work which should be questioned? As with similar studies, it is important to know how many women did not become pregnant. A little doubt springs up around the word 'included' used in the very first sentence of their 'materials and methods' section. The authors say that 'the study included 281 couples'. If this is the entire sample size, then their dropout rate, 21 couples, is very small. If however, they have deliberately used the word 'included' rather than, say, 'consisted of', in order to get round the problem of not reporting on those women who failed to become pregnant at all during the course of the study, then this is a serious omission. In terms of the overall credibility of the results, it would have been helpful to include a table showing in detail what happened to every couple who agreed to join the programme. It would add to credibility if numbers were given for spontaneous abortions, miscarriages and twins. Since at least some of these would occur in any normal sample of 100 conceptions, let alone 281, their omission leaves important questions unanswered.

TESTOSTERONE IN WOMEN

Since testosterone is the linchpin on which the argument of this book depends, some information should be offered on its presence and role in the human female body. As described in Chapter 3, there is already good evidence that testosterone is related to dominance in males, and there is some research which suggests that it is also related to dominance in females. But so far there is nothing in the scientific literature on reproductive physiology to associate the presence or absence of female testosterone with the predetermination of the sex of the infant. As already described above, and in Chapter 4, most of the research effort has gone either into attempts to separate X and Y spermatozoa or on the effects of timing of fertilization.

What follows is a simple description of what is known about female testosterone. It is taken from four standard clinical textbooks on reproductive endocrinology (Greenstein 1994; Griffin and Ojeda 1992; Jeffcoate 1993; Greenspan and Baxter 1994).

As already mentioned in Chapter 3, one of the first things to notice is that the substance that social scientists and journalists casually refer to as testosterone is a great deal more complex than at first appears. Androgens (male sex hormones) take several forms in the body; all have seemingly unpronounceable names – 5 α-dihydrotestosterone, androstenedione, δ-five androstenediol, dehydroepiandrosterone (DHEA) and DHEA sulphate. Of all these different forms, 'only testosterone and dihydrotestosterone have significant androgenic activity' (Greenspan and Baxter 1994, 426).

Another characteristic of testosterone which is not well understood is that it occurs in unimaginably small amounts. Everyone agrees that healthy women have about one-tenth the amount that men do. Jeffcoate (1993, 204) says that serum testosterone concentrations in women are between 0.8 and 2.7 nanomoles per litre (n mol/litre). Healthy men range between 13 and 40 n mol/litre. The mean for women is about 2 n mol/litre; for men it is about 20 n mol/litre. The normal woman of reproductive age produces 200–300 micrograms of testosterone per day, while men generate between 3 and 6 milligrams per day.

The differences between men and women are important. This is one of those rare human dimensions in which men's and women's scores do not overlap. Unlike other measurements such as height, weight or strength, where there is considerable overlap and only the means are consistently separated, here an individual woman's score would never be mistaken for a man's, and vice versa. This is not true of dominance scores on personality tests, however, and if testosterone provides the physiological basis for dominance, then this difference needs to be explained. It presents a problem for the maternal dominance hypothesis, which others have also noticed. In measuring both testosterone and personality dimensions in 200 male and female adolescents, Udry and Talbert (1988) concluded there must be a 'much greater sensitivity of female personality to testosterone'. It may be that women's tissues are more sensitive to testosterone than men's, so a smaller amount has a bigger effect.

A further complication in understanding how testosterone acts in the body is the role of a specific protein in the transport of testosterone through the circulation. This protein is made by the liver and is called sex hormone binding globulin (SHBG). About 45 per cent of the total circulating testosterone is bound to SHBG, 53 per cent is bound to albumin and only about 2 per cent is unbound (or free). Only the free portion is available to enter a target cell and express its hormonal action. In most tissues, testosterone is converted after entering the cell, to the more potent 5 α-dihydrotestosterone which becomes the active hormone.

This whole area of research is so complex that, unless scientists describe which precursor or which form of testosterone they are measuring and under what conditions they have done the measurements, it is difficult to compare results. Differences in procedure can usually account for the somewhat different figures given by different laboratories, but if work is to be replicated researchers must specify the exact form of testosterone they were measuring, how they measured it, where they took their samples from, over what period of time and at what stage in the menstrual cycle.

What is the function of testosterone in women? It is difficult to find an answer to this question. In their main chapter on the subject Griffin and Ojeda say only that testosterone is the 'primary physiologically active androgen in women' (1992, 137). Greenstein says that 'testosterone maintains libido in women' (1994, 62), and this is a view which is backed by clinical evidence. Two Canadian psychologists described 'several investigations which suggest a major role for adrenal androgens, rather than adrenal oestrogens or progestins, in sexual activity' (Gray and Gorzalka 1980). Greenspan and Baxter say that 'the physiologic significance of these small amounts of androgens is not established' (1994, 426). In general it appears there is no way of knowing whether testosterone in women is of little interest or whether it is of very great interest.

A fact of particular importance from the point of view of the maternal dominance hypothesis is where female testosterone comes from. As already mentioned in Chapter 3, in men it comes from the testes, but in women it comes from several different sources. According to Greenspan and Baxter, 'probably about one fourth is formed in the ovary' (1994, 426). Griffin and Ojeda note that in women, although some testosterone is produced in the ovary, more arises in the peripheral tissues. Again there are difficulties for measurement. Simply ascertaining the amount of testosterone in the bloodstream tells one nothing about which particular site it came from. And, as Greenspan and Baxter explain, it is extremely difficult to measure the concentration of the hormone in the blood actually flowing from the gland, or to take a measure of blood flow through the gland itself, without interfering with normal blood flow and gland activity. In general, most scientists appear to think that at least 50 per cent (and probably more) of women's testosterone arises from the peripheral conversion of androstenedione, which in turn comes from the adrenal cortex.

It has long been established that the adrenal cortex secretes the hormones that help the body respond to stress. Again the pathways are complex. Naturally, the initial response to a stressful situation involves the higher centres of the brain. As part of this response the hypothalamus signals the anterior pituitary to secrete adrenocorticotropic hormone (ACTH). The ACTH stimulates cortisol production by the adrenal cortex, thus initiating the body's response to stress. These facts lead to a key question in the maternal dominance hypothesis: Is the production of testosterone also increased in women under stress? (This point is also discussed in the last section of this chapter.)

TESTOSTERONE WITHIN THE OVARY

So far as is known, almost all the research on testosterone in women has involved taking measurements of the level of testosterone in the bloodstream, or of its excretory metabolites in urine. It has been carried out in a variety of research contexts. Most has been done to elucidate mechanisms in reproductive physiology (especially maternal serum testosterone levels during pregnancy), but some has been done in an attempt to show a relationship between behaviour and testosterone (as described in Chapter 3), and some in testing for unfair advantage in athletics and other sports.

But textbooks on endocrinology make it clear that testosterone occurs at much higher concentrations in the ovaries than it does in the bloodstream. The ovaries contain a number of different types of cells, amongst them 'a group of steroid-secreting cells that histologically resemble the Leydig, or interstitial, cells of the testes' (Greenspan and Baxter 1994, 420). The ovary itself actively makes (or synthesizes) and secretes a variety of hormones. It is a major source of oestrogen and progesterone, but it is also 'the source of small amounts of testosterone and other androgens' (1994, 420).

At the beginning of each menstrual cycle an ovum begins to develop in preparation for ovulation. It changes and develops over time, so that descriptions can never be static. Jeffcoate describes it thus: 'The ripening ovum lies within a follicle lined by several layers of granulosa cells. The stromal cells surrounding the follicle form a false capsule – the theca interna. After ovulation the follicle forms the corpus luteum' (Jeffcoate 1993, 204). Testosterone seems to play an important role in these changes. It is 'synthesized by the theca cells'. Further, 'the granulosa cells which line the ripening ovarian follicle utilize the testosterone from the theca interna . . . which in turn prepare the vaginal and cervical mucus for sperm penetration, and the endometrium for implantation of a fertilized ovum' (Jeffcoate 1993, 204). By the time the follicle reaches about 20 mm in diameter it is ready to discharge the ovum it contains from the ovary. The ovum is swept into the fallopian tube, where it is available for fertilization. Meanwhile, in the ovary 'the residual cells of the follicle reform into the corpus luteum . . . the function of which is to support the ovum in the early days after fertilization and implantation into the endometrium, before the placenta is established' (Jeffcoate 1993, 206).

Thus it seems testosterone is actively involved in the development of the ovum. Not only is it secreted by the cells lining the ovary into the follicular fluid that surrounds the developing ovum, but these testosterone-secreting theca cells continue their role as a part of the corpus luteum which helps maintain the developing embryo in the very first days of life.

Like the other authors, Greenspan and Baxter describe the growth of the thecal cells around the developing follicle. They 'align themselves concentrically outside the basement membrane' and thus 'complete the formation of the secondary follicle' (1994, 430). These authors also describe how the thecal cells become part of the corpus luteum after ovulation. They, too, emphasize the importance of the hormones 'within the follicular fluid, rather than the serum concentrations'(1994, 431). It is these on-the-spot hormones that correlate most closely with the development of both the ovum and its support systems. In particular, they note that the two major hormones (luteinizing hormone and follicle stimulating hormone – LH and FSH) are present in lower concentrations in the follicular fluid than they are in the bloodstream; but, in contrast, 'androstenedione, testosterone, dihydrotestosterone and oestradiol may be 10,000–40,000 times higher than their serum levels'. The authors complete their description by saying that it is not known whether all this is part of development, or plays 'an important role in the process that leads to selection of a single preovulatory follicle' (1994, 431).

From the point of view of the maternal dominance theory, these facts provide the context for plausible – and, more importantly, testable – hypotheses. Instead of being distracted by measuring serum testosterone, already shown to be inadequate, the focus of interest could shift to the developing ovum, the level of testosterone in the follicular fluid, the layer of thecal cells surrounding the follicle, the possibility of differential penetrability of the ovum, and the role of the corpus luteum. Ray Haning and his colleagues have already gone some way down this path. In 1993 they wrote that follicular testosterone appeared to be a major regulator of ovulation, playing a critical role in the selection and development of the dominant follicle. The wide range in normal levels of follicular testosterone is particularly helpful to the maternal dominance hypothesis, since it provides a means by which individual levels could range widely. Such inter-individual variability provides the physiological context in which the idea of a threshold amount of testosterone seems more plausible.

A number of authors (for example, Hrdy 1987) have observed that, if there is the potential for maximizing fitness by investing in one sex rather than the other, then the least wasteful time for such a mechanism to occur would be before or at conception. It would make sense for the mother to control the sex of the infant according to the demands of the environment and to do this as early as possible in the reproductive process. If she does so by producing an ovum which is particularly well suited to penetration by either an X or a Y spermatozoon, this would be compatible with almost all the major findings on the sex ratio in both animal and human research.

All of this seems so logical that it raises the question why, if it is as obvious as that, reproductive physiologists have not been doing it already. The answer is, first, that interest in female testosterone is comparatively recent. Second, as described above, scientists today do not get funding for looking in unusual directions – in this case, looking at the possibility for a role for the female in controlling the sex of her infant. And third, someone *has*, but very little attention has been paid to her work.

In 1991 Patricia Saling published a paper in *Biology of Reproduction* entitled 'How the egg regulates sperm function during gamete interaction: facts and fantasies'. Saling, a scientist attached to the departments of Obstetrics and Gynaecology and Cell Biology at Duke University Medical Center, did most of her work with mice. Although her paper is largely a description of molecular mechanisms, beyond the comprehension of lay readers, in the first few paragraphs she describes her work in broad outline. The mouse egg, which provides a good model for almost all mammalian eggs, is covered by two different layers: one is called the cumulus matrix and the other the zona pellucida, and 'Before reaching the egg plasma membrane, the fertilizing sperm must successfully travel through these [two] matrices. The outer layer, the cumulus, appears to function as a filter to select potentially fertile sperm.' Saling acknowledges that no specific interactions have been described, but suggests that characteristics of the sperm's surface might 'determine the sperm's ability to penetrate between the cells . . . ' (Saling 1991). Faulty sperm do not get past the first barrier.

Be that as it may, considerably more is known about the way the mouse sperm interacts with the next layer, the zona pellucida. In spare but elegant prose, Saling describes the complex interaction: what is known, and what remains to be discovered. Once through the outer layer of the egg, a membrane covering the sperm head is used to initiate binding to the next layer. While bound at this surface, a reaction is triggered which results in this outer membrane of the sperm head being 'fused at several sites', and this gives rise to a further chemical reaction. This reaction produces enzymes, which, 'together with the motility of the sperm', make it possible for the sperm to digest a narrow cleft through this inner layer. 'Finally, the sperm gains access to the egg plasma membrane, to which it fuses and thereby initiates fertilization' (Saling 1991).

All kinds of things can go wrong with this process, but the chief limiting factor appears to be the response of the zona pellucida, the second layer of the egg. If this does not respond appropriately the sperm is unable to penetrate. Furthermore, 'it is not unlikely that this single event, crucial to continued reproduction, is under both spatial and temporal control' – again, the narrow window of opportunity. Thus, Saling argues, it is likely that the egg has control over which sperm fertilizes it. In clinics offering assistance in reproductive physiology, this gatekeeping role of the zona pellucida is of course bypassed by artificial means, as scientists inject the sperm directly into the ovum.

There is no mention in Saling's paper of selection on the grounds of sex. Her work is cited to demonstrate the complexity of the process, the amount there is still to discover, and to show that the idea that the mother might have control of the sex of the infant is compatible with what is known in reproductive physiology.

FURTHER CLUES FROM RESEARCH WITH ANIMALS

There are obvious advantages in working with animals. Not only is it much less difficult to gain both ethics approval and access to the appropriate tissues, but the mechanisms may also be simpler – a real advantage when processes appear more and more complex. To be able to describe what happens in the mouse will be an enormously useful step on the way to describing what happens in other mammals, and finally in humans.

Work with animals is also allowing contemporary scientists to try new strategies in tackling long-standing problems concerning the heritability of the sex ratio (see also Chapter 8). Since the maternal dominance hypothesis postulates a biological basis for dominance, albeit one that is highly responsive to environmental influences, one would expect to be able to demonstrate a small inheritance effect. In humans, so much depends on random environmental events that it seems impossible to tease out the varying influences. But in animal research, where scientists have more control, it should be possible to find some evidence for heritability. If the predetermination of the sex of the infant is under the control of the mother through normally occurring variations in testosterone levels, then this ought to be demonstrable by showing how females that are born with higher levels of testosterone conceive and bear more male infants.

In some ingenious work with house mice and gerbils, this is exactly what several different teams of scientists have shown. In these animals, foetuses grow in rows along two arms of the uterus. The sexes are arranged randomly. In this work, each female foetus is designated as belonging to one of three categories, depending on the sex of her neighbours *in utero*. Those which have a male foetus on either side are called 2M mice (or gerbils); those that have a male foetus on one side of them and a female foetus on the other are labelled 1M, and those that have a female on either side, 0M. On the day before full term, Caesarean sections are done, so that each female foetus can be labelled.

Scientists have discovered that 'female foetuses that mature between males are androgenized by testosterone crossing the foetal membranes' (Clark *et al.* 1993). Their article, published in *Nature*, was entitled 'Hormonally mediated inheritance of acquired characteristics in Mongolian gerbils'. Not only were the 2M gerbils androgenized, but, when they matured, these females produced significantly more male infants. Further, 2M females 'produced a significantly greater percentage of sons throughout their reproductive lifetimes' (Clark *et al.* 1993).

John G. Vandenbergh and Cynthia Huggett, of North Carolina State University, found the same phenomenon in house mice. Reporting in the *Proceedings of the National Academy of Sciences* (1994), they said that the sex ratios of their 1M females fitted the theory too, producing an intermediate number of male infants. Of course, no one is suggesting that this is the whole story, even in mice or gerbils. The actual ratios, as always, demonstrate an effect, not a process: 'The sex ratio of the first litter born to 2M females was 58%, for 1M females was 51% and for 0M females was 42%', and the effect on the sex ratio continued into the second litter.

These findings make sense in terms of the maternal dominance hypothesis. Higher maternal testosterone meant higher sex ratios. In addition there is a consistency in subsequent litters which could reflect the limitations of the environment. In animals that are held in a uniform environment, fewer environmentally induced changes in testosterone levels would be expected, and therefore there would be more consistency in the sex ratio of a female's consecutive litters.

But there are still many parts of this puzzle to explore, and answers will not be easy. For example, one might think that the same influence would be seen in humans. After all, Resnick *et al.* (1993) found that women who had once shared the uterus with a male twin had higher scores than other women on sensation-seeking, a personality trait also likely to have a biological basis. All it would take to answer the question would be to ascertain from a good-sized twin register whether women who had a male twin have more sons than women who shared the uterus with a female twin. On a visit to Brisbane to consult with Dr Nick Martin, director of the Australian Twin Register, it took only a few minutes to establish the answer. No, they do not. In fact it was the opposite: women who shared the uterus with a female twin tended to have more sons, though the difference (as always) was very small.

The fault in the thinking probably lay in the fact that opposite-sex twins do not share a placenta, so there is less likelihood of their sharing anything except the uterine space. If this is so, then presumably an environmental explanation would need to be offered for the sensation-seeking opposite-sex female twins. Simply being brought up with a male twin may mean having a more adventurous life. Or perhaps having a mother who was dominant enough to conceive a son at the same time meant that the female twin was exposed to maternal dominance at the male end of the scale from her earliest hours. As to the higher sex ratios for monozygotic female twins, it may be that the dominant twin has more males in the next generation, and that this tendency more than counterbalances any tendency for the non-dominant twin to have daughters. But all this is speculation, for the research has not been done.

TESTOSTERONE AND MATERNAL STRESS

To complete the description of the physiological background to the maternal dominance hypothesis, some mention must be made of the stress response. I think it is most likely that there is a rise of testosterone under stress in females and that this is the proximate cause of skewed sex ratios in both human and animal populations.

Although little is known about actual mechanisms, in principle it looks as though women's testosterone could be playing an important role in keeping the sex ratio in balance through good times and bad. As described in Chapter 8, it is known that an overall rise in the stressfulness of living conditions produces more male births. This is true for both humans and animals. War, famine, disease and (especially in animals) captivity and overcrowding cause the kinds of stress that produce raised sex ratios. It is important to note that it is prolonged stress that is relevant, not the emergency 'fight or flight' short-term reaction. The effect of long-term stress on the production of testosterone is different for the two sexes: in males, it seems to be lowered (Kreuz et al. 1972; Rivier and Rivest 1991), but in females it appears to rise; and this is entirely consistent with the differing sources of testosterone in the male and female bodies, as described above. Since the adrenal cortex is involved in both the stress response and, indirectly, in the production of testosterone in women, the two may be interacting to tip the sex ratio one way or the other.

Although arguments that call on adaptiveness are notoriously slippery, any system which helped females withstand stress by making them temporarily a little tougher during hard times would make intuitive sense. Furthermore, producing more males in tough times makes sense both ways. In most primate and ungulate species, males are both more likely to defend the habitat, risking their lives in the process, and more likely to seek new habitats, again with attendant risks. Thus more males are needed for the species to survive. From the female side, fewer females mean fewer births, which again is more adaptive in terms of having fewer young and inexperienced animals to both feed and defend during hard times. This has been demonstrated in both animal and human research. Such a system can be plausibly argued at the population level, but it needs to be demonstrated at the level of the individual.

Reproductive physiologists already know a little about how the stress response affects reproduction in individual women, although the word 'stress' is used rather broadly. For example, it is known that young women who train strenuously in running, swimming or dancing have delayed menarche as well as secondary amenorrhoea. The same applies to women who are severely undernourished. (For a review of this work, see Gray 1992.) They do not conceive at all. Stress during pregnancy, often related to life events and work pressures, appears to increase the possibility of premature and low birthweight infants. High sex ratios among such births are usually interpreted as part of the male vulnerability package. But some clinicians think that women who experience prolonged stress, particularly of a psychological nature, tend to develop polycystic ovaries which in turn are associated with increased testosterone production. As a consequence, cycles may become irregular and the women are less fertile.

If this is correct, it would provide the middle link in a stepped series that goes from normal conditions, in which testosterone is either normally distributed or only slightly skewed, resulting in normal sex ratios; to slightly higher sex ratios, reflecting slightly more than usual testosterone in a population in which living conditions are tough; to abnormally high sex ratios, seen in some disorders and associated with increased spontaneous abortion; and finally to women's reproductive physiology being so disrupted they do not conceive at all. At the other end of the series, low sex ratios may reflect comfortable times and, in some populations, older mothers (see, for example, Moeller 1996, although he interprets his data differently).

If the facts bear out such a progression, it may provide a clue to the mystery of male vulnerability. In a major article in *Behavioral and Brain Sciences*, Gualtieri and Hicks described how 'males are selectively afflicted with virtually every neurologic, psychiatric and developmental disorder of childhood', and said that 'this phenomenon is largely unexplained' (1985). If more males are conceived at a time when mothers are at the upper limits of conceiving at all, because of stressful conditions, then such males may be disadvantaged from the beginning.

The most persuasive support for such a model comes from animal studies (see Chapter 7, pages 128–31). There is also a little experimental evidence concerning the relationship between stress and testosterone production in pregnant animals. A team of scientists from the University of Missouri-Columbia, led by F. S. Vom Saal, has been working in this area for more than a decade, using the mouse as their experimental animal. In 1990 they published a paper in *Biology of Reproduction* which demonstrated how the known effects of having a male on either side of a female foetus (described in the section above) made no difference to the fact that testosterone rose in all foetuses if the mothers were stressed during pregnancy. Unfortunately, from the point of view of the ideas being presented here, all the mice were sacrificed during the experiment. It would have been interesting to discover whether this procedure, with its associated rise in testosterone, led to higher sex ratios in the next generation. As it is, this research has still to be done. The key result from the work as it stands is that only the testosterone levels changed as a result of the stress. No other hormones were involved.

Thus most of the known changes in both animal and human sex ratios could be explained in terms of the physiological processes underlying them. Under normal circumstances, testosterone levels in the female would remain relatively constant and normally distributed. Those females whose testosterone levels were above the mean would conceive and bear sons; those whose testosterone levels were just below would conceive and bear daughters. Every woman's testosterone levels would vary within a limited range, according to influences from the social and physical environments. Those women whose testosterone levels were either high or low (perhaps outside one standard deviation from the mean) would tend to conceive infants of the same sex in spite of moderate changes in level. For the majority of women, variations of the same order in the level of testosterone would take them either side of the mean, and result in their conceiving infants of both sexes.

But in times of war, famine, disease or other stressful conditions, all women might be required to be a little tougher, just to survive. As already described, the production of testosterone appears to have a toughening effect on personality in both men and women. It is likely that men's greater toughness is, at least in part, a result of their much greater amount of testosterone. The fact that in females (but not in males) the greater proportion of testosterone is produced indirectly through the adrenal cortex – the gland that secretes cortisol, which helps the body react to stress – makes it plausible that testosterone in females would rise under stress. There is both animal and human research which supports this. If a whole community is subjected to prolonged stress this could lead to a slightly higher mean testosterone in women, resulting temporarily in a higher number of male conceptions.

It could also be argued that male foetuses conceived by females who were only temporarily over the critical threshold for conceiving a male, especially during tough times, might be especially vulnerable. As is described in Chapter 7, this suggestion could make sense of the otherwise conflicting results in the animal literature on variations in the sex ratio.

Almost all exploratory ideas in science seem clumsy. They are presented here simply to demonstrate that the maternal dominance hypothesis does not run counter to research in reproductive physiology. In some areas the hypothesis complements the findings, and in others it is highly compatible with them. Such concordance is important because, no matter how much theorizing there is by social scientists it is the reproductive physiologists, and they alone, who will be able to describe what actually happens.

6

DOMINANCE IN ANIMALS

In a book which claims that a biological mechanism within the mother is likely to be the key factor in the predetermination of the sex of the infant, it would add credibility if the same kind of mechanism could be shown to be operating in other mammals. In fact there was a surge of support for this idea in the early 1980s, when zoologists began publishing papers which showed that an animal's position on a dominance hierarchy is related to the sex of the offspring. Some of the highest-profile studies even showed that dominant females produced more male offspring – the same effect as in humans.

On closer inspection, however, the research findings were not as clear as originally thought. In some settings, dominant mothers produced significantly more female infants. Furthermore, it seemed there was confusion about the meaning and usage of the word 'dominant'. Sometimes it was used to mean a quality or characteristic of an animal, but more frequently it was used to describe an animal's position on a dominance hierarchy. This ambiguity meant that the relationship between dominance and sex ratios in animals needed more detailed analysis.

The formal study of dominance in animals goes back to the 1930s. Abraham Maslow, a psychologist who later became famous for his work on self-actualizing human beings, started by describing the role of dominance in the social and sexual behaviour of non-human primates. In 1935 he presented a paper at a meeting of the American Psychological Association in which he outlined the differences in 'dominance-quality' between anthropoid apes, Old World monkeys and New World monkeys.

Maslow's descriptions of dominance were untainted by worries about anthropomorphism. For example, he wrote that in Old World monkeys dominance is 'a powerful, persistent, selfish urge that expresses itself in ferocious bullying', but in anthropoid apes, by contrast, the dominant animal is more like a 'friend and protector'.

The dominant male would often tease the subordinate female to the point of complete exasperation. In such cases she would fly into a towering, screaming rage, and chase him about the cage in an attempt to vent her annoyance on him, he would run away laughing.

(Maslow 1940)

This work was controversial. Because of disagreements between Maslow and 'two notable authorities in the field', its publication was delayed for five years.

The dangers of anthropomorphism are doubtless impressed on every beginning zoologist. Students must be warned against recording what they assume an animal might be 'feeling', much less why it might be feeling it. Here there is an obvious parallel with the emergence of behaviourism in psychology, in which psychologists argued that the only way to make the study of human behaviour scientific was to restrict all analyses to what could be seen and confirmed; in other words to outward, visible behaviour. This would remove the problem of interpretation of feelings and thus bring some much-needed ratifiability to human data. Unfortunately for behaviourists, there are many occasions in the study of both humans and other primates when to ignore the invisible is to ignore what is important.

In this case, shifting from anthropomorphism to behaviourism solved one problem, but gave rise to another. While Maslow appears to have been describing a quality or characteristic of an individual, the change to describing actions led to a subtle shift in the way researchers viewed dominance. Instead of using the word 'dominance' to describe an inherent capacity within the individual it was used to describe a characteristic of a relationship. (This is understandable, since dominance is most easily discerned in the context of a relationship, but since it is inherent it exists independently and may be seen in other contexts, as explained below.) This shift in meaning was later to cause confusion, which, in some quarters, has yet to be dispelled. For example, Moore (1990), having demonstrated that dominant male cockroaches typically produce dominant offspring, described his finding as an example of 'the inheritance of social dominance'. This suggestion was hotly debated in the journal *Animal Behaviour* for several years, but perhaps could have been solved by clarifying the terminology (see Capitanio 1991; Moore 1991; Dewsbury 1991; Moore 1993; Barrette 1993; Dewsbury 1993).

In describing the work on dominance in animals it is necessary, therefore, to differentiate between the ways in which the word has been used. 'Dominance' tends to refer to an inherent capacity of an individual. In writing about the characteristics of a relationship, usually between two animals, the phrase 'social dominance' is often used; when writing about relationships within or between groups, the phrase 'dominance rank' or 'dominance hierarchy' is used. Even with these definitions there is considerable overlap, so it is difficult to be entirely consistent.

At first sight it might appear that defining dominance in animals would be easier than it is in humans. Animals are not self-conscious, and behaviours are generally more basic and open. Experienced zoologists, especially the primatologists and other trained observers of animal behaviour, appear to have little or no trouble in agreeing on the significant indicators of dominance for any given animal species. So the basic reason for the difficulties in terminology is not simply about which behaviours indicate dominance, but about which perspective to take when describing them. Are the behaviours indicative of an inherent capacity, or are they indicative of a particular kind of relationship?

Three further caveats are required in any discussion of dominance in animals. The first is the question about how captivity affects behaviour. It is especially relevant to the interpretation of results in the study of dominance and animal sex ratios (as discussed in Chapter 7) and also to a number of other issues in the study of animal behaviour. Since the late 1980s, for both humanitarian and scientific reasons, researchers like C. T. Snowdon (1994) have developed new criteria for the provision of naturalistic environments. These go beyond physical welfare and provide for psychological wellbeing. This places animal behaviourists in a curious dilemma. Since captivity ('under good but not extravagant conditions' – Beck and Castro 1994, 269) is far less stressful than life in the wild, to what extent should researchers toughen the conditions to mimic those of the wild? This question is of importance in releasing threatened species back into the wild, and may also be important when considering the effects of captivity on dominance. It is likely that social groupings and the way they are constituted will be among the most important environmental considerations.

The second is the different research emphasis adopted by animal behaviourists on the one hand, and psychologists on the other. While psychologists continued to favour environmental explanations of individual differences, animal behaviourists tended to favour physiological explanations. This difference was described by A. H. Buss (1988) in a detailed study of the personality traits which humans share with animals. According to him there are seven. Three of these are concerned with 'activation': activity, fearfulness and impulsiveness. The other four are to do with social behaviour: sociability, nurturance, aggressiveness and dominance. Buss provides a thorough discussion of these attributes, drawing parallels between the human and animal manifestations of each.

One of the best predictors of the strength of some of these attributes is the sex of the animal. As one would expect, nurturance and aggressiveness show the most marked sex differences. Degree of dominance is also affected by the sex of the animal, with males rating higher, on average, than females throughout the primate world.

Buss made an important comment about the way these sex differences were viewed. He said that 'When we find sex differences in personality traits, we are more likely to examine socialization practices, cognitions, and learning for an explanation in humans but more likely to focus on hormones as an explanation in animals' (Buss 1988, 2).

The third caveat is the extent to which the word 'dominance' is used interchangeably with aggression. For example, Higley *et al.* (1996) found a significant positive correlation between free testosterone taken from cerebrospinal fluid and what they called 'different types of aggressive behaviours' in male rhesus monkeys. But, as with the human studies, the relevant behaviours were far more closely related to dominance. The authors said: 'Total aggression included socially assertive behaviours such as displacements, stares, and threats, behaviours which are typically exhibited by animals maintaining or establishing social dominance.'

Aggression may be more closely related to dominance in animals than it is in humans, but it is important to discriminate between them. Whether subjects are human or animal, and whether authors are interested in the hormonal or environmental influences on behaviour, or both, dominance needs to be described with precision.

DOMINANCE AS AN INHERENT CAPACITY OF AN INDIVIDUAL

Comparatively few zoologists have written about dominance as a personality characteristic, but in 1974 Robert A. Hinde, an internationally acknowledged expert on animal behaviour, wrote about it in his book *Biological Bases of Human Social Behaviour*. To describe dominance he drew on the work of S. Richards, who wrote a Ph.D. thesis for Cambridge University in 1972 entitled 'Tests for behavioural characteristics in rhesus monkeys'. Richards used ten different measures to assess dominance in caged animals; 'Four of these depended on priority of access to incentives, and four on behavioural signs of subordinance in the group: the other two involved the winning of agonistic interactions and the frequency of displays' (Hinde 1974, 341). In general these were all highly correlated with one another. In addition to the group observations, Richards tested individual animals in isolation. He found that 'persistence in problem solving' was also related to dominance and wondered whether this persistence might in turn be related to a lack of fear, or greater confidence in the dominant animals.

The tests for dominance done on animals in isolation are of particular interest. While the main emphasis at that time was on dominance rank, the author was describing the characteristics which might contribute to an individual's ability to maintain a high place on a dominance hierarchy.

At about the same time, Irwin S. Bernstein, a primatologist from the University of Georgia, wrote about dominance as he had come to understand it from his observations of animals in the wild. He described how alpha males (the top most dominant males) maintained their dominant positions by the use of superior social skills, not by aggression. These social skills were used primarily to maintain the cohesiveness of a central core or alliance with other males. Subsequently, this group of males from the 'central hierarchy' would 'interfere in prolonged fights within the troop, or respond to external threats from conspecifics or potential predators. What is more, these males were especially vigorous in the defence of infants'. Alpha males also had the ability 'to control the direction of troop travel (whether or not they actually led) and to control the nature of group activities' (Bernstein 1976). Having the support of the other males, they were able to respond actively to challenges to the troop and thus to 'contribute significantly to the survival of infants'. These superior social skills, said Bernstein, may have contributed to their attractiveness to females, thus increasing their reproductive effectiveness.

Several primatologists have made the point that quality of dominance may vary within different primate groups. Robin Dunbar recounts how he changed his mind about the universality of dominance. Having originally thought it was related to aggression, and therefore not relevant to some of the quieter species, he later came to see otherwise.

Despite occasional claims to the contrary, dominance hierarchies have been documented in a wide range of species at all taxonomic levels. Low frequencies of aggression originally led me to conclude that dominance was not an important factor in the social behaviour of the gelada . . . In fact, dominance hier-

archies turned out on more detailed analysis to be a characteristic of all gelada reproductive units, and their consequences
proved to be the fundamental driving force behind many of
the characteristic features of the gelada's social system.

(Dunbar 1988, 208)

Dunbar regarded dominance primarily as a relationship between two
animals. Therefore, he said, it was 'not an inheritable property as such'
(1988, 206). Clearly he did not perceive dominance as a biologically
based characteristic of an individual. Nevertheless, he wrote a most
useful description of dominance in animals, distinguishing between
dominance as a characteristic of an individual, and social dominance as
a characteristic of a relationship.

We do need to be careful to distinguish between the operational use of the term 'dominance' (defined in terms of access
to a given resource) and its use as an explanatory concept (that
summarises certain salient characteristics about an individual).
An animal does not gain access to a resource because it gains
access to a resource, as an operational definition would imply:
defined thus, it merely describes what happens without
offering an explanation. Rather, an animal is dominant
because it can bring greater intrinsic power to bear in keeping
competitors away. Ideally our assessment of dominance ranks
should be independent of resources for which the animals are
competing: that is to say, our estimates of dominance rank
should reflect the animals' respective *capacities* to defeat other
individuals, not simply a statement of whether or not it did so.
Where this capacity (or power) is a simple function of some
biological attribute like size, this obviously poses few problems.
But the ability to dominate another individual often depends
on factors besides sheer physical power: in species as intelligent
as primates, psychological attributes may be just as important,
particularly those that allow animals to draw on extrinsic
sources of power.

(Dunbar 1988, 207)

Other primatologists came to the same conclusion as Dunbar. In a ten-
year study of olive baboons living freely in a national park in Kenya,
Robert Sapolsky and Justina Ray discovered just how sophisticated
dominance behaviours could be. The main reason for their work was to
find out more about the endocrine correlates of stress, having noticed

from other studies that dominant animals in stable hierarchies had 'lower basal circulating concentrations of glucocorticoids, the adrenal hormones secreted in response to stress' (Sapolsky and Ray 1989). In the course of this work they wrote a detailed description of the differing strategies for achieving high status.

While it was clear that all animals had raised levels of glucocorticoids during periods of hierarchical instability, they noticed that even in times of stable hierarchies not all dominant animals had low levels of glucocorticoids. Instead, they said, these low levels were a feature of a subset of dominant males with a particular style of dominance which involved 'a high degree of social skillfulness, control and predictability over social contingencies'. The dominant males were distinguished by an ability to discriminate between neutral and threatening interactions with rivals: in the latter they were most likely to initiate fights, which they then won. They were also the most able to distinguish between winning and losing a fight and, if losing, of displacing the aggression on to an innocent bystander.

Here dominance tends to shade into aggression when circumstances are tougher. Even though Sapolsky and Ray accentuate the social skills involved, they describe them in the context of struggles for status that involve not only dominance but also a repertoire of aggressive behaviours.

In another longitudinal study from the wild, Meikle and his colleagues (1984) described dominance in rhesus monkeys as 'the ability of a social group or individual to control the behaviour of others'. This description is of particular interest because it was related to one of the most accurate definitions of dominance in humans – Fiske's 'acting overtly so as to change the views or actions of another' (1971, 98). It is most unlikely that either Dr Fiske or Dr Meikle would have been aware of the other's work, much less each other's definitions of dominance – which further illustrates how work across disciplinary boundaries can be closely related.

MEASURING SOCIAL DOMINANCE AND DOMINANCE RANK

In much of the work on animals it was never the intention to measure dominance as an individual capacity: the researchers were interested in social dominance or dominance rank, both of which can be measured with fewer complications. To do this, they devise a list of behaviours assumed to indicate social dominance for the particular animal under study, then they observe the animals for lengthy periods and note how often the behaviours occur. This method of measuring dominance has been shown to be reliable, since independent observers produce highly comparable tallies. Its validity is less certain, however; it depends on a number of factors – especially the extent to which the original list of behaviours denotes the kind of dominance being measured.

Sarah Blaffer Hrdy is one of those primatologists who observed animals in the wild over a long period, including nine years in India watching and writing about the sleek, silver Hanuman langur monkeys. She was one of the first to point out that dominance is an important dimension in relationships between females as well as males. She also wrote that a simple definition of dominance in non-human primates was perfectly feasible, because 'dominance hierarchies can be recognized from observations of one-on-one interactions between individuals competing for the same desired resource'. 'Dominant', she said, is the word used to describe the animal that usually wins, 'the animal that typically can approach, threaten, and displace another' (Hrdy 1981, 3). Yet, despite this apparent simplicity, she recognized the limitations of the word. 'No one', she wrote, 'is particularly satisfied with the concept of dominance. Typically, dominance is difficult to assess and highly dependent on context' (Hrdy 1981, 3).

Other primatologists expressed similar reservations. For example, M. J. A. Simpson and A. E. Simpson at Madingley, Cambridge, spent many hours watching, recording and describing the behaviour of captive rhesus monkeys. They said that 'attacking, chasing, displacing, avoiding, fear-grinning and presenting (non-sexual, non-grooming context) between a pair of monkeys' could be regarded as evidence of dominance. But they also made the point that a simple frequency measure would not suffice to designate the most dominant animal. The actual number of displacements or incidents of chasing could be misleading because, although in practice a high-ranking mother was easily recognized as dominating the other females in her group,

> a mother's rank reflects the direction but not necessarily the rate of aggressive behaviour between herself and others. A high ranking female would not be aggressive so long as the others avoided her, but the others could be fighting among themselves at a high rate.
>
> (Simpson and Simpson 1982)

As a general rule, primatologists and other experts in animal behaviour seem to agree that the best indicator of social dominance is a

117

demonstration of priority access to desirable objects. One experienced observer said it was easy to identify the dominant animal – it is the one who gets to lie in the shade after lunch. This is too simplistic, of course, but it captures the spirit of many observations.

Dominance rank (or hierarchy) is an extension of social dominance in that it depends on a series of calculations which relate a number of animals, or even groups of animals, to each other. It is variously described according to which kind of animal is being studied, but is usually some variation of the following. Professor Timothy Clutton-Brock and his colleagues of Cambridge gave their method of calculating ranks in a paper in *Nature* in 1984. First they spent many hours observing the behaviour of each of the red deer hinds in the group. Then they used a formula for calculating exactly where each animal could be placed on a dominance hierarchy.

> The social dominance of each hind is measured by calculating the total number of other hinds more than one year old that she has been seen to threaten or displace, weighted by their ranks, and divided by the total number of hinds that threaten or displace her, again divided by their ranks.
>
> (Clutton-Brock *et al.* 1984)

Thus dominance rank is a relative measure involving relationships between several animals. To assess how dominant a particular animal is, the usual strategy is to calculate its position on a dominance hierarchy. An animal that is seen to displace many other animals in the group is ranked higher and one that is not able to do so is ranked lower.

This way of describing dominance rank provided an acceptable and useful strategy for research in a variety of contexts. But in some areas the terms 'dominance' and 'dominance rank' have come to be used almost synonymously, thus masking the fact that dominance, as opposed to dominance rank, is a characteristic of an individual. Although dominance and dominance rank are usually closely related, this is not a necessary relationship.

Dominance rank is not the only piece of information required for judging the dominance of an animal, for two reasons: the behaviours assumed to indicate dominance may need further differentiation, particularly in discriminating between dominant and aggressive behaviour; and dominance is only one of a number of factors which decide an animal's rank at a particular time.

What other components go to make up rank position? In 1975, E. O. Wilson described them in his book *Sociobiology: The New Synthesis*. He included insects, reptiles, birds, rodents, ungulates and primates in his discussion. Factors known to influence dominance rank are 'age, caste, size, sequence of arrival or emergence (at nest-founding site), victory or defeat in previous encounters, greater defensive ability, persistence and experience, all of which occur in animals below the rank of primate' (Wilson 1975, 291). In principle, Wilson notes, 'the greater the size of the brain and the more flexible the behaviour, the more numerous are the determinants of rank and the more nearly equal they are in influence'. In addition, he says, 'the greater the cohesiveness and durability of the social group, the more numerous and nearly coequal the correlates of rank and the more complex the dominance order' (1975, 291). For example, he says, in ungulates (sheep, deer, etc.) male rank order is especially dependent on size and age. But in baboons and macaques childhood history (mother's rank), membership of a particular coalition, whether the animal has just migrated from another troop, and how experienced an animal is all contribute to dominance rank.

All Wilson's claims about dominance are backed up by citing research from both observers and experimenters. His meticulous documentation leaves little room for argument about the basic facts, though the interpretation of these facts was contentious in some circles. The research shows not only the existence of dominance throughout the animal kingdom, but also the fact that everywhere it has a strong male bias.

DOMINANCE OR AGGRESSION

Dominance is not necessarily related to aggression. Perhaps counter-intuitively, Hinde notes that 'the greater the difference in dominance rank between two individuals in a group, the less frequent are agonistic interactions between them. Indeed the alpha male may show the least aggression of all' (Hinde 1974, 342).

Much depends on the setting in which the observations of dominance are made. The behaviours described above emerge when access to food, water and space is adequate. When these are in short supply, dominance may quickly become aggression, leading some to wonder if dominance does not include the potential to behave aggressively.

In 1984 D. B. Meikle and his colleagues published an article in the *American Naturalist* describing their 11-year study of rhesus monkeys. From 1962, the animals lived on two provisioned islands under the control of the Caribbean Primate Research Centre. The authors and their team of helpers did more than 15,000 hours of observations, noting not only the dominance rank of individual animals, but the rank of the group to which each belonged. They saw that 'all members of one genealogy are either higher- or lower-ranking than all members of other genealogies in their groups', thus documenting the importance of family as well as individual characteristics on dominance rank.

A close reading of the Meikle paper makes it clear that many of the dominance interactions took place in a setting of what some might term a life-and-death struggle. Although in normal times most agonistic encounters involved 'noncontact displacements', when there were shortages of food and water, especially at 'frequently visited feeders', agonistic encounters included vocal threats, chasing, and sometimes physical attacks and wounding.

> During severe resource shortages, lower ranking groups . . . often were forced off the island into adjacent mangrove swamp areas that had no food or water, while members of lower ranking genealogies had low priority of access to food within their groups. In addition, lower ranking animals some- times were badly wounded in violent fights over small amounts of remaining food.
>
> (Meikle *et al.* 1984)

The authors mention a need for euthanasia as well as medical treat- ment. In such extreme settings as this, the frequency of agonistic encounters alone would not be a reliable indicator of dominance.

MEASURING DOMINANCE IN ANIMALS

Since neither rate of aggression nor position on a dominance hierarchy can provide a satisfactory measure of dominance for any individual animal, the problem of measurement has become more complex than originally thought. One way of tackling it might be to follow Dunbar's (1988) suggestion and look for a way of assessing the animal's domi- nance or 'intrinsic power' outside the arena of competition for resources. Or it could be useful to extend S. Richards' early suggestion and test individual animals for characteristics which may be related to dominance, such as persistence (see pages 113–14).

A second strategy might be to construct a series of behavioural measures of dominance based on the observations of Dutch primatol- ogist Frans de Waal. Prompted to write on the topic because 'the view that dominance relationships have an affective component is conspicu- ously lacking from many recent theoretical discussions', he described the behaviours that go to make up what he termed the 'reconciled hierarchy model' of social dominance. Arguing that 'a well-recognized hierarchy promotes social bonds and reduces violence', he showed how specific behaviours both signal the differences in dominance status and maintain harmony.

If de Waal's (1986) categories were used as a starting point, a more detailed qualitative measure of dominance might emerge. On the other hand, care must be taken not to attribute unwarranted cognitive sophistication to animals. For example, in discussing signals of submissiveness in animals, Maestripieri (1996) warned against inferring second order intentionality in animals (that is, the capacity of individuals to attribute mental states or knowledge to others). Even if dominance in animals and humans does have a common biological basis (such as testosterone), the relationships between hormones, cognition and behaviour are likely to be very different.

The difficulties encountered with the behavioural definition of dominance provide an incentive to look for something more solid. And, as noted earlier, when behavioural differences are found in animals, zoologists tend to look to hormones for an explanation. So one might expect to see quite a few studies investigating the relationship between hormones and dominance in animals. In fact there are very few: only a small number of researchers have sought a biological substrate for dominance.

Further, most of the studies which have been done on behaviour and hormone levels sought to elucidate the biological basis of aggression, not dominance. Perhaps because of this, conflicting and negative results have been the norm. However, when dominance has been included among the independent variables, more interesting results have been attained. The reason could be that aggression is far more a matter of environmental influences (or nurture, if that does not seem too ridiculous a word in this context), while dominance is a function of both environment and biology (both nurture and nature).

However this may be, there is good evidence for the existence of a hormonal substrate for dominance in virtually every well-designed study that has attempted to show it. One of the most thorough is by Rose et al., published in Nature in 1971, which was conducted with 34 adult male rhesus monkeys. Because of doubts about how the stress of capture might affect plasma measurement, the researchers took a lot of trouble to accustom their animals to the required procedures. The study began in September 1969 and went on for nine months. For the first month they collected data on dominance and allowed the dominance hierarchies to stabilize. During the next few months they repeatedly caught each animal and then immediately let it go. In the seventh month, each animal was caught and a plasma sample taken.

During all this time the dominance rank remained virtually stable. It is interesting to note in passing that the experimenters were surprised at the very low level of aggression: only 29 of 8000 observations indicated aggression. For the rest of the time dominance hierarchies were maintained by non-contact threat gestures.

Dominance rank correlated significantly with testosterone concentrations. The highest-ranking animals (1–8) had significantly higher levels of plasma testosterone than those in the lower quartiles. A table in the original article shows two medium ranks (animals 9–17 and 18–26) having similar levels, and the lowest-ranking animals (27–34) having the lowest mean concentrations. Mean testosterone concentration was 669 nanograms per 100 millilitres of plasma, and the range was from 200 ng/100 ml to 1560 ng/100 ml.

The authors said it was unclear from their work whether higher testosterone was a precursor or a consequence of higher dominance. On 'anecdotal' grounds their impression was that changes in dominance sometimes preceded altered testosterone levels.

When this study was criticized on methodological grounds, another was done, this time by Rose *et al.* in 1975. In the second report, 'Consequences of social conflict on plasma testosterone levels in rhesus monkeys', published in *Psychosomatic Medicine* in 1975, they summarized their work thus:

> Four adult male rhesus monkeys formed a new social group with 13 adult females. The male who became dominant (alpha) showed a progressive increase in plasma testosterone. The male who became subordinate to the other three males showed an 80% fall in testosterone from baseline levels. After 7 weeks, this group was introduced to a well-established breeding group, and all four males became subordinate to all members of the breeding group. All four males evidenced a fall in testosterone during the first week after introduction, and within 6 weeks their levels were approximately 80% of pre-introduction values. The alpha male of the breeding group showed a large increase in testosterone (238%) 24 hours after he successfully defended his group and became the dominant animal of the larger, newly-formed group. Thus plasma testosterone levels appear to be significantly influenced by the outcome of conflict attendant to alterations in status of rhesus monkeys living in social groups.
>
> (Rose *et al.* 1975)

One of the problems in trying to define a relationship between dominance behaviour and hormone levels is the question of the direction of causality. If there is a relationship between them, does this mean that the presence of more than average amounts of testosterone in the blood increases the potential for dominant behaviour, or does acting in a dominant way lead to the production of more testosterone? At present most scientists appear to believe that the relationship is bidirectional, events from the environment influencing hormone levels which in turn influence the way the individual responds to new events in the environment.

DOMINANCE AND STRESS

An important corollary of the maternal dominance hypothesis is that testosterone in females is influenced by stress, and that higher levels of this hormone contribute to raised sex ratios during hard times. In a system that appears to be so finely balanced, it is of interest that several research teams have found greater physiological reactivity to stress among dominant females. During undemanding times, it appears that dominant individuals may have low cortisol levels, an idea related to the concept of 'comfortable dominance', mentioned in Chapter 2. There is a parallel to this idea in the work on hormones and dominance in animals. High-status males in stable hierarchies are known to have lower cortisol levels than those further down the hierarchy (Sapolsky and Ray 1989). This work was said to demonstrate that being at the top is not as stressful a position as either wanting to be at the top or being at the bottom. It also suggested that low cortisol levels might be associated with dominance.

A study from the late 1970s appeared to corroborate this suggestion. Since so many other factors (age, size, experience and so on) may influence dominance, an early study which bypassed these factors is of special interest. Golub et al. reported in the journal Hormones and Behavior on their work with rhesus monkey weanlings. All the animals were about the same age (6–9 months) and size, and had not yet had any experience in group living. The authors measured plasma cortisol levels immediately before, then shortly after, the infant monkeys were separated from their mothers and placed in small social groups. They found that the dominant animal in each dyad could be predicted from the baseline cortisol levels taken before separation from the mother. They wrote that the relationship was 'very striking; in only 4 of the 31 dyads did the dominant member have a higher baseline cortisol value than the subordinate member'. In other words, no matter what the trauma of separation, those animals whose stress levels were low before separation from the mother were more likely to be the dominant animals in later groupings. But even at this level it is hard to separate nature from nurture. Were low basal cortisol levels before separation due to an accident of birth or to good mothering?

In this study there were equal numbers of each sex and the experimental dyads consisted of half same-sex pairs and half mixed-sex pairs. But the animals were prepubertal and no measures of testosterone were taken. There were no differences between the sexes on measures of cortisol although the range across individuals was wide (82–275 ng/ml).

After puberty there is a relationship between cortisol levels and testosterone levels, and it is different for the two sexes. In the female, an increase in the activity of the adrenal glands means there could be an increase in testosterone. Since the adrenal glands are responsive to environmental stressors, an increase in stress appears to lead to an increase in basal cortisol level, which in turn could lead to increased testosterone output in females. But this is not the case for males. Testosterone in males is secreted by the testes and production is adversely affected by long-term stressors.

Manogue and his colleagues (1975) also demonstrated a relationship between high dominance and low plasma cortisol levels, this time in squirrel monkeys. They too found that the animals high in dominance had the greatest adrenal reactivity to stress.

Very few scientists have tried manipulating hormones in animals to see if this affects dominance. But the few studies there are have been moderately successful. In particular, Marie-France Bouissou at the Station de Physiologie de la Réproduction in Nouzilly, France, has been working on this exact problem for many years. In 1978 she published a paper in the journal *Hormones and Behavior* entitled 'Effects of testosterone propionate on dominance relationships in a group of cows'. In this she demonstrated that 'treatment of ovariectomized or intact adult females (cows, mares, hinds) with androgens consistently raises their social rank'. The effect of the testosterone treatment was that 'dominance relationships between treated and control animals were consistently reversed, whereas relationships among treated animals were not modified' (Bouissou 1990).

In a 1990 study on the effects of oestrogen on dominance relationships in cows, she noted, 'As is the case with androgen treatment, changes in dominance relationships cannot be explained by changes in body weight or aggressiveness induced by treatment.' Bouissou said that changes in dominance status were not related to acts of aggression at all, but rather to a decrease in the number of withdrawals. Animals rose in dominance ranking even though they were not more aggressive.

There are also two series of experimental studies which found an association between testosterone and persistence, a characteristic already known to be related to dominance in humans and possibly, as noted above, also related to dominance in animals. These studies provide examples of the second strategy – that of finding a measurable characteristic related to dominance and seeing if it has a hormonal substrate. The work was done by Andrew and Rogers (1972) and Archer (1977), who trained either chicks or mice to look for food at the end of a straight runway. The experiments consisted of comparing latencies in a variety of conditions involving different kinds of distraction. Comparisons were made between intact males, testosterone-injected castrates, control castrates and females. Results showed convincingly that testosterone increased persistence.

Although the studies cited support the idea that dominance in animals is an inherent capacity of individuals and has a similar biological basis to that of humans, there are still more questions than answers. Dominance hierarchies in most species are well documented, but the relative importance of dominance as a characteristic of an individual has yet to be described. Whatever the relationship between dominance and dominance hierarchies, factors such as age, health and sex influence an animal's status over time. The studies that have attempted to show a hormonal basis for dominance in animals point to testosterone as the hormone of interest. In some circumstances it is likely that animals high in dominance lead a less stressful life than those below them in the hierarchy. Some researchers have suggested that this diminution of stress is reflected in lower cortisol levels. If so, this may be important in the interpretation of studies of low sex ratios in dominant females living in non-threatening circumstances.

Further research using both behavioural and physiological measures will make it easier to judge the extent to which hormones influence both individual characteristics and relationships between individuals. In the meantime, dominance, social dominance and dominance hierarchies need to be clearly distinguished and the effect of stress on the production of testosterone further explored in both sexes.

7

DOMINANCE AND THE SEX RATIO IN ANIMALS

Despite imperfections in the definition of dominance in animals, espe-cially the distinction between dominance as an inherent capacity of an individual and dominance rank, research findings have emerged which show a relationship between maternal dominance and the sex ratio.

As with humans, the term 'sex ratio' is used to describe the ratio of males to females. Unlike humans, however, the sex ratio is 100:100. In his book *The Theory of Sex Allocation* (1982), Eric Charnov gives a brief review of historical material on the sex ratio in animals. The one irrefutable conclusion from the many studies is that the overall birth sex ratio is almost universally 100 females to 100 males for all animals that breed bisexually. Further, as Charnov notes, more than 100 years of agricultural and laboratory research has demonstrated that not only are birth sex ratios almost always equal but they are very difficult, if not impossible, to shift.

For at least two decades much of the work on sex ratios in animals took as its theoretical starting point a paper by Trivers and Willard (1973) published in *Science*, entitled 'Natural selection of parental ability to vary the sex ratio of offspring'. This is a good example of the kind of paper acclaimed by readers in the history of science who have found that a theory's value has as much to do with its ability to generate further research as it does with its ultimate validity.

Judged by this criterion the much-cited Trivers and Willard hypoth-esis must rank as a very useful theory indeed. Robert Trivers, evolutionary biologist, and Dan Willard, mathematician, both of Harvard University, offered the idea that natural selection would favour those parents who were able to manipulate or vary the sex ratio according to their own condition. They argued that 'a male in good condition at the end of the period of parental investment is expected to outreproduce a sister in similar condition, while she is expected to outreproduce him if both are in poor condition'.

Although the main illustrations of their theory were from the animal world, the authors included a comment on human sex ratios. Despite various complications, they said 'the model can be applied to humans differentiated on a socioeconomic scale, as long as the reproductive success of a male at the upper end of the scale exceeds his sister's, while that of a female at the lower end of the scale exceeds her brother's'. Given a sufficiently large sample size, this suggestion is supported by the fact that there are slightly higher sex ratios among higher socio-economic groups than in lower socio-economic groups (see Chapter 8). Whether this has a serious influence on the human sex ratio is open to conjecture, but the matter is of little importance because it was the animal application that caught the imagination of the scientific world and, in particular, that of animal behaviourists, primatologists and evolutionary biologists.

SEX RATIOS, GOOD CONDITION AND DOMINANCE

Looking back, it is difficult to tell exactly where 'good condition' first became 'dominance' in the research literature on animal sex ratios. However, since dominant animals are those which can usually command priority of access to desired resources, it is not hard to imagine that the two groups – dominant animals and animals in good condition – might often be one and the same. But they are not the same, they simply happen to coincide; and this coincidence lies at the base of a flaw in one of the tenets of the Trivers and Willard hypothesis.

The main idea, that natural selection would favour parents that could manipulate the sex ratio to suit the conditions, continues to gather support. But the idea that animals in good condition should produce more males has proved more complex than first thought. Writing only five years after publication of the original paper, Judith Myers (1978) described a computer simulation which showed how the theory did not, and could not, hold for all circumstances; but this did not prevent dozens of papers on the subject from being published over the next 20 years. Some of the papers supported the Trivers and Willard hypothesis; others did not.

The first few publications suggested that high-ranking mothers produced more daughters than sons. These reports were all from leading primatologists. Jeanne Altmann (1980), who had been observing baboon mothers and infants in the wild for several years (1971–8), noticed particularly the high cost of reproduction. Not only did babies and infants die in large numbers, but their mothers did also. So when Trivers and Willard suggested that animals might manipulate the sex ratio in order to maximize their own fitness, Altmann applied this theory to her own work and observations. When so much risk and effort was going into bearing and raising infants, it did not seem unreasonable to suggest that animals would produce infants of the sex that would most easily (or, rather, with the least difficulty) ensure the survival of their genomes into the next generation.

The first formal reports came from studies of caged animals, one at the Californian Primate Research Centre in Davis (Silk *et al.* 1981), and the other at the Unit for Development and Integration of Behaviour at Madingley, Cambridge (Simpson and Simpson 1982). These studies had much in common: both had comprehensive records compiled from thousands of hours of observations over many years; both reported data on maternal dominance rank and the sex ratio of their infants; and both found that higher-ranking females had more surviving female than male infants.

The researchers at Davis worked with a group of caged bonnet macaques. Their data, from 213 births, showed that lower-ranking females had more sons. But there is one curious fact about the sex ratios in this study: *all* the mothers produced more sons than normal. Even the high-ranking females (those producing the fewest sons in this group) had 52 per cent males. There was a significantly high mortality among the sons of lower-ranking females during the infancy period, but newborn female infants of low-ranking mothers suffered the highest mortality of all. Joan Silk and her colleagues wrote that 'all five of the monkeys whose deaths were behaviourally induced were the offspring of low ranking females'. ('Behaviourally induced' means murder, or at the very least grievous bodily assault, as opposed to disease or starvation.) They noticed a general pattern in which unrelated adult females injured the female infants of low-ranking mothers. However, they wrote, 'No young males were seriously wounded during the course of our observations' (Silk *et al.* 1981). They compared their data with a study reported by Dittus in 1979, which described how there had been 'exceptionally high mortality among juvenile female toque macaques during the prolonged drought in Sri Lanka as a result of exclusion from feeding areas'.

Writing about their study a few years later, Dunbar confirmed that lack of food could not have been a factor in the Silk study. Her macaques had unlimited food 'and surplus food was always present at the end of each day' (Dunbar 1988, 66). Dunbar thought the difficulties were best explained by the increased rates of harassment on lower-ranking females as group size increased.

In the second study, Simpson and Simpson reported in *Nature* (1982) on 139 births to 53 mothers. Between 1960 and 1981 the high-ranking monkey mothers had 38 daughters and 15 sons, whereas all the other mothers had 32 daughters and 54 sons. Thus both studies suggested that high-ranking monkey mothers produced more female infants.

A point of interest in the Simpson and Simpson study is the way they related their findings to the Trivers and Willard hypothesis. They said their results supported the hypothesis in that

> mothers potentially able to invest much in offspring should bear and rear the kinds of infants repaying the highest levels of maternal investment most effectively. Such infants could be daughters in some socially living macaque and baboon species although they were believed to be sons in the cases considered by Trivers and Willard.
>
> (Simpson and Simpson 1982)

The living conditions for these animals may also be relevant to the findings. Since the data were collected over a 20-year period, it is likely that most of the animals were born in captivity. The researchers removed the young males before their fifth year, and they excluded data from pregnancies resulting from matings arranged with outside males and pregnancies spent partly away from the group. As described below, comfortable conditions, enhanced by the absence of younger males, may have social effects that are relevant to the maintenance of sex ratios.

STUDIES OF DOMINANCE AND THE SEX RATIO IN THE WILD

Two years later another two papers were published, again one from each side of the Atlantic. This time both studies were done on animals living in the wild, and both showed conclusively that dominant mothers produced more sons. Timothy Clutton-Brock and his colleagues published their now-famous paper on sex ratios and maternal dominance in red deer (1984). Their team was based in the Large Animal Research Group in the Department of Zoology at the University of Cambridge, and their field studies were conducted between 1971 and 1983 on the Isle of Rhum off the coast of Scotland and involved keeping records on about 120 red deer hinds and 100 stags living in four separate groups. In particular they measured the dominance rank of each hind (see Chapter 6) and recorded the sex of every calf born to her.

On analysing their data, these scientists found that 'dominant mothers produce significantly more sons than subordinates' (Clutton-Brock *et al.* 1984). They found the same effect in the four separate geographic areas and also across the seven different cohorts of hinds born during the study period.

This work clearly went beyond the Trivers and Willard concept of 'animals in good condition', and suggested instead that dominance rank was the important factor. At the behavioural level it is not difficult to understand why these two might be related. As described in the last chapter, animals higher in dominance rank tend to be those which have priority access to everything desirable, including food and shelter, so it is hardly surprising that they would be the ones in better condition.

The American scientists working on these problems, Meikle, Tilford and Vessey, published an account of their work in the *American Naturalist* in 1984, the same year as the red deer study. It is important to note that all these studies are of necessity longitudinal, and that the work began many years before the results were published. Again, like many others, Meikle *et al.* (1984) reported on female dominance rank and its relation to the sex ratio of offspring. They described 16 years of work with colonies of rhesus monkeys released on two islands in the Caribbean in 1962, and their data is based on daily observations taken over this period by a team of technicians and investigators. During that time more than 1000 births were recorded. The data show a highly significant relationship between the dominance rank of the mother and the sex of the infant, with higher-ranking females having 60 per cent males and lower-ranking females 40 per cent males. They also show how changes in status over time, both for individual females and for the troop as a whole, had a dramatic effect on the sex ratio of the infants.

Meikle and his colleagues asked themselves what could account for the phenomenon. One idea they considered was that stress (defined physiologically as an increase in adrenocorticotrophic hormone [ACTH] output) might cause higher spontaneous abortion rates, especially of male infants. This idea in turn was based on the theory that primary sex ratios (sex ratios at conception) might be higher than secondary sex ratios. Since humans are known to produce more males, it is sometimes argued that conception sex ratios may be more male-biased than birth sex ratios. If this were so, a higher spontaneous abortion rate might mean fewer male births, as well as fewer births overall.

No matter how the data are explained, the facts observed by Meikle *et al.* were as follows: first, that 'Monkeys that are frequently involved in agonistic encounters appear to have higher rates of abortion and lower production of infants'; and second, that 'adrenal hormones are implicated in the disproportionate termination of males' (Meikle *et al.* 1984).

These findings and their explanations make a lot of sense, both intuitively and in terms of the maternal dominance hypothesis. One would expect that females towards the bottom of the dominance hierarchy would suffer more bite wounds and more stress, particularly when food supplies were low. It is perfectly plausible that frequently harassed and ill-fed monkeys would suffer more spontaneous abortions. If it is more difficult, hormonally speaking, for less dominant animals to conceive males (and carry them to term), then one would expect stress to affect the sex ratio differentially. Given that males are said to be more vulnerable from conception on, it is likely that stressed monkey mothers would lose more male infants, and this too would result in low births overall and low secondary sex ratios.

An important contribution to this problem came from scientists working with a large colony of captive pigtail macaque monkeys at the University of Washington Primate Center. In 1975 Sackett and his colleagues reported on 792 births to 412 mothers during a period of several years. Their figures showed that the 114 pregnant mothers treated at their medical centre, mainly for bite wounds, produced many fewer male infants. These researchers also wondered what was going on to produce such results. Did the mothers who were carrying female infants smell different to the other mothers and thus provoke attacks? Was it a simple matter of dominance rank? Or was it because 'the testosterone produced by the male embryos made their mothers behave so as to avoid attacks'? (Meikle *et al.* 1984, reporting on Sackett 1981).

In response to this last suggestion, Meikle said it was most unlikely, because 'only very small amounts of testosterone are produced by male embryos while very large amounts are usually necessary to cause a change in the behaviour of the females' (Meikle *et al.* 1984). If Meikle's reasoning is correct, his conclusions and his data support the idea that the more dominant females conceived male infants in the first place.

SUMMARIZING THE RESULTS FROM THE
FIRST DECADE OF STUDIES

Two years after the publication of the paper on red deer, Clutton-Brock and Iason (1986) wrote a review of all the papers on sex ratio variation in mammals and, as always, they selected only those papers which reached a defined minimum standard of scientific methodology. They concluded that overall more males are born to higher-ranking, or more dominant, females throughout the animal kingdom. They also noted some well-documented exceptions to this rule, offering ideas about why these might be. They pointed out that the Trivers and Willard hypothesis could not account for all the known variations in the sex ratio and that their ideas about maximizing fitness had taken insufficient notice, they thought, of competition between siblings and parents.

Unlike other evolutionary biologists, who appeared not to concern themselves too much with 'proximate mechanisms' (i.e. how it all might work at the physiological level), Clutton-Brock and Iason (1986) made some suggestions about how the overall findings might be consistent with ideas from other disciplines as well as their own. They wrote: 'In view of the apparent lack of genetic variance in the sex ratio in many species, a hormonal mechanism mediated by environmental factors provides a plausible explanation of many trends' (Clutton-Brock and Iason 1986). This may have been the first time evolutionary biologists mentioned a role for hormones. More than that, they specifically said that the hormones could be 'mediated by environmental factors'.

They went on: 'It may be significant that many of the variables most closely related to the sex ratio are likely to have strong effects on the development of juveniles.' It now appears that at least one of the variables, namely dominance, plays a pivotal role in ensuring the continuation of sex differences throughout the animal world, including humans (see Chapter 9). Finally, they said that 'If environmental factors can influence sex ratio through effects on the parents' early development, it is not surprising that many trends are inconsistent.' This observation highlights a third important effect, namely that responsiveness to environmental change appears to be built into the system. All three ideas are highly compatible with the maternal dominance hypothesis, but the authors came to their conclusions by a completely different route. Their findings from the animal world thus unexpectedly provided further corroborative evidence.

It was not long, however, before there were published accounts of failure to replicate the findings and criticisms of the theory in general. Up till this time observations on dominance and the sex ratio had been done almost entirely on females. The reason for this was not that evolutionary biologists thought that the male has only a minor part to play in the determination of the sex of the infant, but because there was evidence to suggest that facultative adjustment of the sex ratio could be carried out by the female after conception, either within the reproductive tract (e.g. by selective abortion) or in early infancy by means of differential treatment of one sex over the other. Examples of sex ratio manipulation by these means were given by L. M. Gosling (1986), who found that coypu selectively abort entire litters to achieve adaptive control of the sex ratio, and Austad and Sunquist (1986), whose experimental field study of the common opossum led them to suggest that provisioned mothers may assist males rather than females towards functional teats. A number of observers have noted that after birth, particularly where there is local resource competition, 'females will reduce the recruitment of immature females into their group through harassment' (Silk 1983).

There is a good reason why most of the earlier studies of dominance behaviours were done on males, while those investigating the relationship between the sex ratio and dominance were done on females: in most it would have been impossible to ascribe paternity. Only when animals were caged and only one male was present could paternity be determined with the necessary degree of accuracy. But in 1985, Small and Smith reported in the *American Naturalist* on a study they had done entitled 'Sex of infants produced by male rhesus macaques'. They looked at both male and female dominance rank and its relation to the sex ratio of the offspring. Once more the research took place at the Californian Primate Research Center. The macaques were housed in six separate groups; all the groups were in outdoor cages and included males and females as well as their offspring, so paternity had to be determined by blood samples. Dominance was rated in the usual way, 'by recording displacements of one animal by another during agonistic encounters'. Over a period of six years, paternity was established for 374 infants (182 males and 192 females). The researchers found no systematic influence of the father's rank, and that is exactly what the maternal dominance hypothesis would predict.

Nor, however, did they find any influence of the mother's rank on the sex of her infant. They found wide variations between the different cages, some of which showed dominance effects, and some of which did not. So they concluded that:

> The variation among groups and over time in the influence of paternal (and maternal) rank on the infant sex ratio found in this study suggests that sex ratio biases previously reported in individual groups may be the result of sampling error.
>
> (Small and Smith 1985)

They might, or they might not. It seemed too early to dismiss a decade of work, especially since almost all the studies fulfilled the requirements for good scientific methodology.

In 1988 Dunbar, appearing more optimistic, summed up the research on the sex ratio of offspring by saying:

> Available data on neonatal sex ratios are highly variable. Some studies have found that dominant females tend to produce more sons than daughters, with subordinates tending towards the reverse . . . but others have found the reverse relationship . . . and yet others have reported no significant differences. This strongly suggests that the decision is dependent on the biological and social context of the population concerned . . .
>
> (Dunbar 1988, 198)

As a consequence, some researchers came to the conclusion that there was little to be gained from pursuing research on the sex ratio. They said the findings represented little more than chance fluctuations, and that there was therefore little to account for (see, for example, Rawlins and Kessler 1986; Berman 1988; Rhine *et al.* 1992). Others still believed there was something to explain. In recent years several more studies have appeared: of particular interest is a study by Meikle *et al.* (1993), who demonstrated in a tightly controlled experimental study that maternal dominance is related to the sex of the offspring in domestic swine, with high-ranking females again giving birth to a greater proportion of males.

In addition, van Schaik *et al.* (1989) found that high-ranking captive long-tailed macaque females had more sons than lower-ranking females. And an ingenious study of humpback whales living in the Gulf of Maine showed that females in good condition gave birth to significantly more male calves (Wiley and Clapham 1993).

Of those who retained their interest in the topic, many sought a theoretical formulation that could account for the wide variations in the findings. The most prominent of these was the local resource competition hypothesis, an idea originally developed in the late 1970s. Anne Clark, of Johannesburg, based her formulation on three separate sets of data from museum collections, births in captivity and births in the wild. Finding male-biased birth sex ratios in all three, she wrote:

> My explanation of the skewed sex ratio involves a difference between male and female offspring in their use of local, high-productivity areas which are essential for female reproduction. Closely related females compete for this resource during the birth season when their movements are restricted by the

burden of raising offspring. Males are never restricted to these high productivity areas and do not compete intensively for them. I term this 'local resource competition' . . . The term . . . was suggested to me by E. Charnov.

(Clark 1978)

As others have since described in detail, females can thus enhance their own and their daughters' fitness 'by producing sons over and above the number of daughters that can share the local resource' (Clark 1978). Variations occur, consistent with which sex disperses on maturity (see, for example, McFarland Symington 1987; Johnson 1988). A refinement to the model was proposed by Silk (1983), seeking to explain the high behaviourally induced mortality among female infants born to low-ranking mothers. It appeared as though females could be limiting the production of daughters born to other females, thus ensuring better access to resources for their own daughters.

Then in 1991 van Schaik and Hrdy showed how it might be reasonable to assume that the Trivers and Willard hypothesis could take priority when resources were adequate or plentiful, and the local resource competition hypothesis could take priority when resources were scarce: 'By examining the relationship between a female's rank and her birth sex ratio as a function of resource availability', they said, 'we can distinguish between the two models'.

In 1995, Wright and his colleagues suggested yet another idea. They reported on a study of wild opossums in which they concluded that there is a 'first cohort' advantage because first litters were male-biased and second litters were female-biased. This hypothesis, they said, explained the findings better than either local resource competition or the maternal condition. Other researchers have found similar effects, and these too may be incorporated into a model which hypothesizes changes in dominance according to age.

Given the quality of the scientific evidence supporting them, it is possible that all the effects described so far influence the sex ratio in one way or another. The degree of influence will be likely to differ in different species, but all will make sense in terms of maximizing fitness. In the maternal dominance hypothesis, however, more emphasis is placed on the proximate mechanism. Before describing this model, two further dimensions need to be considered: level of nutrition and other factors which can cause stress.

NUTRITION AND THE SEX RATIO IN ANIMALS

Altering sex ratios in livestock has been a subject of interest for at least 150 years, predating Darwin. Most of these older studies found that male-biased sex ratios occur in association with lack of food or 'nutrition stress', as it is frequently called. (Although these studies are clearly related to local resource competition, it is rare to find them cited in the primate literature.)

J. S. Watson, of the University of Western Australia, included some information about the history of this research in his 1982 paper for the *American Naturalist*. He reported on an experiment done in France in 1826 entitled 'A method of obtaining a greater number of one sex, at the option of the proprietor, in the breeding of livestock'. A flock of ewes that had been bred in poor pasture produced 80 male and 55 female lambs; a flock that had been bred in good pasture produced 53 male and 84 female lambs. Thus it was that a century and a half before Trivers and Willard published their theory about animals in good condition (1973), farmers and wildlife experts had noticed a link between level of nutrition and the sex ratio. The old idea, however, was the opposite to the Trivers and Willard theory: these older studies showed that more female infants were born to animals in good condition.

Some contemporary studies show the same effect. One of these is by Louis J. Verme, of the Michigan Department of Natural Resources at Shingleton. In a detailed article in the *Journal of Wildlife Management*, he described how he conducted breeding tests on a penned herd of white-tailed deer over a six-year period (1962–7): 'All the deer were in excellent physical condition when each annual experiment began on October 1st', he wrote.

> Thereafter, approximately half the herd received 3.5 lbs of commercial pelletized food per deer daily, a maintenance ration. The remaining animals were given 2.5 lbs of pellets each per day, or nearly 30 per cent less than the controls. When a doe bred, its food allotment was raised to the higher level.
>
> (Verme 1969)

Thus the experimental animals were on restricted rations for approximately six weeks, from the time they were penned at the beginning of October until they were bred during the November rut. Each year

136

Verme reversed the nutritional regime. Animals that were put into the high diet group one year were put into the low diet group the next. Since deer commonly breed twins, the number of fawns bred was also an important consideration. As expected, deer that had been underfed during the rut produced fewer fawns. But contrary to expectations, they also produced many more male than female fawns.

Over the years, 190 prime-aged does bore 293 young during the breeding experiments: 'Altogether, males comprised 72.1% of the births when productivity averaged only 1.15 fawns per doe because they had been underfed . . . In contrast 43.2% of the progeny were males when production rose to 1.73 fawns per doe under ample pre-breeding nutrition' (Verme 1969).

After all those years of careful work, what did Louis Verme think could explain these striking results? He wrote:

> Variations in fawn sex ratios probably constitute a natural phenomenon which contributes to the self-regulation of a population. As deer are polygamous, limited fawn production coupled with a disproportionate number of male births would markedly depress the herd's annual increment when the range carrying capacity is seriously deteriorating. But if the habitat is capable of supporting a greater deer density, high productivity and more female births would result in a rapidly expanding population . . . But the physiological mechanisms which might account for such a change are poorly understood.
>
> (Verme 1969)

At the Wildlife Research Center in Laurel, Maryland, David Mech found a similar phenomenon in his study, 'Disproportionate sex ratios of wolf pups'. A research officer for the United States Fish and Wildlife Service, he conducted a study of wild wolves from 1969 to 1974 in the Superior National Forest of northeastern Minnesota, and also the east-central and northwestern parts of the state. This is an important detail because the three areas differed in density. The northeastern area was 'saturated' and had a 'stable-to-declining wolf population'. But the other two areas, being highly accessible to hunters and trappers, kept wolf densities lower, because 'the primary prey of wolf in all three areas was the white-tailed deer, supplemented by moose and/or beaver' (Mech 1975).

The overall sex ratio of the pups was 52.7 per cent males, based on 1368 pups from 316 litters. These were the total numbers from all three areas as well as some captive litters. From the high-density area, however, the sex ratio was 66 per cent male. When Mech did a year-by-year analysis his results were even more telling.

> When wolf numbers began to decline in 1972, following a major decrease in deer numbers, and the pups were grossly underweight . . . the sample of pups the following year (1973) contained a greater preponderance of males (82%) than in the four previous years (56%, 70%, 60% and 63%).
>
> (Mech 1975)

Conversely, when densities were lower there was an equal sex ratio or even a preponderance of female pups. Like Verme before him, Mech suggested that the sex ratio variations followed the nutrition status of the animals in a predictable way.

These two studies are representative of a group of studies with similar findings. Both are excellent from the point of view of scientific methodology: their authors have searched for alternative explanations of their data and worried about possible confounding effects, and the reports were read by experts before being accepted for publication. The only reasonable grounds for not accepting their findings would be if one could point to a methodological flaw in the studies that had been missed by the researchers, the reviewers and the editor. At the present stage of knowledge there seems no reason to doubt that among these particular animals, level of nutrition affects the sex ratio. What is not known is how this happens.

STRESS AND THE SEX RATIO

In 1983 van Schaik and van Noordwijk published a paper in the *Netherlands Journal of Zoology* in which they surveyed the primate literature on stress and the sex ratio. They adopted three categories of stressors: 'food shortage, high density and social tension'. For polygynous species, they divided the studies into three categories:

> wild groups . . . of natural composition and thriving on natural foods not provisioned by man . . . captive groups . . . of artificial composition, their food being provisioned by man, usually living in crowded indoor conditions . . . and provisioned groups . . . of natural composition with their food provisioned by man, but generally living in large outdoor compounds.

They hypothesized that the three categories could be expected to experience different levels of social stress.

> The captive artificial groups should experience a high level of stress due to crowding and their artificial composition, the wild groups should have high stress because of the limited availability of food and the resulting social tension ... whereas the provisioned natural groups should experience the lowest levels of social stress.
>
> (van Schaik and van Noordwijk 1983)

Results were entirely in the predicted direction. All stressors gave rise to male-biased sex ratios. (The monogamous captive species did not deviate from the 100:100 ratio.) The authors favoured a behavioural interpretation of their results, citing the well-known studies of Silk *et al.* (1981), Sackett (1981) and Dittus (1979), which all document attacks on female infants by unrelated adults. They used this evidence to argue that altered sex ratios are not, therefore, the result of manipulation of the sex ratio at conception, but are more likely to be the result of 'the disruptive behaviour of conspecifics'.

But high postnatal female mortality is not the only explanation for high male sex ratios, especially since many of these are known to be birth sex ratios. A different interpretation of the findings, based on the maternal dominance hypothesis, would incorporate the physiological aspects of the stress response into the physiological processes surrounding conception.

Louis Verme has also explored this idea. In a comprehensive paper that reviewed all the work on deer, he suggested a possible physiological pathway linking stress and altered sex ratios. The stressors were abnormally high density and disruption to normal family groupings: 'When behavioural displays indicated mounting social tension due to extreme crowding, even prime-age does began producing more male fawns', he wrote. Finding that serum progesterone levels averaged approximately one-third higher among stressed animals, he reasoned thus:

> Because the adrenal gland can be an important source of progesterone ... the higher levels possibly represented some adrenal secretion due to behavioural disorientation induced by absence of family members. This extra progesterone would help maintain pregnancy to term despite adversity, live births being vital to the re-establishment of the family groups. These

findings suggest that social well-being can exert an influence on progeny sex ratio virtually independent of nutrition.

(Verme 1983)

Other workers have drawn attention to the adaptive value of male-biased sex ratios among stressed animals (McGinley 1984). As with human studies, it is likely that the best definitions of stress will incorporate some kind of physiological measure related to the adrenal response.

So the theories about animals in good condition have come full circle. Early observers in agricultural or wildlife settings noticed that animals in poor condition were more likely to have male-biased sex ratios, and these observations have been supported by contemporary scientists. On the other hand, Trivers and Willard argued that animals would invest more in whichever sex could be expected to outbreed the other, manipulating the sex ratio to suit the conditions; and that this would result in male-biased sex ratios among animals in good condition. The local resource competition model predicted that, when males disperse, mothers would produce enough daughters to share the resource and then concentrate on sons. Finally, some researchers have suggested that a low level of nutrition (closely related to local resource competition) can be seen as a stressor, and that stressful circumstances are more likely to tip sex ratios towards a preponderance of males. All these suggestions have been backed up by methodologically good studies, published in reputable scientific journals.

WHAT KIND OF MODEL COULD ACCOUNT FOR THE FINDINGS?

At first it might seem that the only possible theoretical model would be one that drew specifically on ideas about maximizing fitness and provided an overarching view. Instead it may be that the maternal dominance hypothesis, with its emphasis on physiological mechanisms, might explain better many of the puzzling and seemingly contradictory findings in the area of mammalian sex ratios. The reasoning is as follows.

It is likely that testosterone or one of the related hormones is present in female mammals in small but variable amounts, following the principle of normal distribution. Testosterone appears to provide a biological basis for differences in dominance. These differences lead to differences in potential to behave in particular ways, which in turn contribute both to overall physical condition and to dominance rank or status.

Under normal conditions (including sufficient food) and in the wild, maternal testosterone will be normally distributed and will result in a 100:100 sex ratio. Those females whose testosterone levels are above the mean will conceive more males, and those whose testosterone levels are below the mean will conceive more females. Thus, in normal conditions in the wild, and perhaps for most mammals, the dominant females will tend to conceive more male offspring. This is the context for the findings that dominant females (both ungulates and primates) produce more male offspring (Clutton-Brock *et al.* 1984; Meikle *et al.* 1984), and for the conclusion found in their review by Clutton-Brock and Iason (1986) that in general dominant females produce more male offspring.

It has been shown in both male and female animals that testosterone rises and falls in response to changes in the environment, especially those which make demands on the animals' resources. Depending on the individual's response to such events, there will either be a rise in dominance and testosterone or a drop in dominance and testosterone. Such changes, if sufficiently marked or prolonged, will probably also result in changes in status. In both males and females it is likely that environmental, genetic and physiological factors all contribute to natural rises and falls in testosterone. Age is almost certainly one such factor.

Of particular interest is what happens in response to prolonged hardship or stress. In males, testosterone production is adversely affected. But in females, the production of testosterone is associated with the adrenal cortex, the gland which is simultaneously responsible for coordinating the body's response to stress. At present it seems likely that in stressful circumstances, or when times are tough, at least some females produce a little more testosterone than usual. Such a process may be adaptive even at the level of the individual, since by producing slightly more testosterone than normal a female may become temporarily slightly tougher and more able to survive. At the same time the extra testosterone could shift the threshold level (temporarily) beyond the critical amount needed to conceive a male infant.

If there is a critical threshold in the amount of testosterone needed to conceive male offspring, then any stressful circumstance (including nutrition stress, being held captive, overcrowding or, in the case of humans, war or epidemic) which results in a rise in testosterone across a whole population would result in an increase in the number of males conceived. This process could account for the findings in the wildlife studies (Verme 1969; Mech 1975), as well as the human and other studies documenting higher sex ratios in hard times. Silk *et al.*'s (1981) study may be a particularly apt illustration of this phenomenon: not only were more males conceived at all levels of the dominance hierarchy, but the sex ratio at the top, where it is less stressful, was less distorted than it was at the bottom, where socially stressed monkey mothers conceived even more males.

If conditions improve during pregnancy (if, for example, the food supply improves or if captive animals are housed differently), then more males will be born. If conditions stay adverse during pregnancy, two different factors will operate: first, many 'threshold' mothers will lose their ill-conceived male infants early in pregnancy for physiological reasons (that is, there will be many more spontaneous abortions of male infants); and second, many low dominance mothers, usually carrying females, will lose theirs for behavioural reasons, as documented by Dittus (1979) and Sackett (1981).

In conditions that are abnormally comfortable or completely lacking in challenge (for example, when animals are born in captivity, have plenty of food, and no effort is required either for foraging or for interactions), testosterone drops below what is normal for the wild and sex ratios go down. For example, Perret's (1990) study (described in Chapter 4) documents low sex ratios in prosimian primates housed in isolation.

PROBLEMS AND QUESTIONS

As indicated in preceding chapters, some of the most important questions about the maternal dominance hypothesis are about the definition and measurement of dominance. Is dominance a biologically based behavioural characteristic and, if so, is testosterone its basis? A related question concerns the importance of differences between mammals in the way testosterone acts at the physiological level. If testosterone underlies dominant behaviour in primates, is it reasonable to suppose that this is true for ungulates? Is it wrong to assume that a dominant red deer hind and a dominant macaque would have a common physiological basis for their behaviour? At present there appears to be no means of knowing this, much less how the hypothesized testosterone levels might act to control the sex of the offspring in different species.

Another major issue is the extent to which it is relevant to consider environmental influences on behaviour. How exactly does being caged affect behaviour in primates? And how do different degrees of control of the environment make a difference to observations in this area? Does 'semi-free-ranging' mean that animals behave as though they were not in captivity? And does this mean their behaviour is different to those that are caged? Some observers have noted that dominance hierarchies are more marked in caged environments. Does this mean that stressors associated with the wild (such as lack of food, predators and so on) are simply replaced by alternative stressors such as overcrowding and social tension? If so, how does that affect dominance and its hypothesized physiological underpinning?

Jeanne Altmann has given a straightforward answer to some of these questions. In the introduction to her book *Baboon Mothers and Infants* (1980), she describes the differences in lifestyle between baboons in the wild and those in captivity, based on ten years following groups of baboons across the African savannah. Keeping a constant watch for predators animals must spend 65–70 per cent of their time walking and feeding. In captivity, these activities take up only 10–20 per cent of the day. Altmann writes:

> It is impossible to ignore these activities when animals walk several kilometres a day in the hot sun . . . and laboriously dig bulbs or grass corms from the ground for much of the day, and when their rest periods seem necessary to recover from fatigue, rather than just a response to boredom.
>
> (Altmann 1980, 1)

This is in sharp contrast to animals, even on a small provisioned island, where they must do nothing more than pick prepared food pellets out of a hopper. Altmann is certain that having to spend three-quarters of every day just making a living affects all baboon behaviour – not just from the point of view of time, but in other more complex ways. Presumably the extent to which the environment is or is not important is already widely debated by primatologists and leads to differences in their own behaviour – namely whether to make the sacrifices involved and go off to the jungle or savannah to observe behaviours in the wild. It is likely that the benefits from such work are nowhere near exhausted.

Measurements of dominance may all be affected in important ways by differences in how and in what circumstances the data were collected. To make sense of a theory that suggests that testosterone levels fluctuate in response to environmental stressors, much more needs to be known about what is stressful for animals and what is not, whether in the wild or in captivity. Contemporary thought about what constitutes an appropriate 'naturalistic environment' includes consideration of how much work should be involved in feeding, and even whether minimum levels of stress should be incorporated into the daily round. In addition to the opportunity to practise foraging skills, Snowdon suggests, 'captive animals might be given appropriate predator avoidance experience' (1994, 223). Social groupings may need to reflect those that occur naturally. If there are only one or two things that test an animal's dominance in captivity (for example, access to the food hopper or swing), measures of dominance are likely to be inadequate.

On the other hand, primatologists who have spent thousands of hours observing their subjects almost certainly develop a feel for how the animals adapt to specific situations, as well as for the social dynamics of any particular grouping. Primatologists have often reported that it is not difficult to discern which animals are dominant. Do the behavioural records, either theirs or their technicians', always confirm their hunches? More than ever it seems important to take full account of the potential impact of the social environment on the behaviour of mammals.

With so many areas of uncertainty, it could be argued that any hypothesis is premature. On the other hand, a plausible hypothesis will sometimes give rise to researchable questions that have the potential to advance understanding.

So far as mammalian sex ratios are concerned, it is likely that a finely balanced homoeostasis is at work, at both the individual and population levels. This is far from being a novel idea, having been thoroughly explored by many theorists. It is perhaps most closely related to Maynard Smith's 'frequency-independent' evolutionarily stable strategy, being what he considered a 'game against nature' in which the payoff to a strategy is independent of the frequency with which it is played (Maynard Smith 1982, 55). Such novelty is linked rather to the proximate mechanism, which provides a potential vehicle for the theory.

Where individuals are concerned, a genetically determined, normally distributed, baseline level of female testosterone which fluctuates adaptively in response to environmental pressures ensures that each mother conceives offspring of the sex she is at that time suited to raise. At the population level, where a common stressor could affect all mothers, a general rise in testosterone could produce an overall increase in male offspring. Conversely, in the absence of war, famine or disease, there might be a general drop in testosterone and an increase in female offspring.

Such a system could be summarized at both levels by referring to psychological toughness. For individuals, being forced by circumstances to be psychologically tougher means an increased likelihood of conceiving a male offspring; for populations, tough times mean more males. This theory would make sense of a large proportion of the published studies in the area of both animal and human sex ratios.

The theory has arisen out of a consideration of biological and behavioural studies. It is not a 'top-down' theory. But it would also be adaptive in the sense of maximizing reproductive fitness, for at least two reasons. First, it provides a built-in mechanism for adapting the number of animals to what the environment can support. As Louis Verme made clear in interpreting his results (1983), this mechanism works perfectly to regulate population numbers in accordance with resources. Second, as with humans, it appears as though this grand-scale homoeostasis ensures that dominance does not get out of hand. Or, as Dunbar (1995) so neatly put it, such a process would mean that 'the evolutionary advantages of winning in competitive mating systems . . . do not lead to evolutionary arms races in which individuals become ever more aggressive'. Dunbar was commenting on reasons for the apparently excessive loss of infants to high-ranking females, whereas my reasoning refers to the phenomenon that under normal circumstances dominant females conceive males. Such a mechanism would ensure that the powerful influence of maternal dominance behaviours on early development are confined to young males (see Chapter 9).

It is interesting to see how comparable ideas have already been described in the scientific literature. For example, Nancy Burley of the Department of Ecology at the University of Illinois had clearly thought hard about the Trivers and Willard hypothesis and found it wanting. So what is going on? she asked herself. Thus began a line of reasoning that went like this. 'Assume', she said, 'that only females manipulate the sex ratio. Individuals inherently superior at producing one sex could be selected to preferentially produce that sex. Such individuals can be termed predisposed sex-ratio manipulators.' Of course genetic explanation would be ridiculous, she wrote, but

> if variables other than quantity of parental investment affect offspring reproductive success, then it becomes plausible for individuals to specialize in rearing one sex . . . It seems reasonable to expect that facultative mechanisms would exist to modulate a genetic tendency to produce a particular sex.
>
> (Burley 1982)

These suggestions may come to be viewed with increasing respect as more is discovered about the mechanisms that control the sex ratio.

8

THE SEX RATIO IN HUMANS

Demographers and statisticians working on the sex ratio assume that the sex of the infant is a matter of chance. Therefore they argue, since X- and Y-chromosome-bearing spermatozoa are produced in equal numbers, the chances of having a boy or a girl ought to be 50:50. If this were so, the mathematical model for working with sex ratio data would be the same as the classic coin-tossing model. But boys and girls are not born in equal numbers, and herein lies a mystery. How can this be? What could possibly explain the fact that for every 100 baby girls there are 105 baby boys?

Demographers have spent thousands of research hours trying to find answers to this question. Hundreds of scientific papers have been written offering clues about what might be going on. As a consequence much is known about the distribution of the sexes in human populations, and many theories have been offered to explain minor or localized variations in the sex ratio. Much of the work, especially that using huge sample sizes, is scientifically and mathematically impeccable. So to be plausible the theory that maternal dominance leads to the conception of sons has to be compatible with the findings in demography. As it happens, not only is it compatible but it also helps to explain some otherwise inexplicable findings which have perplexed scientists for years.

Throughout this book the term 'sex ratio' is used as a shortened form of the more accurate 'secondary sex ratio'. This is the term most frequently used to describe the live-birth sex ratio. Sometimes it includes stillbirths of known sex, but usually it does not. It must be distinguished from the primary (or conception) sex ratio. At present, no one knows what the primary sex ratio is, in spite of many efforts to establish it. This point was discussed in Chapter 5, and will also be discussed later in this chapter.

For the most part, the sex ratio is the same everywhere across all populations, at all times and in all places. Its very intractability has proved the despair of researchers. Genuine variations are described below, but these do not include some well-publicized variations which are due to artificial causes. For example, new technologies have made some procedures widely available which only a short time ago were restricted to research laboratories. Richard Tomlinson, a freelance writer stationed in Beijing, reported in the *British Medical Journal* that

> The use of ultrasonographic equipment to identify the sex of a fetus is increasingly common, especially in the countryside, where female fetuses are then aborted and couples try again for a son ... In the city of Zhangye in north west Gansu province the ratio of newly born boys to girls is 131:100.
>
> (Tomlinson 1994)

This highly aberrant ratio implies thousands of female abortions.

In countries where there is a strong preference for male infants, reports of high sex ratios across an entire population must be regarded with suspicion. It is most unlikely that these occur by chance. In almost every case the figures mask female infanticide – 'almost' because anthropologists have hinted that extremely tough living conditions, such as occur in North Alaska, may have given rise to naturally occurring male-biased sex ratios (see, for example, Smith and Smith 1994). If so, this might mean that Inuit tribes have a false reputation for female infanticide. But this is an exception, and by far the majority of claims to population-wide male-biased sex ratios are better explained by female infanticide or negligence. It could be argued that the advent of high technology to rural areas had improved the situation, because early abortion is less repugnant than infanticide. But one could also argue that things are worse because the end result is that there are more female terminations than ever.

To understand the research in population sex ratios it is necessary to recognize what is, and what is not, a significantly different ratio. Basically the question is: How high would the numbers need to be before doubt was eliminated? For example, suppose someone claimed to have discovered a way of predicting which way a coin would fall. Suppose, further, that the method, though ingenious and theoretically plausible, still needed further refinements before it demonstrated perfect prediction. At what point would sceptics be convinced that the method was worth pursuing because the results were not attributable to chance alone?

This is the sort of reasoning that operates in deciding whether changes in the basic sex ratio are likely to be meaningful. If a coin is tossed many times, there will almost certainly be some sequences that look significant even though they are not. The coin would have to be tossed hundreds of times more for these sequences to be counterbalanced by sequences showing the opposite effect. This is what statisticians call 'confidence limits'. How many boys would need to be born, per hundred girls, for a statistician to be sure that the effect was not a chance one? Fortunately, the calculations have all been done. If it is assumed that the normal sex ratio is 105 boys to 100 girls, there would need to be more than 157, or fewer than 71, boys (in a sample of 200 children) to be 99.9 per cent sure that the ratio reflected a real influence (Stern 1973, 530).

Because bigger numbers tend to iron out chance effects, the larger the numbers the smaller the differences need to be to indicate statistical significance. So, for example, if the sample consists of more than 10,000 births, a significant ratio for male births (normally 105:100) would have to be either below 100.9:100 or above 109.2:100. If the sample was more than 1,000,000, the corresponding levels of confidence would fall within the range 104.5 and 105.4. So much of this is counter-intuitive that it is no wonder many researchers rely on professional statisticians to help interpret complex data.

In other primates the sex ratio is 100:100, so why is it permanently and universally skewed in favour of males in humans? So far there seems to be no improvement on the answer given by J. P. Sussmilch in 1741. According to him, the 105:100 sex ratio demonstrates the wisdom of God, who ensures

> that four to five per cent more boys than girls are born, thus compensating for the higher male losses due to the recklessness of boys, to exhaustion and to dangerous tasks, to war, to sailing, to emigration, and Who thus maintains the balance between the two sexes so that everyone can find a spouse at the appropriate time for marriage.
>
> (cited in Chahnazarian 1988, 214)

In the 21st century, thinkers may wish to modify Sussmilch's pronouncement by substituting or adding evolutionary forces to the wisdom of God, but overall no better explanation has yet been offered.

Since the middle of the eighteenth century, the vulnerability of males has been extensively documented. Males are subject to greater difficulties, both physical and psychological, at every step from conception onwards. Everywhere they are more prone than females to disorders, diseases and disasters. In 1985, two researchers from the

University of North Carolina wrote a paper for *Behavioral and Brain Sciences* entitled 'An immunoreactive theory of selective male affliction', in which they reviewed the evidence. They found that 'the sex differential works unequivocally to male disadvantage' and that 'the phenomenon is largely unexplained' (Gualtieri and Hicks 1985). Whether it is reasonable to associate this fact with the difference in the numbers of male and female births is still unknown.

WHAT INFLUENCES THE SEX RATIO?

In their search for the solution to the problem of the unequal sex ratio, demographers have investigated a wide variety of factors. Some have wondered whether the eldest child is more likely to be a boy; some have wondered if the age of the mother might be relevant; still others have sought seasonal or occupational effects.

It is important to note the variability in the quality of research in this area. Especially in the past, there were often claims of an important finding, but when the data were analysed in the appropriate manner, the effect did not stand up to scrutiny. That is to say, the apparent effects were due to chance after all.

Sometimes the defects in the research originate in deficiencies in the data set. Before starting on the analysis, a demographer checks the raw data: it must be either indisputably representative or, better still, include every case. Finding and gaining access to complete accurate data sets is one of the primary research problems in this area. When such data sets are found, they become famous and access to them becomes a privilege.

An early data set that became very well known is 'the Swedish set', which was used by Professor A. W. F. Edwards of Cambridge University, and consists of information about the offspring of 5477 Swedish ministers of religion. In a paper in the *Annals of Human Genetics* in 1960, Edwards and his coauthor M. Fraccaro presented the set credentials thus:

> The data are in the files of the Institute of Medical Genetics, Uppsala and have been extracted from a series of collected biographies of the ministers ... [each of which] gives the years of birth and death of the parents and of the children. The data include neonatal deaths, and those stillbirths whose sex was recorded, and are only for families in which both parents were alive at the end of the reproductive period, which was taken to be when the mother was 45 years old. The period

covered by the sample is from the end of the sixteenth century to 1920 . . . the data are homogeneous both socially and genetically by virtue of the single occupation of the propositi, and the family tradition of ordination. It is interesting to note that the ministers themselves were registrars of births, so that the records of the births of their own children may be expected to be accurate.

(Edwards and Fraccaro 1960)

In this way, all the important qualities of the data are declared, the most important points being their likely completeness and accuracy. Another attractive feature of this data set from the point of view of research on the sex ratio is that the entire sample was collected in the days before contraception. Thus, for example, if researchers were investigating the possibility that children born to younger mothers were more likely to be one sex and children born to older mothers the other, this would be a good sample on which to test their hypothesis. If, however, they were looking for racial or occupational effects, obviously the sample would not be suitable, since the set is homogeneous for both of these.

It is possible that this was the first large data set to be 'placed on punched-cards'. In population statistics, as in so many other disciplines, the advent of computers to do the calculations made an immeasurable difference. Before the late 1950s, a statistician had to be a person who enjoyed doing lengthy and difficult calculations by hand. Since then, equations that used to take months to solve are done in minutes.

Another notable aspect of Edwards and Fraccaro's paper on the Swedish family data is that the complete set of numbers is given in the appendices. In the first appendix is the sex distribution for every family size from the smallest (1 child) to the largest (18 children). The second appendix shows the actual structure (i.e. including birth order) for every family with seven or fewer children.

One of the issues that gave direction to Professor Edwards' work was the search for genetically controlled variability and heritability of the sex ratio. Did some couples produce all girls or all boys in greater numbers than would be expected by chance? Some researchers had found what they thought was evidence for an inherited tendency to bear male children only, but the claim needed further investigation (see Chapter 4, pages 72–5). The Swedish data (as well as two or three other large data sets) were carefully analysed for anything and everything that might provide a hint of heritability, but not a single result was significant. In a later paper Edwards wrote: 'The conclusion drawn from the

Swedish data is easy to record, for there is no evidence for any departure from a chance determination of sex.' Among other things, they had searched for parity effects (birth order), for correlations between consecutive births and for 'the influence of the sexes of previous births on whether or not procreation was continued' (Edwards 1962). In this data set there was no evidence for anything except random effects. Edwards' conclusion from an extensive review of his own and others' data was that 'little progress has been made in establishing the heritability of the sex ratio', and 'it must be concluded that, if genetic variability exists, it is of a very low order of magnitude' (Edwards 1962).

This conclusion remained unchallenged for more than 30 years until William H. James (1996) described a new way of conceptualizing and analysing the data. His work means that there may, after all, be evidence for a genetic effect (see Chapter 4).

There are two reasons why the early work did not show the small sex ratio effects that are generally accepted today. First, the sample sizes were still too small and, second, some of the effects that have since been discovered were not sought at that time – for example, the effect of race on the sex ratio.

SMALL EFFECTS ON THE SEX RATIO

In 1972, Michael S. Teitelbaum of the Office of Population Research at Princeton University wrote a chapter entitled 'Factors associated with the sex ratio in human populations'. In it he listed 75 different research papers published between 1931 and 1970, all investigating the possible influence of various factors on the sex ratio. Ideas ranged far and wide. Some of these were the relative ages of father and mother, ancestral longevity, baldness of father, cigarette-smoking, coffee-drinking, blood groups, physique and temperament, birth control, seasonal variation, geographical and climatic conditions, illegitimacy, urban–rural differences, and high-speed stresses. Most of these are now considered to be irrelevant to the sex of the infant. A possible exception is physique, which may have an indirect effect (see pages 166–7).

Why would all these researchers in different parts of the world have been so intent on investigating factors affecting the sex ratio? There were probably several reasons. People have always been interested in what influences whether a woman will give birth to a girl or a boy. Computer technology had also made it much easier to check the results of earlier studies as well as to investigate new hunches. But for serious demographers the main source of concern appears to have been the possibility that genetic damage may have resulted from radiation, and in the 1950s and 1960s they studied the Japanese populations of Hiroshima and Nagasaki. After many years, researchers concluded that if there was an effect associated with radiation it was very small and soon disappeared.

In the process, however, some factors were found that did have a small effect. The demographers were looking for radiation effects on the sex ratio and found nothing; instead they found some small but important influences they were not looking for. These were race, birth order or parity effects (associated with age of parents), and socio-economic status. They found that there is a slight tendency, detectable only in very large sample sizes, for eldest (first-born) children to be male.

A comprehensive contemporary account of these effects is given by Anouch Chahnazarian, of the Department of Population Dynamics at Johns Hopkins University. In 1988 he published a paper in *Social Biology* entitled 'Determinants of the sex ratio at birth: review of recent literature'. In this paper, he summarized the findings of 30 studies that met rigorous methodological requirements. All the demographers had used 'vital registration data' from countries which, as Chahnazarian put it, had 'high quality birth registration systems'. The countries with these 'clean records' were Norway, the Netherlands, the United States of America, England, Wales, Scotland, Japan, Italy, France, Australia and Belgium. Almost all the studies used sample sizes of several million births; altogether they add up to more than 400 million births. Although there were minor variations in the findings, taken together their results are dependable.

Chahnazarian divided his review into two parts according to whether the researchers were investigating socio-demographic or biological influences on the sex ratio. Both sets of data are relevant to the idea that dominant women conceive more sons – the biological data through the varying effects of the hormones of reproduction, and the socio-demographic data through indirect effects (as explained below).

The strongest effect on the human secondary sex ratio is race, 'black populations having consistently lower sex ratios at birth than white populations'. In his summary, Chahnazarian wrote that some researchers think that the sex ratio is 'determined by the level of maternal hormones circulating' at the time of conception. 'This hypothesis', he said, 'would explain the differences between the races'.

On the basis of his own and others' studies, Teitelbaum (1972, 103) also said that 'After adjusting for the confounding effects of the socio-economic factor, the difference between white and Negro sex ratios in the present analysis remained significant.' Both researchers were aware that their results were limited by the characteristics of their samples, hence Teitelbaum's emphasis on 'the present analysis'. Even though sample sizes were very large, were they representative so far as race was concerned? Probably not.

Because methodologically sound studies of population sex ratios all use data from countries with reliable registration systems, data on sex ratios by race are usually available only for ethnic groups living within a multicultural environment. Where the same groups live in monocultural settings, sex ratios show the opposite effect. For example, although they were working with comparatively small numbers, both Alexandra Brewis (1993) and Jane Underwood (1993) found unusually high sex ratios in Micronesian atoll populations. This, too, would fit the maternal dominance hypothesis. As others have remarked, sex ratios are low in disadvantaged groups – that is, where a group as a whole is dominated by another, this is likely to be reflected in average hormone levels. When the group gains or regains independence, hormone levels rise. Such environmental responsivity is an essential component of the maternal dominance hypothesis and is compatible with the findings on the sex ratio and ethnicity.

After race, the strongest socio-demographic effect on the sex ratio is parity or birth order. It has proved difficult to extract this finding from the data because it is so highly correlated with other socio-demographic factors. Obviously the mother's age, father's age and the order in which the babies arrive are all closely related. When researchers working on the statistical analysis of data confront problems like this they must use sophisticated mathematical techniques such as multivariate analysis to extract the true meaning from the data. These techniques allow researchers to discover which of the various factors is making the most important contribution to the overall correlation and which are making lesser contributions. In this case, earlier univariate studies appeared to indicate that mother's age was the strongest factor related to the sex of her infant, but more sophisticated techniques suggest that the most important effect is birth order. Eldest children are more likely to be male. Again, however, the size of the effect is very small and can be seen only in large data samples. Demographers generally describe it as a 'small negative effect of birth order', which means that as more babies are born (to the couple) there is an increasing likelihood that the child will be female.

This is exactly the kind of effect one would expect from the maternal dominance hypothesis. When Raymond Cattell investigated his core personality traits, he went to considerable trouble to test large numbers of people from a wide variety of backgrounds. He found that women's scores not only differ from men's (Cattell 1965, 260), but decline with age as well (Cattell 1970, 72). In the culture in which he standardized his tests (the United States), older women were found to be less dominant than younger women. This decline in dominance as measured by Cattell's Factor E – small though it is when taken over large populations – exactly reflects the decline in the sex ratio as a woman has more children. This could reflect a basic biological phenomenon involving a decline in the production of hormones. Alternatively, it could be a psychological phenomenon. Women might gradually run out of energy as they bear more children, and this may lead to a lower production of the relevant hormone. Whichever of these mechanisms is operating, or even if both are, they fit the maternal dominance hypothesis.

Some researchers have found that the father's age shows slightly more influence on the sex ratio than the mother's, which at first sight seems odd. But in terms of the indirect influences of mate selection (see pages 165–7) it would make good sense. The portion of the lifespan available for procreation is shorter in women than it is in men, because women cease to be able to bear children from their late 40s, whereas men can sire children for another 20 or 30 years after that. It is possible that the kind of woman that appeals to the older man is less dominant, more nurturant and thus daughter-bearing.

The last major influence on the sex ratio is socio-economic status: people who have higher status tend to have more male infants. This idea has a long history and has been the subject of several research papers dating back at least to 1931. Interest in the conception of sons has been particularly high in families where property and other indicators of wealth and status are handed down through male heirs. Many years ago demographers wondered if the birth of a male heir or two (the contemporary 'heir and a spare') meant that couples would be less likely to continue to have children than if they had daughters only. In the earlier part of the twentieth century this delicate matter was referred to as 'parental instinct', and evidence to support or refute the hypothesis was sought through the records of European royalty.

H. W. Norton, of the Galton Laboratory at University College London, took a particular interest in this issue. In 1940 he wrote a paper for the *Journal of Heredity* in which he criticized the work of a contemporary scientist who had written a paper full of inaccuracies and untenable conclusions. In a no-holds-barred conclusion he wrote that

> the study of data regarding royal families is arbitrary and
> subjective in the case of 'large' families, and fallacious in the

study of 'small' families. His data for small families are examined and it is found that there is no association between family size, sex, birth order, and rank . . . and that the data show no tendency for the youngest children to be male. Finally it is shown that the observed sex ratio of 137:100 exceeds the value of 105:100, usually observed, at the one per cent fiducial level.

(Norton 1940)

This was one of the first studies to show the much-debated socio-economic status effect, assuming that royal families are particularly apt examples of high status. But the numbers were small (278 males to 203 females) and the possibility of a chance effect could not be ruled out. The topic was taken up again in the 1970s by Michael S. Teitelbaum and Nathan Mantel, who were interested in exploring it for two reasons. The first was for the same reason as the earlier papers on parental instinct, a search for a male 'stopping' effect. Do parents stop having children once they have had one or two sons? But by this time the context was different: contraceptives had become widely available and people had much more control over family size than they had ever had before. The second reason was the one associated with the hypothesized differential male vulnerability, especially during pregnancy. It seems almost certain that the primary sex ratio, or sex ratio at conception, is higher than the secondary sex ratio. If it is, then anything that has an effect on the health of the foetus might influence the sex ratio at birth. Researchers wondered if higher socio-economic status meant better health, nutrition and antenatal care, and thus less loss of male foetuses.

As already mentioned, perhaps the most difficult thing about research in this area is that of finding and gaining access to a good data set. Methodologically it is not good enough to simply take a sample of either low or high socio-economic status people and compare their secondary sex ratios with population norms, because there is no way of accounting for unknown factors. One needs a large sample covering the full socio-economic range in order to make legitimate within-group comparisons. In this case, Teitelbaum and Mantel had access to data describing 40,000 participants taking part in a collaborative study of neurological disorders.

Another problem was the definition and measurement of socio-economic status. As noted by Teitelbaum and Mantel, 'sociologists are wary of assigning social status on the basis of a single criterion' (1971). Again computer technology made it feasible to work with multidimensional indices, giving a more complete representation of socio-economic status than could have been achieved earlier. The most commonly used indicators of socio-economic status are occupation, income and educational attainment – Teitelbaum and Mantel used all three. In their conclusion they said:

> our clearest finding . . . is of a significant positive effect of socio-economic status upon the sex ratio at birth. This is true even when the effects of race and gravidity are taken into account . . . it is of the order of 8–9% . . . [and] it may be operative only over the low-to-moderate portion of the socio-economic scale.
>
> (Teitelbaum and Mantel 1971)

In spite of the above seemingly unequivocal findings, there is still uncertainty in this area, most of which originates from continuing ignorance about the primary sex ratio. It is likely, however, that the higher numbers of male infants born to women of moderate as opposed to low socio-economic status reflect the presence or absence of dominance rather than the presence or absence of good nutrition and antenatal care. In addition, it looks as though stressful circumstances are counterbalanced by biological responses relevant to the conception of male infants (see below). Psychological factors seem more plausible and could be related to the position of women in downtrodden circumstances and to the determination of those struggling to improve things for themselves and their families.

A number of smaller studies have reported that high social status is associated with higher sex ratios. These studies range from studies of royalty to studies of high-status wives in polygamous marriages. The latter, in turn, cover a range of situations, from contemporary Mormon marriages to primitive tribal groups, and were discussed in Chapter 4. Dominance appears to be the common characteristic, which is shared by the favoured wife (confident of her charms) and the heiress (confident of her status and wealth).

MORE BOYS IN TOUGH TIMES

The best-known, best-documented and most reliable variation in the human sex ratio occurred during and immediately following the First and Second World Wars. Although many researchers have described this effect, the most frequently cited paper is by Brian MacMahon and Thomas F. Pugh, of the State University of New York and the Harvard University School of Public Health respectively. Writing in the *American*

Journal of Human Genetics in 1954, they showed how the sex ratio in the United States changed during the Second World War, but not during the First. Because some investigators had found non-confirmatory results, MacMahon and Pugh were very thorough in both their work and the presentation of their findings. Since the effect is so important it is described in detail; the following is taken from the introduction.

> The sex ratio increased in practically all the belligerent European countries during the First World War and in the succeeding two or three years. Complete data have not been collected for the period of the Second World War, but certainly in England and Wales a most marked increase occurred. During the years 1941–46 the English live birth sex ratio was the highest ever recorded in that country since the introduction of birth registration in 1841 . . . No change in sex ratio was noted in the United States during the First World War . . . This is hardly surprising, since at most 4 per cent of the United States population was under arms at any one time, and this only for a short period, whereas in the principal European populations from 15 to 22 per cent were so mobilized, in most instances for the entire duration of the war. The Second World War, however, affected the social structure of the United States to almost as great an extent as some of the participating European countries, and if no change in sex ratio occurred in the United States it would certainly bring into question the validity of the generalization regarding sex ratio and war.
>
> (MacMahon and Pugh 1954)

Having thus set the scene, MacMahon and Pugh proceeded to demonstrate beyond any doubt that the sex ratio in the United States rose significantly during the war years, reaching a striking peak in 1946, the year following the signing of peace treaties. In arriving at this conclusion, they dealt with the possible confounding effects of incomplete reporting of stillbirths, and with some noticeable differences in sex ratio by state. As so many demographers have been obliged to do, they omitted all but white births because of inadequacies in reliability. Like others they addressed the possibility of confounding effects of both mother's age and father's age, but found nothing that could account for the wartime effect.

MacMahon and Pugh expressed the differences they found in the form of percentages rather than ratios. Another way of describing the data in this area is to say that male births constitute 51.4 per cent of all births, instead of using the ratio 105:100. People are sometimes surprised when they see the actual figures, forgetting that since the population numbers are very large (several million in each category) quite small differences in the percentage or ratio are statistically significant and reflect large differences in the population. For the years 1942–6, the sex ratio was 51.481 per cent, whereas for the 20-year period 1930–49, it was 51.406 per cent.

MacMahon and Pugh, again like so many others, sought an explanation for their findings. They wrote:

> These data support the belief that some factor or factors associated with war, or the end of war, influences the secondary sex ratio in man. A belief in the wisdom of Divine Providence in increasing the proportion of males born at such times is not essential to the rationalization of this relationship, although it must be admitted that no more satisfactory explanation is yet available.
>
> (MacMahon and Pugh 1954)

Neither a belief in the wisdom of Divine Providence, nor an intellectual commitment to evolutionary biology, nor even a wish to see the latter as the means by which the former's goal was achieved, preclude the explanation being offered here: that dominance in women leads to the conception of male infants. The reasoning is as follows. In times of war when, in the absence of their men, women are required to take over male roles, there is a temporary shift in average dominance. For a short time, these social changes mean that there is a rise in dominance and its hormonal underpinnings, which is likely to be further accentuated by the rise in female testosterone during times of long-term stress. With this increase some women who were close to the hormonal threshold for conceiving male infants tip over it. Hence the temporary rise in male births, which readjusts itself as everyone settles back into more normal circumstances.

If this is the mechanism by which sex ratios are adjusted and maintained, then, one might ask, surely it would be obvious in other settings in which women are required to be tougher than normal. As it happens, in the few scraps of evidence available to investigate this idea, exactly this effect is shown. And one of the first of these scraps of evidence is also in MacMahon and Pugh's paper.

In the course of their work they had become concerned that the rising wartime sex ratios might be being confounded with a continuing overall rise in sex ratio across the entire country for the whole period 1915 to 1950. When they looked more closely at this phenomenon, they noticed that the overall sex ratio was being distorted by the figures from the newer states. On noticing this, they started all over again and re-analysed their data, using only the population figures from those states with stable conditions – and found an even more striking effect for the rise in wartime sex ratios than they had for the country as a whole. In describing their reasons for excluding the newer states, they wrote that:

> prior to 1933 the Birth Registration Area was constantly shifting its geographical boundaries as states were admitted to and dropped from the Area. It was frequently observed that newly admitted states had high sex ratios. This may . . . have its explanation in the greater completeness of male reporting in under-reported areas.
>
> (MacMahon and Pugh 1954)

In other words, the reason for the high sex ratios in the frontier states was said to be the under-reporting of female births. But surely any live birth would be seen as a success and made welcome in the tough frontier conditions? There may simply have been more male births. Further research on existing data might help support or refute this suggestion.

A recent finding from anthropology provides another clue. In 1994, John Martin of Arizona State University published a paper in *Current Anthropology* entitled 'Changing sex ratios: the history of Havasupai fertility and its implications for human sex ratio variation'. In this paper Martin described the fluctuations in sex ratio which occurred over a period of nearly 100 years (1896–1988) in a small group of Havasupai Indians. He gave all the demographic data for each of 1087 individuals. It is rare to find a study such as this that looks completely accurate and tracks families through several generations. The data show wide varia-tions in the sex ratio over time and, although the numbers are small, they are consistent with the idea that tough times for women lead to more male births. Martin described how slave raiders, raids by other Indian groups and epidemics all took their toll on the population. During these times life was very hard, especially for the women. Best documented is the period 1896–1905, when a series of epidemics reduced the population by 34 per cent. All these deaths produced many widows and widowers who 'quickly remarried'. The sex ratio of births to these unions was high. For the period 1906–20, when things were calmer, there was a correspondingly lower sex ratio.

The editor of *Current Anthropology* provides a system of comment and analysis on papers that present major work. Most of the commentators on this study focused on Martin's interpretation of his data, criticizing his idea that coital frequency might explain the changing sex ratios. (This suggestion is discussed in Chapter 4.) John H. Moore, of the University of Florida, took a more positive approach. He wrote:

> Martin is too modest about the significance of the relationship he has discovered. It represents one of the few empirically identified feedback mechanisms between sex ratio and environmental factors: higher adult male mortalities produce more males in the next birth cohorts.
>
> (Moore 1994)

Moore was probably not writing about any specific mechanism; he was simply commenting on what looked like a solid piece of evidence that could lead to a theory about maintaining or stabilizing the sex ratio. It looks as though there could be a kind of large-scale homoeostasis with feedback loops. The means by which this might be accomplished are as follows. Although testosterone is present in only small amounts in women, it is none the less normally distributed, most women having an average amount. But there are fluctuations in this amount over time, occurring in response to social and other events. It looks as though the amount of testosterone might be very sensitively regulated by mechanisms which are both biological and environmental. The biological mechanisms probably set the ceilings or limits on the amount of testosterone in either direction for each individual woman, and may be genetically regulated. The environment probably provides the stimulus for change. Thus women's sensitivity to social conditions may be reflected in the hormones of reproduction; in particular the small variations in the amount of testosterone underlying both the conception of sons and dominant personality.

If this were true it would provide an explanation for a few years of very high sex ratios in a small industrialized town in central Scotland. This phenomenon was discovered by the Lloyds and their colleagues of the University of Dundee Medical School. In a meticulously documented study they found that a sharp rise in the sex ratio for the five years from 1967 to 1971 was accompanied by an equally sharp rise in the standardized mortality rate. This in turn was caused by a rise in both malignant and non-malignant lung and chest disease, later attributed to emissions from the local steel foundry. The area of the town downwind from the foundry was particularly severely affected, and the authors wondered if 'changes in the sex ratios of births may be an early indication of changes of general mortality or morbidity resulting from chemical or biological stresses in the environment' (Lloyd *et al.* 1984).

From the graphs and figures supplied by the authors, it did look as though the rates rose at the same time, which is why the authors suggested that the rise in the sex ratio was an 'early indication' of difficulty. The maternal dominance hypothesis would suggest a slightly different interpretation. Death from lung cancer is not a sudden occurrence: it usually involves a long period of severe illness requiring intensive nursing care. One of the few details that the Lloyds and their colleagues did not give was the sex ratio of the deaths. But whether or not it was predominantly the men that died, the horror of the epidemic and the demands associated with the care of the sick may well have provided the context for an overall rise in dominance for the women of the town, already coping with a far from easy life.

If it is true that tough times lead temporarily to more dominant women and more male births, then it may be possible to suggest a solution to a longstanding puzzle from Ireland. In 1981, Dr Leonard Walby and his colleagues published a paper in the *Ulster Medical Journal* describing a mysterious dip in the Irish live-birth sex ratio. They set out the figures as follows. (In this extract a decimal point has been inserted in the ratios, relating them to base 100 rather than 1000 as the authors did in the original version.)

> Between 1913 and 1977 the mean sex ratio of live births registered in the six counties and the two county boroughs of Northern Ireland was 106.3 males per 100 females. The lowest ratio was 103.4 in 1913 and the highest 109.6 in 1941. In 1978 the very low ratio 100.7 was recorded. In 1977 the ratio was 107.0, and in 1979 it was again close to normal at 105.8.
>
> (Walby *et al.* 1981)

At the time of publication, Dr Walby was director of the Research and Intelligence Unit of the Department of Health and Social Services in Belfast. He and his colleagues investigated every possible explanation for this sudden drop in the number of male births. They analysed the figures county by county, and found that 'in 1978 a ratio of less than 100 occurred in 10 districts, 8 of which, including Belfast, were in the eastern half of the country'. Like other parts of the British Isles, Ireland was expecting a rise in population in 1978. But the number of male births rose by only 14, whereas the number of female births rose by 788. 'It seems therefore', the authors wrote, 'that the low sex ratio in

1978 may reflect a deficit of male births rather than an excess of females'. In England, Wales and Scotland, no such fall occurred. After exhausting all avenues of enquiry the authors wrote:

> We have been unable to think of a likely explanation for the 1978 ratio . . . The fact that it was confined to a single calendar year does not make it easier to understand, but made us look for some form of artefact as a possible cause. This we did not find . . . The departure from the expected sex ratio in 1978 will be noticed when this cohort of Northern Ireland children reaches school age and a number of boys sufficient to fill several schools are [sic] missing mainly from the east of the province . . .
>
> (Walby et al. 1981)

A plausible explanation for this otherwise inexplicable dip may lie in the social history of the time. In 1977 'Right to Life' movements in a number of different countries were at the peak of their influence. As Linda Bird Franke wrote in her book *The Ambivalence of Abortion*, 'In a stunning reversal for the pro-choice forces, the Supreme Court [in the United States] upheld the right of individual states to deny public funding for elective abortions among the poor' (Franke 1978, 244). The annual Right to Life march in Washington DC drew 35,000 marchers in 1977.

> On New Year's Day in 1977, Pope Paul VI not only called abortion a threat to world peace but branded women who have abortions killers who 'freely and consciously murder the fruit of their womb', and in August of the same year, the National Conference of Catholic Bishops announced a new offensive to ban all abortions and family-planning.
>
> (Franke 1978, 249)

In the Irish Republic, because of the strong influence of the Roman Catholic church, both the sale and importation of contraceptives had been illegal since the passing of the Criminal Law Amendment Act in 1935. But in the late 1970s it had become the object of new attention. The Republic had joined the European Community in 1973 and in so doing accepted the compulsory jurisdiction of the European Court of Human Rights. The extent to which the church should or should not proscribe certain behaviours (chief among them being contraceptive practices) for both believers and non-believers was debated with passion. As Roger Sawyer wrote, 'in the Republic there is only a thin line between consensus rule and majority tyranny' (1993, 113). During 1977 the opponents of change made it even harder to acquire contraceptives through illicit channels. The difficulties ended with the passing of the Health (Family Planning) Act in 1979, 'the so-called Irish solution to an Irish problem', because it said that

> contraceptive devices might only be obtained from registered pharmacists if a doctor's prescription was produced; and the Act contained a conscience clause enabling doctors or pharmacists to refuse to co-operate should they have moral or religious objections to such methods of family planning.
>
> (Sawyer 1993, 115)

It seems possible, therefore, given the social, political and religious climate in Ireland during 1977, that only the very determined, tough young women (and probably those living nearer the eastern ports) were able to make it across the Irish Sea to abortion clinics in other parts of Britain.

OCCUPATION AND THE SEX RATIO

The relation between occupation and the sex ratio has fascinated researchers for many years. One of the first was Marianne Bernstein (1954), who found a significant relationship between the occupations of parents listed in *Who's Who in America* and the sex of their children. The more 'masculine' the occupations, as judged by the ratio of men to women working in them, the greater the likelihood of male infants.

The Australian W. R. Lyster also published a number of papers in reputable journals reporting unusual and statistically significant findings. Typical of Lyster's work is a letter to the *Lancet* in 1982 entitled 'Altered sex ratio in children of divers'. During May and June of that year Lyster collected sex ratio data from 58 licensed divers for abalone working on the southeast coast of Australia. 'These self-employed men', he said, 'work on average some 20 hours a week under water, at depths of 10 to 25 metres'. Lyster limited the information on the sexes of offspring to those who 'were engendered after their fathers had become divers'. They had among them 85 daughters and 45 sons, a proportion which would occur by chance less than once in 1000 times. The fact that the data came from a small group of men all working in the same occupation prompts the question: What could be going on?

All through the 1960s and 1970s a number of researchers had

published data on similar themes, the best known of which was prob- ably the sex ratios of airline pilots' offspring. According to Goerres and Gerbert (1976), Lyster's basic working hypothesis was that 'men in so- called stress professions . . . including the pilots of high-performance military aircraft, would be predominantly "girl-fathers"'. By the mid- 1970s, military personnel in Germany considered these 'rumours' to be sufficiently serious to warrant an official investigation. In July 1975 they commanded the director of the German Air Force Institute of Aviation Medicine to look into it. Their findings were reported in a paper published in *Aviation, Space and Environmental Medicine* in August the following year. (This detail alone is enough to make contemporary researchers green with envy. There was no messing around for months applying for approvals in the military of the 1970s!) Another historic aspect of what the authors termed 'this somewhat curious study' was the possibility that pilots might have to be compensated for damages if their 'procreative capacity had been detrimentally affected . . . in the line of duty' (Goerres and Gerbert 1976). This last point was consid- ered important enough to be included in the abstract.

Several explanatory hypotheses had been advanced, the most popular being 'that radiation affecting jet pilots via radar equipment would alter spermiogenesis to such an extent as to cause more X- than Y-chromosome carrying spermatozoons to be present in the ejaculum'. Today there is nothing to suggest that either X- or Y-chromosome- carrying spermatozoa are more vulnerable to stress than the others; nor was there any evidence at that time. But in the absence of any other explanation this was the concern.

In the German investigation, 863 jet and helicopter pilots completed questionnaires. Results were analysed in terms of number of flying hours. ('Why?' one might ask.) Sex ratios were presented in groups, divided into those pilots who had completed 1000 hours of flying and those who had completed 2000 hours. Only in the latter groups did the pilots have significantly more daughters. Since the first 1000 hours of flying is by common consensus far more stressful than the second, stress could not, therefore, be a factor. *Quod erat demonstrandum.*

The 'rumour' might have been laid to rest for a time, but a decade later the worrying thought occurred again, this time in the context of even higher-status men – astronauts. A team of investigators, headed by Bertis B. Little of the Division of Clinical Genetics, Southwestern Medical School, Texas, published a paper in the same specialist journal entitled 'Pilot and astronaut offspring: possible G-force effects on human sex ratio' (1987). This time pilots were divided into two groups according to their exposure to G-forces (a measure of gravitational pull). The paper has an appendix which gives the exact amounts and times of exposure for each of the four groups that took part in the study. Non-rated officers and non-tactical pilots (who suffered either no exposure or little exposure to G-forces) were in one group and tactical pilots and astronauts in the other. These men suffered exposure to forces ranging on average from −2 to +6. 'While combat maneuvering flight could greatly exceed the frequency of exposure to G-forces shown . . . other training flights are not so stringent . . . the frequency represents the average over many flights' (Little *et al.* 1987).

This was clearly a careful study. A number of alternative interpretations of the data were investigated, but none could explain the differences. The results showed that the tactical and astronaut pilots had many fewer sons than daughters (66:100), and that the other pilots had equal numbers of sons and daughters. So once more there was convincing documentation of an effect of fathers' occupation on the sex ratio of their offspring. Pilots were not the only fathers to be investigated: there is evidence that anaesthetists and policemen also have more daughters, and these occupational effects are strong enough to reach statistical significance even in small samples.

The cumulative results of these studies, especially those done over the years on pilots, do need to be accounted for. If the maternal dominance hypothesis is right and women play an important part in controlling the sex of the infant, how is it that there is a continuing effect of father's occupation at least in some groups?

There may be a plausible explanation for these findings in the phenomenon psychologists call 'assortative mating', which describes the fact that most people marry or mate with people who are very like themselves in a number of ways. The overall finding from the studies, most of which were done during the 1980s, was that there are low (but consistent) positive correlations between partners on physical characteristics, cognitive abilities and personality dispositions. This means, for example, that people who are rather tall tend to marry one another, as do people of similar intelligence and so on. This is in addition to the more obvious partner-matching that occurs at the level of race, religion and geographic location.

But when researchers looked for evidence of assortative mating for dominance, there was none, even though there is for other personality traits. This finding was curious enough to cause further work to be done on the relationship between partner selection and dominance. In 1987, Edward Sadalla *et al.* published a paper called 'Dominance and heterosexual attraction'. By working through a series of ingeniously designed studies, they were able to show that while dominant behaviour increases the sexual attractiveness of males it has no effect on the sexual attractiveness of females. Put another way, females are sexually attracted to dominant men, but only half the men find dominance attractive in women. The remaining males prefer non-dominant women.

In the introduction to their paper, Sadalla and his colleagues remind readers that 'dominance is a phylogenetically conservative trait within the primate order, occurring in all primate species', and note that 'one explanation for the evolution of dominance hierarchies in primate societies is that males are compensated for their competitive striving by an increase in their sexual attractiveness to females' (Sadalla *et al.* 1987). If this was the only mechanism at work it would indeed mean, as the authors suggest, that there would be an increase in the proportion of competitive males in each successive generation. But, since this has not been observed, there must be a balancing factor. Although there is as yet little direct evidence to support it, it seems likely that, at the extremes, very dominant men prefer nurturant, 'womanly' partners – non-dominant women. One of the confounding factors here is physical attractiveness, an element in sexual attraction for both sexes, but particularly important in a man's view of a woman's sex appeal. Since being a pilot, diver or police officer probably requires more dominance or toughness than other occupations, it is likely that these men would be above average on dominance and thus sexually attractive to the majority of women. In competitive situations, the majority of such men tend to choose the most beautiful woman, not the most dominant. Evolutionary psychologists have explained these phenomena in terms of 'evolved motivation' (Buss 1994, 97). Both males and females have struggled to acquire certain characteristics (for example, dominance in men and physical attractiveness in women) because members of the opposite sex have signalled a preference for them (Barber 1995).

This indirect effect could form the basis of an explanation. Male occupations, including sports, in which high dominance or toughness is needed to succeed, tend to lead to more daughters in the next generation. Conversely, there is a tendency for more intellectual or artistic men to be attracted to dominant women, who produce more sons (Bernstein 1981).

There are two pieces of research documenting this phenomenon, published nearly 40 years apart. In 1954, Clark W. Heath of Harvard University reported on a relationship between physique, temperament and sex ratio. He was part of a team who followed up on the work of Sheldon and Stevens (1942), by taking further measurements 10 to 15 years after the original 'somatotyping' and 'psychotyping' had been done. During a study of pulse rates, he noticed that 'Men having the lowest pulses had more daughters than sons when they later married and had families, whereas men with the fastest pulses had more sons than daughters' (Heath 1954). Pulse rate had already been found to be related to physique, very athletic men having quite slow pulse rates. Heath found that, whereas men who were not mesomorphs had sons and daughters in equal numbers, mesomorphs had a significantly greater number of daughters.

Intrigued by this finding, he pursued it further. The choice of major topic of study, which had originally shown a correlation with physique, also showed a relationship with the sex of offspring born many years later. Although not statistically significant, there was a trend for men who did 'natural sciences' to have daughters, and for those who did 'arts, letters and philosophy' to have sons. Heath checked his findings by repeating them with the next class, and by looking at first-born infants only. In those, the trends were stronger than for second and later-born children. He also investigated additional measures of physique associated with mesomorphy, such as 'tidal air (volume of air per inspiration at rest)' and a 'recovery index'. He summarized his findings thus: 'The relationship of these various factors with sex of offspring is consistent with the hypothesis: muscular and active fathers tend to have more daughters than sons; thin and intellectual fathers tend to have more sons than daughters' (Heath 1954).

Beck (1992) took a different approach. Controlling for possible bias in reporting he found that artists whose names were included in the British publication *Who's Who in Art* were more likely to have sons than daughters. The word 'artists' in this case appears to be short for 'artists, designers, craftsmen, critics, writers, teachers and curators'. Unfortunately the sex of the artist is not given, so it is not known whether these were the mothers or the fathers; presumably they were predominantly fathers.

The overall trend for men who are more dominant than other men to have more daughters – and for dominant women (whether or not they are married to 'artistic' or 'intellectual' men) to have more sons – appears to be related to the grand-scale homoeostasis mentioned earlier. Such evolutionary fine-tuning could ensure that personality and other psychosexual attributes stay within reasonable bounds and do not go off into extremes. Without such balancing mechanisms it would take only three or four generations for extreme personality attributes to develop, including dominance. Instead, there seem to be a number of factors operating at an almost subconscious level, many of them incorporated into the mysteries of mate selection. I believe there is still much to discover about the processes involved in selecting or rejecting a potential sexual partner.

9

EARLY EXPERIENCE AND EVOLUTIONARY ADVANTAGE

Almost all psychologists agree that early experience influences behaviour in later life. Both psychoanalysts and behaviourists place considerable emphasis on the infant's experience, albeit for very different reasons. At the simplest level, learning theory provides a scientific explanation for the well-known observation that what happens to the baby influences the adult, which is why psychologists seeking to throw more light on individual differences in adults go back to childhood to try to discover how the differences might have arisen in the first place. This universal truth is summed up in folklore in the sayings 'As the twig is bent so grows the tree' and 'The child is father to the man'.

These two sayings also illustrate the two different perspectives on the process whereby this happens. The first, 'As the twig is bent so grows the tree' could be said to imply training. That is, an active agent bends the twig in a particular way, thus influencing the direction of all future development. The second saying, 'The child is father to the man', implies an inherited component, thus emphasizing the biological or natural part of the process.

These two views on growth and development have provided the setting for fierce arguments in the social sciences. The controversy is variously described as 'the nature–nurture debate' or 'heredity versus environment'. Sometimes those who argue that nature is the more important influence on behaviour appear to have the upper hand. At other times those who emphasize nurture have the edge. So far as psychosocial sex differences are concerned, it was assumed until recently that biological influences were the strongest. In the 1970s and 1980s, however, the pendulum swung the other way and many social scientists considered environmental influences to be much more important than biological influences. Now, with the rise of evolutionary psychology and the renewed respect for behaviour genetics, especially the persuasive evidence from twin studies, the pendulum is beginning to swing again towards a more serious consideration of biological influences. One of the main arguments of this book is that each must be given due weight – that any theory which does not incorporate both nature and nurture is unlikely to be useful.

During the 1970s and 1980s the biological perspective on psychosocial sex differences came in good measure from the primatologists. But according to Sarah Blaffer Hrdy their work lacked proper consideration of the full range of attributes. She said that

> theories explaining the nearly universal dominance of males fall into two categories: hypotheses that are either biologically oriented and informed by stereotypes . . . or those that eschew the primate evidence altogether and thereby ignore much that is relevant to understanding the human condition.
>
> (Hrdy 1981, 3)

As an example of the way in which primatologists had oversimplified, she said that early research had 'focused on the way adult males manoeuvre for dominance while females attend to the tasks of mothering: it [had] neglected the manifestations of dominance and assertiveness in females themselves' (Hrdy 1981, 2).

But if primatologists at that time were guilty of biological stereotyping, the psychologists were among those whose tactic was to 'eschew the primate evidence altogether'. They resolutely set themselves the task of demonstrating how nurture, rather than nature, was the chief influence on later behaviour. They said they believed that boys and girls were not born different: they were trained to be different. The basic working hypothesis was that differences in the achievements of men in comparison with women were the result of receiving different treatment by adults while they were children. Psychologists had a hunch that parents and teachers took more notice of boys and provided a more stimulating environment for them, thus enabling them to achieve more in later life. If that was true, the situation could be corrected. To accomplish this, it was necessary to describe in detail exactly how this training was being carried out, then it would be possible to change the attitudes of parents and teachers, modify the training, and thus eliminate psychosocial sex differences.

In fact, psychologists found much more than they were looking for. They had expected adolescents to be treated differently because there are such pronounced differences in physical development during the teenage years. But they had not realized the extent to which prepubertal children experience the world differently according to sex. At every age the differences in the way adults treated children were so strong that psychologists were drawn further and further back in time to see whether these differences were occurring in younger and younger children.

The work involved thousands of hours of observations. In dozens of universities across the world, postgraduate students studying developmental and educational psychology formulated thesis protocols designed to establish whether or not sex stereotyping among children was the reason for later psychosocial sex differences.

The most popular method was to watch mothers and teachers interacting with children in both school and home settings. Researchers would spend weeks with clipboards and check lists, noting the number of occasions and the total amount of time adults attended to boys in comparison with girls. In addition to quantity of time, they noted aspects of the interactions which would indicate how the time was being used. For example, they recorded such details as who initiated the interaction; whether it was for 'positive' or 'negative' reasons; whether the interaction resulted in further information, guidance or encouragement for the child, and so on.

After several years a considerable body of information had been assembled. When the results of all these studies were pooled and analysed, it became clear that the social environment experienced by boys is very different from that experienced by girls. Particularly in classroom settings, interactions between adults and boys on the one hand, and adults and girls on the other, have been shown to be both quantitatively and qualitatively different. Wherever researchers looked, adults were unconsciously differentially reinforcing what they deemed to be sex-appropriate behaviours. They found that children and young people are actively guided into behaving in particular ways according to whether they are female or male. Correct behaviours are approved and rewarded (by smiles, warmth, affection, attention), and incorrect behaviours are either not rewarded (ignored) or, in some instances, punished.

Stanford University professors Eleanor Maccoby and Carol Jacklin wrote the definitive summary of work in this area. They found that 'Boys seem to have more intense socialization experiences than girls' (Maccoby and Jacklin 1974, 348). They also said that boys have more pressure put on them to behave in sex-appropriate ways. For example it is more acceptable for a girl to be a tomboy than it is for a boy to be a sissy. Maccoby and Jacklin found that boys receive more punishment than girls do, and also more praise. They wrote that 'adults respond as if they find boys more interesting, and more attention-provoking than girls' (1974, 348), and wondered if this could be most simply explained by the fact that the boys were more active than the girls. But there is no reliable sex difference in total activity level, so researchers were left wondering whether there was something about boys' activity which was more attention-getting than girls'. Whether there is or not is still unknown.

When developmental psychologists found that even toddlers are treated differently according to sex, they went back to the very beginning to look for the origin of these sex differences. Contrary to expectations, researchers found sex differences in the way even babies experience the world. When sex is assigned at the moment of birth, the pattern is set for all future interactions. After that, people have different expectations about how the child should grow and develop. If children and young people behave in ways which are contrary to these expectations, they create uneasiness in those around them. This happens everywhere. Across all human cultures, children are taught to behave in sex-appropriate ways.

Up till now the explanation for this phenomenon has been solely in terms of gender-role socialization and sex stereotyping on the part of parents and care-givers. An alternative view is that sex stereotyping, powerful as it is, is not the whole story. The personality of the mother, and in particular the extent to which she is or is not dominant, appears to be relevant not only to the predetermination of the sex of her infant but also to the way she interacts with him or her after birth. If there are personality differences between women who conceive sons and women who conceive daughters, and if dominance is relatively stable over a period of months, then newborn babies whose experience of the world is so intimately associated with their mothers will experience that world differently according to sex.

This is a testable hypothesis. All it needs is for someone to watch mothers interacting with their newborn infants and record the behaviours. Differences in the mothers' personalities ought to result in differences in their behaviour towards their infants. Of course, the people who do the observations should not know about the theory beforehand. In that way one could be sure that the observations were not influenced by what the observers hoped or expected to see.

Because of the prolonged and intense interest in the origin of psychosocial sex differences (described above), this work has already been done. All that remains is to describe the ways in which researchers made the observations and look at their results.

OBSERVATIONS OF MOTHERS AND BABIES

After finding sex differences in interaction at every age level, researchers were finally left with the necessity to observe mothers interacting with their babies within hours of birth. To the surprise of many, every researcher who did a properly designed study of mother–infant interaction and published the findings found significant sex-of-infant differences in mothers' behaviours, whether they had been looking for them or not.

One of the most important methodological concerns is to be sure that the babies themselves are not behaving differently. If baby boys behave in specific ways that baby girls do not, then any differences in the mothers' behaviours might simply be a consequence of responding appropriately to different events. In almost every study, however, researchers found no differences in the behaviour of male and female babies. Those who did (two found that male infants cried more) controlled for this in the analysis of their results.

The first study in this area, and one of the most influential, was done by Howard Moss of Stanford University. In 1967 he published his findings in the prestigious *Merrill Palmer Quarterly*, in an article entitled 'Sex, age, and state as determinants of mother–infant interaction'. In the mid-1960s he had established a research team to discover more about what goes on between mothers and their babies in normal everyday settings. He sent out highly trained observers to watch mothers with their first-born babies in their own homes. The mothers were told that they were part of a study on how normal infants behave in the home environment. They were asked simply to carry on as usual, as though the observers were not there. Two groups of observations were made of each mother and infant, the first during the first month of the infant's life and the second during the third month. A group of observations consisted of two three-hour observations and one eight-hour observation. An ingenious way of recording the behaviours was devised, and of course the study fulfilled a number of strict methodological criteria including inter-observer reliability and allowance for the baby's state and level of activity.

Moss found that the differences in the mothers' behaviours according to the sex of their infants were most pronounced at the three-week observations, and still significantly different at three months. Of the 16 maternal behaviours that were measured (things like 'holds infant close', 'burps infant' and 'talks to infant'), there were strong sex differences on three. The variables 'stresses musculature' and 'stimulates/arouses infant' were performed significantly more frequently by the mothers of sons, and the variable 'imitates infant' significantly more frequently by the mothers of daughters:

> In general, these results indicate that much more was happening with the male infants than with the female infants. Males slept less and cried more during both observations and these behaviours probably contributed to the more extensive and stimulating interaction the boys experienced with the mother, particularly for the 3-week observation.
>
> (Moss 1967)

Even after irritability was controlled for, the male infants still received much more stimulation and arousing behaviour from their mothers than did the female infants. And female infants received much more imitative behaviour from their mothers. In most cases 'imitative' behaviour referred to the mother repeating a vocalization made by the baby.

Moss discussed his findings in detail. He wondered whether the male infants were getting more stimulation from their mothers because they cried more. Then, since the mothers of irritable male babies tended to respond less frequently to their crying as time went by, he suggested that mothers kept on responding to the infant girls' cries, but not to the boys', because that was 'in keeping with cultural expectations'. Moss suggested that 'the mother is initiating a pattern that contributes to males being more aggressive or assertive, and less responsive to socialization'.

From then on, developmental psychologists began a series of investigations, all looking at the nature of the interactions between mothers and their infants. Between 1967 (when Moss first published his findings) and 1988, more than a dozen papers were published giving details of sex-of-infant differences in mother–infant interactions. The papers were all from teams of independent researchers working in a variety of settings, predominantly in the United States, but also in Sweden and France.

Of these papers, nine are particularly well carried out in terms of the methodological criteria necessary to ensure the validity of the results. For example, all the researchers ensured that only full-term, normal babies were included in the sample; that drugs during delivery were within a stated minimum; that mothers and babies were behaving as naturally as possible, and that inter-observer reliability trials reached 90 per cent agreement.

Even so, there were variations in the way data emerged from the various programmes. The most important reason for this was that all the research teams were completely independent; another that all the researchers had different reasons for carrying out their projects. This meant that the study of sex-of-infant differences in mother–infant interaction was not their only goal – nor even their most important one.

These goals were not necessarily fulfilled either. Sometimes the hypotheses they were testing proved supportable and at other times not. The striking thing, however, was that every one of them found significant differences in the ways mothers of male infants interacted with their babies compared with mothers of female infants, whether they were looking for them or not (for a full account, see Grant 1994b).

In 1972 Michael Lewis, a meticulous researcher, reported his results. He had been especially careful to note whether or not there were differences in the babies' behaviours which might account for the differences in the mothers' behaviours. He said he could find no group differences (boys versus girls) in the babies' behaviours. But, he wrote,

> Not so the behaviour of the mothers. These seem to be determined by the sex of the infants. In general mothers of boys held, touched and rocked their children more than mothers of girls. Mothers of girls however, tended to vocalize and look at their children more than mothers of boys.
>
> (Lewis 1972)

In 1966 Peter Wolff found some minor differences in the behaviours of newborn baby girls and newborn baby boys, but these were not sustained beyond the first few days of life and were largely reflexive in nature. All the researchers since then have found (like Howard Moss and Michael Lewis) that mothers respond differently to male and female infants even though from the point of view of the babies there seems no reason to do so.

THE NATURE OF THE DIFFERENCES IN MOTHERS' BEHAVIOURS

When one looks in detail at what all these researchers found, some common themes emerge. In general, Moss's original observation that boys received more stimulation in a variety of ways is borne out. In a programme based at Stanford University in the early 1970s, Evelyn Thoman's team (Thoman *et al.* 1972) found that male infants received more 'general stimulation' than female infants, while mothers talked to female infants more. In 1975 Josephine Brown, of Georgia State

University, reported on the interactions of 45 African-American inner-city mothers with their healthy full-term newborn infants. For the first time, workers on her team had used an efficient electronic digital recording system to collect their data. They found that mothers of male infants both stimulated and talked to their babies more than mothers of female infants did (Brown *et al.* 1975).

At Umea University in Sweden, Jan Winberg and Peter de Chateau (1982) found that middle-class mothers of male infants also stimulated their infants more than mothers of female infants. They did this by looking, holding the infant's hand, playing, smiling and kissing. In Göteborg, Sweden, Carl-Philip Hwang (1978) worked with first-time mothers at a maternity hospital. He found that mothers of female infants had more skin-to-skin contact with their babies, and smiled and talked to them more. Mothers of male infants had more contact with their babies through clothed parts of the body.

In 1982, Monique Robin, working in Paris and recording the interactions of both full-term and premature babies with their mothers, found that mothers of female infants stroked and caressed their infants more than mothers of male infants. Their findings were similar to those of another team of French workers from Besançon (Millot *et al.* 1988). And at Louisiana State University a team of developmental psychologists (Gottfried *et al.* 1987) summed up their findings by writing that 'Mothers held first-born sons upright in tactual contact with the trunk, whereas daughters were held supine on the lap and exposed to frequent maternal smiling.'

Taken as a whole, there is a high degree of uniformity in the results. Where there is an element of disagreement it is primarily in the details, and even this may be reduced by demonstrating that these small inconsistencies occur in areas where there is not quite enough information in the original reports on exactly what the researchers were measuring. For example, if researchers simply wrote that mothers 'touched' their infants more, this is too general to be able to make a proper comparison. Some touching can be very gentle and may occur while the baby continues sleeping; other touching, as Robin wrote in her report, might be more stimulating and 'intended to provoke a reaction in the baby' (1982).

In addition to all these studies, there have been informal accounts of similar findings of sex-of-infant differences in mothers' behaviours. In 1977 a team of developmental psychologists at Edinburgh University was studying very early reflexive behaviours. In this context 'reflexive behaviour' is a way of describing certain actions of a very young baby which look as though they might be purposive, but which are not, because the neurological networks which would make them purposive are not yet mature. For example, sometimes a baby no more than two or three days old will appear to be smiling. But this is not true responsive smiling – it is as though the muscles were just practising, without yet knowing what they were doing.

The psychologists studying early reflexive behaviours were interested to see if such behaviours could be maintained beyond the neonatal period. The two reflexive behaviours selected for study were 'reaching' and 'imitation'. Bower (1977) reports that mothers were given no special instructions and were assumed not to be practising either behaviour with their babies in between sessions. One of the researchers, however, found a massive (approaching 100 per cent) sex difference – 'the girls gave up reaching and the boys wouldn't imitate'. The researchers said that 'it was clearly an artefact of the mothers' pattern of interest rather than a true sex difference'.

An alternative interpretation is that the mothers were behaving normally, and that 'normal' behaviour for mothers of girls differs slightly from 'normal' behaviour for mothers of boys. It was especially interesting that these two behaviours were consistent with those which discriminated mothers of boys from mothers of girls in so many other studies of mother–infant interaction.

In another so-called fluke finding, developmental psychologists in Nashville, Tennessee, also found an impressive sex-of-infant difference in the behaviour of mothers. This time it was the mothers' behaviours before the birth of the child. The researchers were trying to establish the antecedents of good mothering, and as part of this study the authors administered a personality subscale to mothers early in their pregnancies. They reported that those who later gave birth to male infants 'demonstrated more positive personality characteristics than did mothers of female infants'.

When asked for further information about this, one of the researchers, Dr W. A. Altemeier, replied as follows:

> This must just be on the basis of chance alone . . . The personality scores of the mothers were taken very early in pregnancy before she had any idea whether she was carrying a boy or a girl, and it is hard to understand how personality characteristics would have been influenced by the baby she was carrying. The data are also only based on 85 subjects.
>
> (Altemeier 1984)

At the same time as he offered this explanation, Dr Altemeier was kind enough to share information on the personality questionnaire he had used. The questions were very similar to others used by personality theorists to measure dominance. For example, one question read: 'Does it spoil your day when someone criticizes you or puts you down?' (Dominant, or 'strong' people as Dr Altemeier called them, tend to answer 'No'.) Another question read: 'Who makes the decisions in your household?' Again the power of decision-making, or the power to delegate decision-making, has often been used as an indicator of dominance in personality research.

This kind of informal evidence must not be given the same weight as the more formal scientific research reports. Nevertheless, both pieces of evidence came from the laboratories of reputable researchers and it is appropriate to take them seriously. No similar but contrary pieces of evidence have been found. The upshot is that more than a dozen developmental psychologists have found that mothers of male infants behave differently from mothers of female infants. Mothers of males are pushier, initiating interactions with their babies; mothers of female infants are gentler and more responsive.

THE SEARCH FOR EXPLANATIONS

When a number of different researchers, working independently in different parts of the world and at different times, all come up with similar results, both researchers and theorists begin to take the findings seriously. What all these psychologists showed is that although there are at most only very minor differences in babies' behaviours in the first few weeks and months of life, there are strong and consistent differences in mothers' behaviours according to whether the baby is a girl or a boy. What, they asked, could possibly explain this?

As mentioned earlier, most theorists decided that this was the strongest evidence so far of the pervasiveness of sex stereotyping. It was argued that women who have recently given birth would hold these beliefs about gender role development as strongly as anyone else in the community, and that therefore the differences in mothers' behaviours were no more than should be expected. When these differences were found to be consistent across studies, researchers looked again at the exact nature of the stereotypes to see how they would fit.

They found, as expected, that in most societies boys are brought up to be more aggressive, more competitive and more interested in things, whereas girls are brought up to be more submissive, more emotionally expressive and more interested in people. One of the most widely accepted descriptions of the contrasting social roles was Hoffman's, written in 1977. He found that females are required to be responsive to the needs and feelings of others, to express empathy, to be kind, unselfish and loving; and that males are encouraged to acquire such attributes as mastery and problem solving, and that they are urged, more frequently than females, to be independent, self-reliant and strong-willed.

No one who has thought about it would doubt the deep pervasiveness of sex stereotyping. Appropriate gender role socialization is a very important part of a child's adaptation to the community in which he or she lives. But is a mother within hours of the birth of her baby intent only on preparing her child for future society? Could this be the total explanation for the findings? The sex-of-infant differences in mothers' behaviours towards their infants have proved to be so consistent over time and place that some additional explanation seems warranted.

The maternal dominance hypothesis claims that in one important respect the mothers themselves are different. As well as holding ideas about sex-appropriate ways of behaving, mothers are also interacting with their newborn babies in ways which are completely natural for them. If dominant women conceive more sons, then infant boys are more frequently exposed to the interactive styles of dominant women, rather than to those of less dominant women.

DOMINANCE MAKES THE DIFFERENCE

Because of the early work on the definition of dominance, it is possible to describe the sorts of differences likely to occur in the interactions of more and less dominant woman with their babies. For example, Fiske's definition of the core of dominance was 'acting overtly so as to change the views or actions of another' (1971), while Cattell's definition (1965) included self-assertive and vigorous behaviour. Accordingly, a dominant mother would probably be more interactive, perhaps initiating interactions more frequently. She may even be a little tougher on her baby than a non-dominant mother would be. A less dominant mother might be less willing to interfere with her baby, content to respond to the baby gently, perhaps even to soothe and caress baby more. On the whole she would tend to be more accepting and to intervene less.

Thus the specific nature of the differences in the mothers' behaviours supports the maternal dominance hypothesis. Or, to put it round the other way, the differences in mothers' behaviours that one would expect to find if the hypothesis were sound are the very ones which the researchers found. They are consistent not only in that mothers *do* behave differently according to the sex of their infant, but also in the independent descriptions of the nature of the differences.

It should also be noted that because of specialization in the academic world very few psychologists working in the area of personality theory would be aware of what was going on in developmental psychology. Those personality theorists (Fiske, Cattell, Russell and Mehrabian) who have offered carefully thought-out definitions of dominance were probably totally unaware of the findings on mother–infant interaction. Yet their descriptions of what constitutes dominant behaviour in women have enabled others to make easily ratifiable predictions about the differences one would expect in the ways mothers of boys would interact with their infants compared with mothers of girls. The concordance in the findings has been a surprise to everyone.

Some might argue that even if mothers of boys are interacting with their babies differently to mothers of girls, the differences are relatively minor. All babies are handled in similar ways by both care-givers and parents. Whether they are boys or girls, they sleep and feed, cry and interact with their mothers or care-givers in very much the same ways. Does it really make such a difference in the long term?

On this point there is no real disagreement. Not only do all major psychological theories emphasize the critical role of early interaction, but contemporary researchers continue to find systems of great complexity in the development of the human infant. And everywhere tiny differences in mother–infant interaction lead to important differences in the adult. The detailed intertwining of nature and nurture contributes to the wide individual differences seen in adults. For example, Trevarthen described the complexity of the vocal interaction between mother and infant in the first few days and weeks of life. His research showed that the infant's care-giver (usually the mother), who 'enters into an intimate supportive relationship' with the infant, 'has to have intuitive emotional responses and behaviours that are unconsciously controlled and cannot be learned' (1993, 74). In support of this he writes:

> The extraordinary similarities that appear in different cultures, for example, in the intonation, timing, pitch and rhythms of mothers' vocalizations to babies, and the similar but less marked features observed when men or children attempt the same contact with a baby, are evidence for both the universal needs of babies and some universal motivation in all human brains to meet these needs.
>
> (Trevarthen 1993, 74)

In addition to the decades of work in this area by developmental psychologists, personality psychologists with an evolutionary perspective have emphasized that both biological and environmental influences on behaviour are likely to be important. Commenting on a series of experiments which showed how dominance increases the sexual attractiveness of males, but not of females, Sadalla *et al.* (1987) said: 'Specific relations between dominance and attraction are predicted both by sociobiological theories that emphasize evolutionarily determined behaviour tendencies and by sociocultural theories that emphasize socialization practices and sex role expectations.'

If dominance adds to a man's sexual attractiveness but not to a woman's, it seems reasonable to postulate an adaptive mechanism behind the maternal dominance hypothesis. In suggesting that psychological sex differences have their origins in the different problems faced by our male and female ancestors, evolutionary psychology provides a framework that renders the whole idea more plausible. There would need to be a mechanism by which sex role development is initiated and maintained. To maximize reproductive success, mothers would need to train their male offspring to be dominant, but not their female children. How could such an end be achieved except through a link between reproductive physiology and behaviour? The association between female testosterone and dominance provides such a link. The very nature of the differences in the mothers' behaviours endorses the idea that dominance in the mother is not only relevant to the conception of a male infant, but also to laying the groundwork for the kinds of behaviours which will later characterize the man.

It is also of interest that male dominance is not imposed by males, but is accomplished by females. There may be an irony here, in that it appears that women themselves, by their very nature, are the ones who maintain psychosocial sex differences.

This kind of theorizing raises many more questions than it answers, not least among them: Why so early? Why would these critical influences on later sex role development need to be instigated within hours and days of birth? The findings give more weight than ever to the two sayings from folklore quoted at the beginning of this chapter.

Discoveries about sex role development in the rat add one final irresistible piece of evidence. Beyer and Feder (1987), in their work on brain sex differentiation, wrote that 'Mother–infant relationships during the first week of postnatal life in rats appear to permanently alter organization of the neural substrates underlying sexual behaviour. The key finding is that mothers spend more time with male than with female pups.' The authors think that sex steroids probably alter some stimulus characteristics of the pups to which the mothers respond.

> These interesting behavioural observations suggest that expo-
> sure to neonatal sex steroids, besides producing organizational
> changes in brain tissue, may also alter maternal behaviour
> toward male pups, leading to an increase in the rate of sensory
> stimulation during the critical postnatal period . . . [This]
> maternal stimulation may produce optimal masculinization.
>
> (Beyer and Feder 1987)

In support of these claims, the authors cite the work of others – especially Moore and Morelli (1979) who made the original observations. If
there are differences of this magnitude and importance in early
mother–infant interaction in rats, it would not be surprising if even
more was happening in humans. It is likely that we are only beginning
to see the importance of it all.

10

SEX PREFERENCES AND SEX SELECTION

Throughout recorded history there is evidence that people have been interested in being able to select the sex of their infant and, from ancient times until today, by far the greatest part of the advice concerns how to get a boy. Not surprisingly, feminist writers have done the best job of documenting the history of son preference. One of these is Gena Corea, a founding member of the Feminist International Network of Resistance to Reproductive and Genetic Engineering (FINRRAGE) and author of *The Mother Machine* (1985). In a hard-hitting chapter she presents the evidence for son preference down the ages and across cultures. It is very convincing and provides strong support for the existence of son preference as an almost universal phenomenon.

Prescientific suggestions about how to conceive a son go back at least to 800 BC (Wells 1990). Some have been recycled through the ages and modern versions of them are still current. Ideas with a long history are those that offer advice on the seasons or weather, diet, having intercourse on odd or even days, specific behaviours or positions during intercourse, and timing of orgasms.

While methods of sex selection were based on mere folklore, they attracted little attention from researchers. But serious attempts to document son preference have increased since the late 1960s, reflecting the perceived efficacy of the latest sex selection techniques.

Articles about the possible social effects of sex selection began to appear in the mid-1970s in response to the wave of publicity about L. B. Shettles' work (see Chapter 4). One of these was entitled 'What happens when we get the manchild pill?'

> Sex control appears finally to be inevitable and unstoppable . . . Too many scientists are working on it for it to go away, and no doubt the work itself is fascinating and

compelling. The commercial market for sex control would be tremendous.

(Campbell 1976)

The article illustrates the confidence and excitement that the issue of sex selection provoked at that time, but it was not long before caution replaced the excitement. An article in *Science* (Westoff and Rindfuss 1974) reported on son preference in the United States. Their research was carried out on women who had yet to begin their reproductive lives, and was said by some to document only the fact that the whole culture was male-biased. Later research showed that a majority of women (but again nulliparous students) would prefer a boy first and a girl second. Further studies carried out on white populations in the United States found that men desire sons more than women do; but women themselves want a boy first, and if the number of children is not even they want more boys than girls. In Western cultures overall, the most frequently desired family unit is said to be a boy first and then a girl.

Developmental psychologists tend to be wary. Some say that such a family structure is far from ideal. It appears to owe more to some misplaced romanticism than it does to what is known about child development. Feminist writers have also explored the issue, citing the literature on the known benefits of being first-born. They too have made it clear that universally relegating women to the position of second-born would not be a good idea.

Since much of the research in this area is based on what people said they wanted before they had started their own families, it was a real step forward when demographers began their research on 'stopping rules'. This branch of enquiry looks at the question: Do people with single-sex families continue reproduction until they have had a child of the other sex? And if so, is there a difference between those couples who have all-male families, and those who have all-female families? If there were a strong preference for a male infant throughout a particular culture, the argument goes, then surely it would be demonstrable at a population level. Families with a number of girls would continue having children in the hope of achieving a boy. This in turn would give rise to a preponderance of sibships in which several girls were followed by 'finally a boy', rather than the opposite pattern: several boys followed by 'finally a girl'. In fact it is hard to find evidence to support either pattern. Some studies have shown a preponderance of all-male single-sex sibships (see Chapter 4), but these may be confined to a particular time and a particular geographical area.

Although the reliability of the data in biostatistics is usually very high, its interpretation can be most difficult. In this case, one can easily think of a number of factors which would influence a couple's behaviour. One of the most important of these is the availability of contraception. Was the data for the study collected before or after contraceptive techniques became widely available? In addition, there are issues about religious beliefs, whether or not a couple actually practised contraception reliably, what their attitudes are towards larger families, and the state of their marriage.

In spite of all these difficulties in research and interpretation, social scientists have built up a picture which suggests there is still good evidence for son preference in Western cultures. In reaction to this, some feminist groups are making a point of articulating a daughter preference, but this is probably insufficiently widespread to make a noticeable difference to the overall pattern, which remains persistently son-preferring.

SON PREFERENCE IN ASIAN CULTURES

For a long time it has been clear from anthropological sources that female infanticide was widely practised in some cultures, particularly some Asian cultures. It is likely that this practice is now greatly reduced, at least in the majority of areas. According to most commentators, however, the reason for the reduction in female infanticide is not due to the greater acceptance of girls, but to the introduction of amniocentesis facilities, and the wide availability of early abortion for sex selection. In the last 10 to 15 years, well-trained and concerned Asian demographers have been collecting new data on sex ratios, and what they have found is evidence of a stronger-than-ever trend towards son preference.

In 1980, A. Ramanamma and U. Bambawale published an article in *Social Science and Medicine* entitled 'The mania for sons'. They presented data taken from the records of three hospitals in a large city in India which gave clear evidence of sex-selective abortion. Of the 450 women carrying female infants, 430 chose to terminate the pregnancy, but not a single woman carrying a male foetus chose to do so, even when there was a risk of genetic defect.

The authors described how these findings are consistent with a long tradition that 'values the birth of sons and devalues daughters in South Asia'. They elaborated on this cultural tradition by explaining what happens:

Economically, a female child is considered a drain on the family purse. She takes away considerable money in the form of wedding expenses and dowry. As she grows up a girl is trained in the parental home to take up the role of housewife, but when she takes the role she has been groomed for, she becomes an asset in the house of the in-laws. The burden of rearing a girl falls on the parents, but there is no material gain in their endeavour.

(Ramanamma and Bambawale 1980)

Although the data was collected at hospitals in 'a large city in India' it is not entirely clear what the authors mean by 'South Asia'. What is known from a number of other sources is that at least the largest and most prominent Asian cultures, and probably some of the smaller ones too, do have a tradition of favouring males. If the reasons for doing so are similar to the economic reasons described above, it is not hard to understand why the older generation might believe they were acting in their children's best interests if they advised against the birth of a daughter. There have been reports that it is the grandmother or grandmother-in-law who acts against the conception or birth of a female infant, not the mother herself.

In some countries the situation has been exacerbated by government demands to limit each couple's reproduction to one child. If, for cultural and economic reasons, there is a strong son preference in a particular country, and then superimposed on this there is a restriction on the number of children, it is not surprising that people become desperate and resort to desperate measures.

WOULD PARENTS WANT TO CHOOSE?

Given the evidence for son preference, it is likely that some parents would want to select the sex of their infant if it were possible to do so. But how many parents would actually avail themselves of such an opportunity? Suppose, for the sake of the argument, that the preselection of the sex of the infant were a simple matter – that there was, as Colin Campbell suggested, a 'manchild pill' or a 'womanchild' pill that people could afford. How many couples would want to design their families, and how many would prefer to leave this matter to chance?

This is a similar kind of question to the one asked when contraception first became available, only now it concerns a characteristic of the children. As with contraception, some would doubtless welcome it and use it immediately, claiming that theirs was the responsible course of action. Every planned child would be even more wanted than before. Those concerned about world population and related ecological problems might be especially pleased, believing that if people could have one child of each sex they would limit their families to two children. Others would claim it was against the laws of nature, or against the wishes of God, and that it was wrong to interfere in something so profound as the creation of another human being. Such issues would be discussed at the personal level as a matter of individual conscience. Some might see it as a matter that concerned only the couple involved.

So far as the maternal dominance hypothesis is concerned, however, all these issues would be overridden by the idea that a particular woman was psychologically suited to conceive and bear a child of a particular sex. If the processes involved in the predetermination of the sex of the infant are as complex and wide-ranging as it now appears they may be, this would become another important factor in the decision.

One could argue that if the mother could artificially alter her hormonal status in order to conceive a boy or a girl, then her personality would change too in the direction appropriate to the sex of the infant she planned. But even if this were possible it may be unwise, given that there are so many things we still do not know about the conception, birth and development of the human infant. It may seem preferable for women who have given birth to all-girl or all-boy families to view themselves as specialists in one sex or the other and be proud of that, instead of trying for an infant of the sex they are not so suited to raise.

If the maternal dominance hypothesis were confirmed, one might also want to think about its implications for adoption, especially when parents seek to adopt a child of the sex they have been unable to conceive naturally. Theoretically it would be unwise to do so, particularly in terms of the child's early development. But this, too, is a researchable question. It would help in making decisions about this to know whether those adoptions which were made to provide a child of the other sex in an otherwise single-sex sibship were ultimately as successful as those which were undertaken for other reasons.

A PROBLEM FOR SOCIETY

Although couples might believe the problem was a personal one, to be solved by discussion with one's spouse or partner, it is all too possible that it would shortly become a societal problem as well. As noted above, it is likely that the ability to preselect the sex of the infant would result in more boys being born. This would mean a fundamental change in the sex ratio, the consequences of which would be hard to predict. Although distorted sex ratios would almost certainly be more pronounced in some cultures than in others, they would probably occur in almost all.

As so often happens when new ideas are introduced in reproductive technology, some people want the research stopped. In 1968 the editors of *Science* gave prominence to a lengthy paper by Amitai Etzioni, then Professor of Sociology at Columbia University. He had addressed the International Symposium on Science and Politics at Lund, Sweden in June of that year on the topic 'Sex control, science and society'. After reviewing what was known at that time, he said there was 'no specific reason we could not have sex control five years from now or sooner'. This being the case, he addressed himself to the question: Are there any circumstances under which society could justify some limitation on the freedom of science? His was not a philosophical treatise; rather it surveyed the scientific findings and social evidence for sex preferences and came down on the side of restrictions. Since technology 'is largely already socially guided ... the argument that its undesirable effects cannot be curbed because it cannot take guidance is a false one', he declared, and he recommended setting up committees to deal with the matter. 'Such bodies could rule, for instance, that whereas fertility research ought to go on uncurbed, sex-control procedures for human beings are not to be developed.'

Neither science nor society heeded this call. The only noticeable consequence was that scientists learned to step in quickly to calm people's fears, often with superficial reassurances. Or they claimed that scientists cannot be blamed for what society does with their results. Some of the most energetic discussion on this issue took place in the 1970s, when it seemed that parents everywhere would soon be able to preselect the sex of their infants by timing intercourse (see Chapter 4).

In 1979, in response to some of the misgivings that were being expressed, Joe Leigh Simpson wrote an editorial on the topic for the *New England Journal of Medicine*, saying: 'alarming possibilities notwithstanding, it seems unlikely that sex preselection would have profound long-range implications ... ' The ostensible reason for his equanimity was his certainty that any problem of imbalance would be short term because the 'under-represented sex' would soon become more desirable. 'Common sense', he declared 'and biologic selection would eventually regain what nature had evolved a sex ratio nearly equal to one'. Since he presented no evidence at all to support his views, one cannot help wondering whether he was simply seeking to ensure that scientific research could proceed without objections from the more conservative members of the public.

In contrast, social scientists were taking the problem seriously and had set about conducting a series of studies. In 1983, Gary H. McClelland wrote a chapter on 'Measuring sex preferences and their effects on fertility', in which he explained how sex selection had the potential to make three major changes in population structures. These would be overall fertility rates (people might have fewer children if they could be sure of having both sexes), sex ratios (there would probably be a greater number of males) and birth order of the sexes (more boys would be born first, more girls second). Information about the cultural and religious values of the particular population studied, including the prevalence of the use of contraceptives, give studies like this more validity than some of the earlier ones.

McClelland based his findings on an analysis of 'parity progression ratios', the proportion of women at a given parity who have an additional child. By examining existing family compositions, and noting which ones had lower than average progression ratios, it was possible to come to a conclusion about which was the preferred sex in any given population.

Mathematically elegant though this method is, it is not without interpretive difficulties, as McClelland himself pointed out. The figures alone cannot explain why parents might decide against continuing to have children, even if the sex of the child were the only consideration (which it clearly is not). McClelland cited the gambler's fallacy as one of the confounding factors – parents might believe that if the first three children are girls, then the family is due for a boy. Or parents might believe the opposite, what McClelland calls the 'trend fallacy'. In fact there is some evidence for this: 'If the first three children are boys, then the probability of a fourth boy rises from 0.513 (the probability of a boy on the first birth) to 0.534' (1983, 19). But on the whole,

> Inaccurate subjective probabilities for sex of next birth further complicate interpretation of parity progression ratios. For example a couple may stop even though they are not satisfied because they 'know' incorrectly that their next child will be of the undesired sex.
>
> (McClelland 1983, 31)

Overall, most commentators conclude that not enough is known to be sure about any of the longer-term social consequences of free availability of sex selection. Although there is evidence for a strong son preference in some cultures, and a moderate son preference in others, we cannot predict what effects this might have even in the foreseeable future, let alone in the next generation.

THE ETHICS OF SEX SELECTION

The debate on this topic needs to be separated into two parts, depending on the method of sex selection. The first, involving early amniocentesis and abortion, has been going on vigorously ever since the technology became readily available. The second, called more accurately the ethics of sex preselection, comes to the fore whenever it looks as though reproductive physiologists may have devised a way to preselect the sex of the infant at or before conception. In the first, the issues are closely tied to the abortion debate. In the second, the problems are related to balancing the rights of the individual with the good of society. So far as the first is concerned, there is a further division between those who would allow abortion and those who do not. Naturally those of the latter view would not countenance sex selection by abortion under any circumstances.

Amongst those who do believe that abortion should be available to women who seek it is Joseph C. Fletcher, an American philosopher and ethicist. By being open about the way he has changed his mind over the years, he has given a historical perspective to the debate. In 1979 he wrote a piece for the *New England Journal of Medicine* in which he described his thinking up till then. Originally, like most, he said his reaction to sex-selective abortion was one of 'queasiness'. Building on this gut reaction, he argued that although early abortion could be justified if the foetus were abnormal or carried a sex-linked hereditary disease, it could not be justified on the 'frivolous' grounds of sex choice alone.

But, he said, he had had the opportunity to rethink the issues and had come to a different conclusion. The change in his thinking came about after a re-examination of his (and others') major reason for supporting abortion at all – namely that the overriding factor was the woman's right to choose. American courts did not critically evaluate any particular woman's reason for having an abortion, but simply expected her, like everyone else, to act in a moral way. Why then should the rules be different in this case?

> My major argument is that it is inconsistent to support an abortion law that protects the absolute right of women to decide and, at the same time, to block access to information

about the fetus because one thinks that an abortion may be foolishly sought on the basis of the information.

(Fletcher 1979)

But feminists tackling the same problem came to exactly the opposite conclusion. The complexities of the 'woman's right to choose' argument, evidence about sex preferences and the likely outcome of being able to choose the sex of one's infant made for a very difficult problem indeed. Dorothy Wertz argued that sex selection 'would increase sexism, and sex role stereotyping, undo advances of the women's movement and lead to restrictive laws against abortion'. On the other hand, she would not want legal prohibition of sex selection, since this would threaten the gains women had made in reproduction rights. Being caught thus between two most undesirable positions, she opted, with the support of others, for the withholding of information: 'The practice would be best discouraged by not routinely providing information on fetal sex' (Wertz and Fletcher 1992, 251).

In a reassuring extension to this conclusion, she also argued for the information to be withheld from doctors. Since 'withholding information is a feminist issue', and information equals power in so many settings, the best suggestion would be for laboratories not to pass the information on to doctors in the first place. Neither doctor nor patient would know, thus bypassing the power differential problem.

If the request for sex selection by early abortion had become widespread, this constructive suggestion might well have passed into custom. On the whole, however, with the exception of some Asian countries, this particular technology has not led to large numbers of women using early abortion to select the sex of their children. Since Fletcher wrote his careful analysis, most countries have changed or modified their abortion laws, depending on the cultural and religious values of the contemporary majority. And, as suggested by Wertz and Fletcher, even where the legal entitlement stands, local laboratories sometimes use subtle methods to make the information difficult to obtain. In other countries decisions have been taken to disallow amniocentesis if the only reason for it is to select the sex of the infant.

Beyond all this debate, however, it is possible there is a more important phenomenon. Most women find the idea of an abortion for any reason an occasion for fear, if not dread. No matter how safe the techniques or kindly the staff, it is still a physical, psychological, emotional and spiritual ordeal, and one that very few undergo lightly. It is probably an indicator of the strength of localized social pressure to have a boy that women ever submit to this procedure for reasons of sex selection.

THE ETHICS OF SEX PRESELECTION

If it became technically easy to preselect the sex of one's infant, then the ethical issue would cease to be complicated by the abortion issue, but would stand as a problem in its own right. There would be scarcely any reason not to make the technology readily available to all if it were not for the problem of the potentially disrupted sex ratio and birth-order problems. Two of the expected outcomes – limitation of family size and the control of sex-linked genetic diseases – would probably be welcomed by most.

But what of the possibility of changes in the sex ratio and changes in birth order according to sex? Would the forebodings about these become reality? What would be the social consequences if many more boys were born and women became comparatively scarce? In the past feminists have been divided in their views on the extent to which the new reproductive technologies have or have not benefited women. Some argued that they have empowered women by enhancing their reproductive success; others said they have further exploited and abused women's bodies. On the subject of sex selection, however, there is a degree of unanimity.

In her sometimes strident book *Gendercide*, Mary Anne Warren considered the consequences of the scarce women scenario: 'Although women sometimes profit from a shortage of their own sex, the rarity value of women often leads to imprisonment rather than power' (Warren 1985, 2). Unfortunately this sounds all too plausible, especially in cultures where women are seen as possessions. Given men's greater strength, and knowing what they do with other scarce but valuable possessions, it is possible that a scarcity of women would lead to restrictions and not to freedom. A parallel scenario has already been explored in Margaret Atwood's horrifying *Handmaid's Tale* (1986). On the other hand, a shortage of women may have worked to their advantage in other settings. The cinematic representations of frontier towns provide some information on this point.

Science fiction and Westerns notwithstanding, it is difficult (if not impossible) to predict what would happen if sex preselection became readily available. Some thoughtful commentators have wondered if most people would find the decision too difficult. In 1983 Nathan Keyfitz of Harvard's Department of Sociology wrote: 'choosing could be a burden for many; if forced to choose they might toss a coin! The X and Y chromosomes being nature's equivalent of a coin, indifferent parents would simply disregard the new technology.'

At the other end of the spectrum, liberal writers speak of 'ending reproductive roulette', and say they would welcome the advent of widely available techniques for preselecting the sex of the infant. Some said that it would not be long before society's values changed, and girls would be more welcome because they 'read more books, commit fewer crimes, go to more plays, are more religious, and do more about the moral education of the young' (Etzioni, cited in Fletcher 1988, 110).

It is perhaps not too surprising that some of the most carefully thought-out responses to the problems should come from an Indian woman philosopher. In an article entitled 'Should one be free to choose the sex of one's child?', Dhama Kumar argued against permitting sex preselection. She took as her starting point the argument that if one could preselect the sex of one's infant every child would be wanted and there would thus be an increase in overall happiness.

But Kumar was more concerned with longer-term consequences.

> The little boy may be happier than the little girl would have been, but this difference in happiness is much less than his unhappiness in a world where he cannot find a wife, where other men are aggressive, and so on, not to mention the unhappiness of other people. Of two societies with equal numbers, the one where people can choose the sex of their child, and end up with far more boys than girls, is less happy than one where they cannot choose, and which therefore has a more balanced population. Many people therefore draw the conclusion that individual freedom of choice in the matter of the sex of one's children is not desirable, and hence that policies to ban tests or discourage them are desirable.
>
> (Kumar 1987)

On the other hand, Kumar was aware of the incidence of female infanticide and would sooner women had access to safe, early abortion than go back to this practice. She argued this on the grounds that in many instances women's lives, and the lives of their daughters, are much better if they have produced at least one son.

Kumar also cited one of the two most creative solutions to the problem. It is an attempt to find a logical outcome within the liberal dictum 'freedom with fairness'. Kumar said the idea originally came from G. K. Boulding in an article entitled 'Marketable licenses for babies'. In pursuit of a way of combining maximum individual liberty with control of overall population numbers, a good outcome for society, he advocated giving each girl approaching maturity 'a certificate entitling her to 2.2 children (or whatever number is needed for the desired rate of growth); certificates could be bought, sold or gifted'. This meant that those who did not want to have children could transfer their entitlement by one means or another to those who would like a large family.

Kumar wondered if a similar system might solve the problems in the preselection of the sex of the infant. Instead of the certificate giving entitlement for 2.2 children, it might give entitlement for 1.1 girls and 1.1 boys. Having a working association with the Delhi School of Economics, she could of course see that the price of boy certificates might become very high in son-preferring cultures. A way would need to be found to ensure that women from poor families were not immediately pressured into selling their boy-entitlement.

A second creative suggestion was put forward by workers from the Faulkner Center for Reproductive Medicine in Boston. Their idea, 'Gender distribution – not sex selection', was similar in spirit to the one above, but set in the context of today's technology (not in the context of preselection being easily available to all). They noticed how more couples every year are seeking to select the sex of their infants. But they said:

> Prenatal diagnosis using amniocentesis or chorionic villus sampling and pregnancy termination on the basis of gender is, in our opinion, morally wrong and could have adverse and potentially unanticipated implications on the composition of societies. Similarly, preimplantation genetic diagnosis for the sake of gender selection only with destruction of the resulting embryos would seem, at best, a tremendously inappropriate use of technology.
>
> (Seibel *et al.* 1994)

Their ingenious solution was to offer pre-implantation genetic diagnosis for sex selection only to those couples who 'agreed to donate the resulting embryos of the undesired sex to an infertile couple needing embryo donation'. Since almost 70 per cent of childless couples wishing to adopt express a preference for a daughter, their scheme could work very well.

This seems an eminently sensible way of tackling the problem. But any such measures are interim and the main problem, son preference and the likelihood of imbalanced sex ratios, has yet to be solved. There are still two distinct aspects to this core problem: Would the presumed son preference in fact lead to imbalanced sex ratios and, if so, what ought we to do about it?

The first is a researchable question. Already there has been a sufficiently long time for an imbalance of the sexes to have occurred in locations where amniocentesis for sex preselection has been readily available. Is there in fact an imbalance of the sex ratio in these locations such that young men are unable to find partners? If there is, is there evidence of an increased demand for girls or even a diminishing demand for boys? The social experiments already carried out in some societies might provide information about the type of society likely to result, and the longer-term consequences for everyone. It is to be hoped that well-trained social scientists or demographers will turn their attention to these problems.

As to the second question, if it can be shown that sex selection techniques would lead to an imbalance of the sex ratio and that this would disadvantage everyone in the long term, then much serious thinking remains to be done. As Matt Ridley put it in *The Red Queen*,

> It is a tragedy of the commons: a collective harm that results from the rational pursuit of self interest by individuals. One person choosing to have only sons does nobody any harm. But if everybody does it, everybody suffers.

> (Ridley 1993, 122)

Many commentators would concur with Nancy Williamson who, in 1983, concluded a thorough review of 'Parental sex preferences and sex selection' with the comment that 'we should consider ourselves fortunate that sex selection techniques are not yet widely available'. Years later, they are still not available and, instead of regretting the slow advance, many express relief. The delay means there is more time to study the problem.

GOING WITH NATURE INSTEAD OF AGAINST

If the maternal dominance hypothesis has anything to contribute to the discussion, it is on the question of suitability. A woman conceives an infant of the sex she is more suited to raise. It could be argued that the child's development will proceed more smoothly if this situation is maintained. Parents everywhere seek the best for their children, and many now see this task in terms of creating the physical, social and psychological environment in which the children can grow up to fulfil their potential. The natural synchrony of interaction between mother and child may be one of the important aspects of this environment.

Parental acceptance also seems important. If parents who have completed their families are asked about sex selection, they usually say they are content with what they have. Even those with several children of one sex and none of the other say they would not have things any other way. Occasionally one of them, more frequently the father, may express regret at the absence of a child of a particular sex, but the large majority of parents express satisfaction at the makeup of their families.

The maternal dominance hypothesis would suggest that there is a reason for this. A man selects the type of woman he feels most comfortable with. She conceives an infant of the sex she is psychologically suited to raise. In the absence of strongly adverse indications from the social environment, parents would feel a psychological or emotional satisfaction that things were as they should be.

Another way of approaching the sex selection dilemma is to ask why males should be preferred. For many years psychologists sought to minimize psychological sex differences (Eagly 1995), in order to promote the claim that men and women are 'equal'. In a variety of social and political contexts this word is commonly used as an abbreviated form of 'deserving equal respect' or 'equal under the law'. No one would seriously question these forms of equality, and most would go further and say that all should have equality of opportunity, especially opportunity to develop their potential.

The fallacy in the 'all are equal' proposition comes with one of its most popular extensions – namely that everyone has the same potential. But that is demonstrably absurd. The fact that every human being is unique underlines the fact that there are individual differences, and these differences mean that people are born with different biological potentials. It is most unlikely that an ectomorphic girl would ever become a sumo wrestler, just as it is most unlikely that an intellectually handicapped person would ever become a Nobel prize winner. (It is still necessary to say 'most unlikely', because human beings will always have the capacity to surprise.) Ideally no one should be prevented from exploring their potential or interests to the fullest extent possible, consistent with equal opportunity for all.

While confirming the importance of treating men and women with equal respect and dignity, it ought also to be possible to acknowledge the existence of biologically based, physical and psychological sex differences. If, instead of denying their existence, these differences were accepted and valued, we might create a climate in which those areas in which women have the advantage become the focus of as much interest and admiration as those areas in which men have the advantage.

Why should 'different' mean 'inferior'? This seems to be the point which needs urgent exploration. Why do people everywhere appear to believe that the things men are somewhat better at than women are inherently more valuable than the things women are somewhat better at than men? This misperception (if that is what it is) appears to underlie the reluctance of women to stop trying to compete with men in those areas where men are known to be biologically advantaged, and to begin to explore those areas in which women have the biological advantage. Why do women think it is so important to beat men at their own game? Why not develop a *new* game? Why do not both men and women simply strive for personal excellence, developing whichever characteristics or abilities they were fortunate enough to be born with? Some philosophers and theologians believe that one has a duty to develop one's natural gifts, to work towards the fulfilment of one's potential. Some view this as the path to happiness.

If one were to accept that the varying domains of expertise are equally valuable, one might come to a conclusion about the development of these different domains which is distinctly unflattering to women. In comparison with all the time and energy that women have spent in trying to compete with and outdistance men in their areas of expertise, they have been very slow to take up sophisticated, formal exploration of their own areas of expertise. If women really wanted to employ their talents for the betterment of the human race, surely the best thing to do would be to develop those potentials that are unique to women.

An Auckland lawyer, Janet Leman, has suggested redefining our definition of 'success':

> Could it be that notions of merit objectively measured by career advancement, financial rewards, and power, position and responsibility are male standards and that some women (and men, for that matter) pursue different goals? A life apparently stunted in terms of career advancement may in fact be rich in subjective intangible criteria such as intellectual achievement, creative fulfilment, positive relationships, and a balance between spirituality and materialism. Why should the marks of success be confined to those measurable only by the narrow determinants of power and wealth? . . . The riddle of why educated intelligent women do not succeed may be solved if attention were given to a broader definition of success.
>
> (Leman 1993)

It is a measure of the difficulties that so few have given attention to defining women's special skills. In 1976 Jean Baker Miller published a book entitled *Toward a New Psychology of Women*, in which she talked about women being able to illuminate the path for others, because of their special knowledge. 'Women', she said, 'have the ability to tolerate, recognize and work *with* feelings', which is a strength. 'Much current literature, philosophy and social commentary focuses on the lack of human connection in all our institutions' (1976, 25). She claimed that women's special areas of expertise included sexual, emotional and physical frankness, a knowledge of human development, and an interest in humanizing society. If she is right, exploring these skills may be particularly timely. It is likely there will be an increased need for such expertise as people become more physically isolated from one another in the wake of technological and information revolutions.

In similar vein Sally Helgesen described what women might do to contribute to the commercial world in their own special way. They should not 'play the game the way men play it', but instead retain their basic values. These, she said, include 'an attention to process instead of a focus on the bottom line; a willingness to look at how an action will affect other people instead of simply asking "what's in it for me?"; [and] a concern for the wider community' (Helgesen 1990, xviii).

If those societies which currently overvalue males and undervalue females were to promote the idea that the development of biologically based potentials would benefit society as a whole, then going with nature rather than against might create a society in which women's special skills were valued, and sex preferences disappeared.

A person who has actually been present at the birth of a healthy baby tends to speak of awe as much as of joy. Even today, with all the advanced technology and expertise, it is an occasion for profound wonder. The first question people ask after the 'Is everything all right?' question is, 'Is it a boy or a girl?', and this is a persistent, cross-cultural phenomenon. At one point in my own research I wondered if it would be possible for a doctor or midwife to withhold this information from everyone, even for an hour or so. Would people be able to interact naturally with the baby without knowing its sex? But this is an impossible piece of research, because no one would countenance such a suggestion.

The sheer unimaginability of the suggestion is thought-provoking. Why should this be? Knowledge of one's sexual identity runs very deep: it is the first part of all self-knowledge to come into awareness (before the age of two) and the last to go (in Alzheimer's disease). Not only is it the first part of self-knowledge, it is almost always the first part of knowledge about others. It comes before age or race, occupation or status. We find it difficult to interact with a person whose sexual identity we do not know.

I think now that there is something more profound about the pre-determination of the sex of the infant than anything we have so far imagined. It is likely that at conception a woman is particularly suited to conceive an infant of one sex and not the other. Her body, her personality and her behaviour are all appropriately tuned for the conception of a male or a female infant. Furthermore, this condition is maintained during pregnancy and usually into the first few weeks or months of the baby's life, mothers of baby boys interacting differently with their babies from mothers of baby girls. These differences between mothers ensure the continuation of psychological sex differences, thereby laying the foundations for interpersonal relationships and maintaining the basic structure and richness of human society.

APPENDIX

Simple adjective test (includes the scoring key)

Date .... Name ....

I quite often feel:

hopeful	☐		depressed	☐	C
shy	☐	C	awed	☐	C
sad	☐	C	influential	☐	A
relaxed	☐		vigorous	☐	A
admired	☐	B	carefree	☐	B
strong	☐	A	protected	☐	C
aggressive	☐	A	feeble	☐	C
thankful	☐		fearful	☐	C
cruel	☐	B	pain	☐	C
excited	☐	B	proud	☐	B
humiliated	☐	C	serious	☐	B
despairing	☐	C	quiet	☐	
confused	☐	C	sheltered	☐	C

199

arrogant	☐	B	upset	☐	
troubled	☐	C	guilty	☐	C
kind	☐	A	crushed	☐	D
domineering	☐	A	lucky	☐	B
dignified	☐	A	responsible	☐	B
bored	☐	C	powerful	☐	A
joyful	☐	B	rejected	☐	C
capable	☐	B	frustrated	☐	C
timid	☐	C	self-satisfied	☐	A
affectionate	☐		helpless	☐	C
bold	☐	A	useful	☐	B
alert	☐	B	concentrating	☐	B
terrified	☐	C	masterful	☐	A
discouraged	☐		enjoyment	☐	B
distressed	☐	C	defeated	☐	C
controlling	☐	A	inhibited	☐	C
free	☐	B	triumphant	☐	A
friendly	☐	E	happy	☐	B
insecure	☐	C	alone with responsibility	☐	B

REFERENCES

Allen, B. P. and Potkay, C. R. (1981) 'On the arbitrary distinction between states and traits', *Journal of Personality and Social Psychology* 41, 916–28.

Allport, G. W. (1937) *Personality*, New York, Holt.

Allport, G. W. and Odbert, H. S. (1936) 'Trait names: a psycholexical study', *Psychological Monographs* 47 (whole no. 211).

Altemeier, W. A. (1984) Personal communication.

Altmann, J. (1980) *Baboon Mothers and Infants*, Cambridge, MA, Harvard University Press.

Andrew, R. J. and Rogers, L. (1972) 'Testosterone, search behaviour and persistence', *Nature* 237, 343–6.

Archer, J. (1977) 'Testosterone and persistence in mice', *Animal Behaviour* 25, 479–88.

Atwood, M. (1986) *The Handmaid's Tale*, Boston, Houghton Mifflin.

Austad, S. N. and Sunquist, M. E. (1986) 'Sex-ratio manipulation in the common opossum', *Nature* 324, 58–60.

Baker, R. R. and Bellis, M. A. (1995) *Human Sperm Competition*, London, Chapman and Hall.

Barber, N. (1995) 'The evolutionary psychology of physical attractiveness – sexual selection and human morphology', *Ethology and Sociobiology* 16, 395–424.

Barrette, C. (1993) 'The "inheritance of dominance" or of an aptitude to dominate?', *Animal Behaviour* 46, 591–3.

Baucom, D. H., Besch, P. K. and Callahan, S. (1985) 'Relation between testosterone concentration, sex role identity, and personality among females', *Journal of Personality and Social Psychology* 48, 1218–26.

Beck, B. B. and Castro, M. I. (1994) 'Environments for endangered primates', in E. F. Gibbons, E. J. Wyers, E. Waters and E. W. Menzel (eds) *Naturalistic Environments in Captivity for Animal Behavior Research*, New York, State University of New York Press.

Beck, R. A. (1992) 'Artists' offspring', *Nature* 356, 189.

Beernink, F. J., Dmowski, W. P. and Ericsson, R. J. (1993) 'Sex preselection through albumin separation of sperm', *Fertility and Sterility* 59, 382–6.

Berman, C. M. (1988) 'Maternal condition and offspring sex ratio in a group of free-ranging rhesus monkeys: an eleven-year study', *American Naturalist* 131, 307–28.

Bernstein, I. S. (1976) 'Dominance, aggression and reproduction in primate societies', *Journal of Theoretical Biology* 60, 459–72.

Bernstein, M. E. (1954) 'Evidence of genetic variation of the primary sex ratio in man', *Journal of Heredity* 45, 59–64.

Bernstein, M. E. (1981) 'Sex distribution in sibships according to occupation of parents', *Genus* 37, 179–81.

Beyer, C. and Feder, H. H. (1987) 'Sex steroids and afferent input: their roles in brain sexual differentiation', *Annual Review of Physiology* 49, 349–64.

Booth, A., Shelley, G., Mazur, A., Tharp, G. and Kittok, R. (1989) 'Testosterone, and winning and losing in human competition', *Hormones and Behavior* 23, 556–71.

Bouissou, M. F. (1978) 'Effects of testosterone propionate on dominance relationships in a group of cows', *Hormones and Behavior* 11, 388–400.

Bouissou, M. F. (1990) 'Effects of estrogen treatment on dominance relationships in cows', *Hormones and Behavior* 24, 376–87.

Bower, T. (1977) Personal communication.

Brewis, A. A. (1993) 'Sex ratios at birth in a Micronesian atoll population', *Social Biology* 40, 207–14.

Bromley, D. B. (1977) *Personality Description in Ordinary Language*, London, Wiley.

Brown, J., Bakeman, R. B., Snyder, P. A., Fredickson, W. T., Morgan, S. T. and Hepler, R. (1975) 'Interactions of black inner-city mothers with their newborn infants', *Child Development* 46, 677–86.

Burley, N. (1982) 'Facultative sex-ratio manipulation', *American Naturalist* 120, 81–7.

Buss, A. H. (1988) *Personality: Evolutionary Heritage and Human Distinctiveness*, Hillsdale, NJ, Lawrence Erlbaum.

Buss, D. M. (1994) *The Evolution of Desire: Strategies of Human Mating*, New York, Basic Books.

Buss, D. M. (1995) 'Psychological sex differences: origins through sexual selection', *American Psychologist* 50, 164–8.

Buss, D. M. and Craik, K. H. (1983) 'The act frequency approach to personality', *Psychological Review* 90, 105–26.

Campbell, C. (1976) 'What happens when we get the manchild pill?', *Psychology Today* 10(3), 86–91.

Capitanio, J. P. (1991) 'Levels of integration and the "inheritance of dominance"', *Animal Behaviour* 42, 495–6.

Carducci, B. J. and Zimbardo, P. G. (1995) 'Are you shy?', *Psychology Today* 28, 34–41, 64, 66, 68, 70, 78, 82.

Cashdan, E. (1995) 'Hormones, sex and status in women', *Hormones and Behavior* 29, 354–66.

Castle, W. E. (1922) 'The Y-chromosome type of sex-linked inheritance in man', *Science* 55, 703–4.

Cattell, R. B. (1965) *The Scientific Analysis of Personality*, Harmondsworth, Penguin.

Cattell, R. B., Eber, H. W. and Tatsuoka, M. M. (1970) *Handbook for the Sixteen Personality Factor Questionnaire*, Champaign, IL, Institute for Personality and Ability Testing.

Chahnazarian, A. (1988) 'Determinants of the sex ratio at birth: review of recent literature', *Social Biology* 35, 214–35.

Charnov, E. (1982) *The Theory of Sex Allocation*, Princeton, NJ, Princeton University Press.

Chedd, G. (1969) 'Struggling into manhood', *New Scientist* 118, 524–6.

Clark, A. B. (1978) 'Sex ratio and local resource competition in a prosimian primate', *Science* 201, 163–5.

Clark, M. M., Karpluk, P. and Galef, B. G. (1993) 'Hormonally mediated inheritance of acquired characteristics in Mongolian gerbils', *Nature* 364, 712.

Clutton-Brock, T. H., Albon, S. D. and Guinness, F. E. (1984) 'Maternal dominance, breeding success and birth sex ratios in red deer', *Nature* 308, 358–60.

Clutton-Brock, T. H. and Iason, G. R. (1986) 'Sex ratio variation in mammals', *Quarterly Review of Biology* 61, 339–74.

Corea, G. (1985) *The Mother Machine*, New York, Harper & Row.

Crouchley, R., Davies, R. B. and Pickles A. R. (1984) 'Methods for the identification of Lexian, Poisson and Markovian variations in the secondary sex ratio', *Biometrics* 40, 165–75.

Cui, K. and Matthews C. D. (1993) 'X larger than Y', *Nature* 366, 117–18.

Dabbs, J. M., Frady, R. L., Carr, T. S. and Besch, N. F. (1987) 'Saliva testosterone and criminal violence in young adult prison inmates', *Psychosomatic Medicine* 49, 174–82.

Dabbs, J. M., Ruback, R. B., Frady, R. L., Hopper, C. H. and Sgoutas, D. S. (1988) 'Saliva testosterone and criminal violence among women', *Personality and Individual Differences* 9, 269–75.

Davis, R. O., Thai, D. M., Bain, D. E., Andrew, J. B., Siemers, R. J. and Gravance, C. G. (1992) 'Accuracy and precision of the cell form human automated sperm morphometry instrument', *Fertility and Sterility* 58, 763–9.

de Waal, F. B. M. (1986) 'The integration of dominance and social bonding in primates', *Quarterly Review of Biology* 61, 459–79.

Dewsbury, D. A. (1991) 'Genes influence behaviour', *Animal Behaviour* 42, 499–500.

Dewsbury, D. A. (1993) 'More on the inheritance of dominance relationships: extending the concept of the phenotype', *Animal Behaviour* 46, 597–9.

Dittus, W. P. J. (1979) 'The evolution of behaviours regulating density and age-specific sex-ratios in a primate population', *Behaviour* 69, 265–302.

Dunbar, R. I. M. (1988) *Primate Social Systems*, Ithaca, NY, Cornell University Press.

Dunbar, R. I. M. (1995) 'The price of being at the top', *Nature* 373, 22–3.

Eagly, A. H. (1995) 'The science and politics of comparing women and men', *American Psychologist* 50, 145–8.

Edwards, A. W. F. (1962) 'Genetics and the human sex ratio', *Advances in Genetics* 11, 239–72.

Edwards, A. W. F. and Fraccaro, M. (1960) 'Distribution and sequences of sexes in a selected sample of Swedish families', *Annals of Human Genetics* 24, 245–52.

Ehrenkranz, J., Bliss, E. and Sheard, M. (1974) 'Plasma testosterone: correlation with aggressive behavior and social dominance in man', *Psychosomatic Medicine* 36, 469–75.

Eisenbach, M. and Tur-Kaspa, I. (1994) 'Human sperm chemotaxis is not enigmatic anymore', *Fertility and Sterility* 62, 233–5.

Ericsson, R. J. (1994) 'Sex selection via albumin columns: 20 years of results', *Human Reproduction* 9, 1787–91.

Ericsson, R. J., Langevin, C. N. and Nishino, M. (1973) 'Isolation of fractions rich in human Y sperm', *Nature* 246, 421–4.

Eriksson, C. J. P., Fukunaga, T. and Lindman, R. (1994) 'Sex hormone response to alcohol', *Nature* 369, 711.

Etzioni, A. (1968) 'Sex control, science and society', *Science* 168, 1107–12.

Evans, D. J., Hoffmann, R. G., Kalkhoff, R. K. and Kissebah, A. H. (1983) 'Relationship of androgenic activity to body fat cell topography, fat cell morphology, and metabolic aberrations in premenopausal women', *Journal of Clinical Endocrinology and Metabolism* 57, 304–10.

Eysenck, H. J. (1967) *The Biological Basis of Personality*, Springfield, IL, C. C. Thomas.

Eysenck, H. J. (1981) *A Model for Personality*, New York, Springer-Verlag.

Fiske, D. W. (1971) *Measuring the Concepts of Human Personality*, Chicago, Aldine.

Fiske, D. W. (1974) 'The limits for the conventional science of personality', *Journal of Personality* 42, 1–11.

Fletcher, J. C. (1979) 'Ethics and amniocentesis for fetal sex identification', *New England Journal of Medicine* 301, 550–3.

Fletcher, J. C. (1988) *The Ethics of Genetic Control: Ending Reproductive Roulette*, New York, Prometheus Books.

Foote, R. H. (1977) 'Sex ratios in dairy cattle under various conditions', *Theriogenology* 8, 349–55.

France, J. T., Graham, F. M., Gosling, L. and Hair, P. I. (1984) 'A prospective study of the preselection of the sex of the offspring by timing intercourse relative to ovulation', *Fertility and Sterility* 41, 894–900.

Franke, L. B. (1978) *The Ambivalence of Abortion*, New York, Random House.

Gledhill, B. L. (1988) 'Selection and separation of X- and Y-chromosome bearing mammalian sperm', *Gamete Research* 20, 377–95.

Goerres, H. P. and Gerbert, K. (1976) 'Sex ratio in offspring of pilots: a contribution to stress research', *Aviation, Space and Environmental Medicine* 47, 889–92.

Golub, M. S., Sassenrath, E. N. and Goo, G. P. (1979) 'Plasma cortisol levels and dominance in peer groups of rhesus monkey weanlings', *Hormones and Behavior* 12, 50–9.

Gosling, L. M. (1986) 'Selective abortion of entire litters in the coypu: adaptive control of offspring production in relation to quality and sex', *American Naturalist* 127, 772–95.

Gottfried, N. W., Seay, B. M. and Wismar, K. (1987) 'Neonatal sex and birth-order effects on behaviours of mothers and temporary caretakers during bottle-feeding', *Journal of Genetic Psychology* 148, 479–87.

Grant, V. J. (1990) 'Maternal personality and sex of infant', *British Journal of Medical Psychology* 63, 261–6.

Grant, V. J. (1992) 'The measurement of dominance in pregnant women by use of the Simple Adjective Test', *Personality and Individual Differences* 13, 99–102.

Grant, V. J. (1994a) 'Maternal dominance and the conception of sons', *British Journal of Medical Psychology* 67, 343–51.

Grant, V. J. (1994b) 'Sex of infant differences in mother–infant interaction: a reinterpretation of past findings', *Developmental Review* 14, 1–26.

Grant, V. (1996) 'Sex determination and the maternal dominance hypothesis', *Human Reproduction* 11, 2371–5.

Gray, A., Jackson, D. N. and McKinlay, J. B. (1991) 'The relation between dominance, anger, and hormones in normally aging men: results from the Massachusetts male aging study', *Psychosomatic Medicine* 53, 375–85.

Gray, D. S. and Gorzalka, B. B. (1980) 'Adrenal steroid interactions in female sexual behavior: a review', *Psychoneuroendocrinology* 5, 157–75.

Gray, J. A. (1982) *The Neuropsychology of Anxiety: An Inquiry into the Functions of the Septo-Hippocampal System*, Oxford, Clarendon Press.

Gray, R. H. (1992) 'Stress and reproduction: an epidemiological perspective', in K. E. Sheppard, J. H. Boublik and J. W. Funder (eds) *Stress and Reproduction*, New York, Raven Press.

Greenspan, F. S. and Baxter, J. D. (eds) (1994) *Basic and Clinical Endocrinology* (4th edition), London, Prentice-Hall.

Greenstein, B. (1994) *Endocrinology at a Glance*, Oxford, Blackwell Science.

Griffin, D. K., Abruzzo, M. A., Millie, E. A., Feingold, E. and Hassold, T. J. (1996) 'Sex ratio in normal and disomic sperm: evidence that the extra chromosome 21 preferentially segregates with the Y chromosome', *American Journal of Human Genetics* 59, 1108–13.

Griffin, J. E. and Ojeda, S. R. (1992) *Textbook of Endocrine Physiology*, Oxford, Oxford University Press.

Gualtieri, T. and Hicks, R. E. (1985) 'An immunoreactive theory of selective male affliction', *Behavioral and Brain Sciences* 8, 427–41.

Gubbay, J., Collignon, J., Koopman, P., Capel, B., Economou, A., Munsterberg, A., Vivian, N., Goodfellow, P. and Lovell-Badge, R. (1990) 'A gene mapping to the sex-determining region of the mouse Y chromosome is a member of a novel family of embryonically expressed genes', *Nature* 346, 245–50.

Guerrero, R. (1974) 'Association of the type and time of insemination within the menstrual cycle with the human sex ratio at birth', *New England Journal of Medicine* 291, 1056–9.

Gustafson, M. L. and Donahoe, P. K. (1994) 'Male sex determination: current concepts of male sexual differentiation', *Annual Review of Medicine* 45, 505–24.

Haig, D. (1991) 'Developmental asynchrony and environmental sex determination in alligators', *Journal of Theoretical Biology* 150, 373–83.

Haning, R. V., Hackett, R. J., Flood, C. A., Loughlin, J. S., Zhao, Q. Y. and Longcope, C. (1993) 'Testosterone, a follicular regulator: key to anovulation', *Journal of Clinical Endocrinology and Metabolism* 77, 710–15.

Hassold, T., Quillen, S. D. and Yamane, J. A. (1983) 'Sex ratio in spontaneous abortions', *Annals of Human Genetics* 47, 39–47.

Heath, C. W. (1954) 'Physique, temperament and sex ratio', *Human Biology* 26, 337–42.

Hedricks, C. and McClintock M. K. (1990) 'Timing of insemination is correlated with the secondary sex ratio of Norway rats', *Physiology and Behavior* 48, 625–32.

Helgesen, S. (1990) *The Female Advantage: Women's Ways of Leadership*, New York, Doubleday.

Hewitt, D., Webb, J. W. and Stewart, A. M. (1955) 'A note on the occurrence of single-sex sibships', *Annals of Human Genetics* 20, 155–8.

Higley, J. D., Mehlman, P. T., Poland, R. E., Taub, D. M., Vickers, J., Suomi S. J. and Linnoila, M. (1996) 'CSF testosterone and 5-HIAA correlate with different types of aggressive behaviors', *Biological Psychiatry* 40, 1067–82.

Hinde, R. A. (1974) *Biological Bases of Human Social Behaviour*, New York, McGraw Hill.

Hoffman, M. L. (1977) 'Sex differences and related behaviours', *Psychological Bulletin* 84, 712–22.

Hrdy, S. B. (1981) *The Woman that Never Evolved*, Cambridge, MA, Harvard University Press.

Hrdy, S. B. (1987) 'Sex-biased parental investment among primates and other mammals: a critical evaluation of the Trivers–Willard hypothesis', in R. J. Gelles and J. B. Lancaster (eds) *Child Abuse and Neglect: Biosocial Dimensions*, New York, Aldine De Gruyter.

Hrubec, Z. and Robinette, C. D. (1984) 'The study of human twins in medical research', *New England Journal of Medicine* 310, 435–41.

Hwang, C. P. (1978) 'Mother–infant interaction: effects of sex of infant on feeding behaviour', *Early Human Development* 2, 341–9.

Jacklin, C. N., Maccoby E. E. and Doering, C. H. (1983) 'Neonatal sex-steroid hormones and timidity in 6–18 month old boys and girls', *Developmental Psychobiology* 16, 163–8.

James, W. H. (1971a) 'Cycle day of insemination, coital rate, and sex ratio', *Lancet* 16 January, 112–14.

James, W. H. (1971b) 'Excess of like sexed pairs of dizygotic twins', *Nature* 232, 277–8.

James, W. H. (1987a) 'The human sex ratio. Part 1: a review of the literature', *Human Biology* 59, 721–52.

James, W. H. (1987b) 'The human sex ratio. Part 2: a hypothesis and a programme of research', *Human Biology* 59, 873–900.

James, W. H. (1992) 'The current status of Weinberg's differential rule', *Acta Geneticae Medicae et Gemellologiae* 41, 33–42.

James, W. H. (1995a) 'Sex ratios of offspring and the causes of placental pathology', *Human Reproduction* 10, 1403–6.

James, W. H. (1995b) 'What stabilizes the sex ratio?', *Annals of Human Genetics* 59, 243–9.

James, W. H. (1996) 'Evidence that mammalian sex ratios at birth are partially controlled by parental hormone levels at the time of conception', *Journal of Theoretical Biology* 180, 271–86.

Jeffcoate, W. (1993) *Lecture Notes on Endocrinology* (5th edition), Oxford, Blackwell Scientific.

Jeffcoate, W. J., Lincoln, N. B., Selby, C. and Herbert, M. (1986) 'Correlation between anxiety and serum prolactin in humans', *Journal of Psychosomatic Research* 30, 217–22.

Johnson, C. N. (1988) 'Dispersal and the sex ratio at birth in primates', *Nature* 332, 726–8.

Keyfitz, N. (1983) Foreword, in N. G. Bennett (ed.) *Sex Selection of Children*, New York, Academic Press.

Krackow, S. (1995) 'The developmental asynchrony hypothesis for sex ratio manipulation', *Journal of Theoretical Biology* 176, 273–80.

Kreuz, L. E., Rose, R. M. and Jennings, J. R. (1972) 'Suppression of plasma testosterone levels and psychological stress', *Archives of General Psychiatry* 26, 479–82.

Kuhn, T. S. (1970) *The Structure of Scientific Revolutions* (2nd edition, enlarged), Chicago, University of Chicago Press.

Kumar, D. (1987) 'Should one be free to choose the sex of one's child?', in R. F. Chadwick (ed.) *Ethics, Reproduction and Genetic Control*, London, Routledge.

Leman, J. (1993) Letter to the editor, *New Zealand Herald*, 3 May.

Levin, R. J. (1987) 'Human sex pre-selection', *Oxford Reviews of Reproductive Biology* 9, 161–91.

Lewis, M. (1972) 'State as an infant–environment interaction: an analysis of mother–infant interaction as a function of sex', *Merrill-Palmer Quarterly* 18, 95–121.

Little, B. B., Rigsby, C. H. and Little, L. R. (1987) 'Pilot and astronaut offspring: possible G-force effects on human sex ratio', *Aviation, Space and Environmental Medicine* 58, 707–9.

Lloyd, O. L., Lloyd, M. M. and Holland, Y. (1984) 'An unusual sex ratio of births in an industrial town with mortality problems', *British Journal of Obstetrics and Gynaecology* 91, 901–7.

Lobel, S. M., Pomponio, R. J. and Mutter, G. L. (1993) 'The sex ratio of normal and manipulated human sperm quantitated by the polymerase chain reaction', *Fertility and Sterility* 59, 387–92.

Loehlin, J. C. (1992) *Genes and Environment in Personality Development*, Newbury Park, CA, Sage.

Lorrain, J. (1975) 'Pre-conceptional sex selection', *International Journal of Gynaecology and Obstetrics* 13, 127–30.

Lyster, W. R. (1982) 'Altered sex ratio in children of divers', *Lancet* 334, 152.

McClelland, G. H. (1983) 'Measuring sex preferences and their effects on fertility', in N. G. Bennett (ed.) *Sex Selection of Children*, New York, Harper & Row.

Maccoby, E. E. and Jacklin, C. N. (1974) *The Psychology of Sex Differences*, Stanford, CA, Stanford University Press.

McFarland Symington, M. (1987) 'Sex ratio and maternal rank in wild spider monkeys: when daughters disperse', *Behavioral Ecology and Sociobiology* 20, 421–5.

McGinley, M. A. (1984) 'The adaptive value of male-biased sex ratios among stressed animals', *American Naturalist* 124, 597–9.

MacMahon, B. and Pugh, T. F. (1954) 'Sex ratio of white births in the United States during the Second World War', *American Journal of Human Genetics* 6, 284–92.

Maestripieri, D. (1996) 'Primate cognition and the bared-teeth display: a reevaluation of the concept of formal dominance', *Journal of Comparative Psychology* 110, 402–5.

Manning, J. T., Anderton, R. and Washington, S. M. (1996) 'Women's waists and the sex ratio of their progeny: evolutionary aspects of the ideal female body shape', *Journal of Human Evolution* 31, 41–7.

Manogue, K. R., Leshner, A. I. and Candland, D. K. (1975) 'Dominance status and adrenocortical reactivity to stress in squirrel monkeys (Saimiri sciureus)', *Primates* 16, 457–63.

Martin, J. F. (1994) 'Changing sex ratios: the history of Havasupai fertility and its implications for human sex ratio variation', *Current Anthropology* 35, 255–66.

Martin, R. H. (1994) 'Human sex pre-selection by sperm manipulation', *Human Reproduction* 9, 1790–1.

Maslow, A. H. (1940) 'Dominance-quality and social behaviour in infra-human primates', *Journal of Social Psychology* 11, 313–24.

Maynard Smith, J. (1982) *Evolution and the Theory of Games*, Cambridge, Cambridge University Press.

Mazur, A. (1994) 'A neurohormonal model of social stratification among humans: a microsocial perspective', in L. Ellis (ed.) *Social Stratification and Socioeconomic Inequality*, vol. 2, *Reproductive and Interpersonal Aspects of Dominance and Status*, Westport, CN, Praeger.

Mazur, A. and Lamb, T. A. (1980) 'Testosterone status and mood in human males', *Hormones and Behavior* 14, 236–46.

Mazur, A., Booth, A. and Dabbs, J. M. (1992) 'Testosterone and chess competition', *Social Psychology Quarterly* 55, 70–7.

Mealey, L. and Mackey, W. (1990) 'Variation in offspring sex ratio in women of differing social status', *Ethology and Sociobiology* 11, 83–95.

Mech, L. D. (1975) 'Disproportionate sex ratios in wolf pups', *Journal of Wildlife Management* 39, 737–40.

Meikle, D. B., Tilford, B. L. and Vessey, S. H. (1984) 'Dominance rank, secondary sex ratio, and reproduction of offspring in polygynous primates', *American Naturalist* 124, 173–88.

Meikle, D. B., Drickamer, L. C., Vessey, S. H., Rosenthal, T. L. and Fitzgerald, K. S. (1993) 'Maternal dominance rank and secondary sex ratio in domestic swine', *Animal Behaviour* 46, 79–85.

Miller, J. B. (1976) *Toward a New Psychology of Women*, Harmondsworth, Penguin.

Millot, J. L., Filiatre, J. C. and Montagner, H. (1988) 'Maternal tactile behaviour correlated with mother and newborn infant characteristics', *Early Human Development* 16, 119–29.

Mittwoch, U. (1989) 'Sex differentiation in mammals and tempo of growth: probabilities vs. switches', *Journal of Theoretical Biology* 137, 445–55.

Mittwoch, U. (1996) 'Differential implantation rates and variations in the sex ratio', *Human Reproduction* 11, 8–9.

Moeller, H. (1996) 'Change in male:female ratio among newborn infants in Denmark', *Lancet* 348, 828–9.

Moore, A. J. (1990) 'The inheritance of social dominance, mating behaviour and attractiveness to mates in male Nauphoeta cinerea', *Animal Behaviour* 39, 388–97.

Moore, A. J. (1991) 'Genetics, inheritance and social behaviour', *Animal Behaviour* 42, 497–8.

Moore, A. J. (1993) 'Towards an evolutionary view of social dominance', *Animal Behaviour* 46, 594–6.

Moore, C. L. and Morelli, G. A. (1979) 'Mother rats interact differently with male and female offspring', *Journal of Comparative and Physiological Psychology* 93, 677–84.

Moore, J. H. (1994) Comment on Martin's 'Changing sex ratios', *Current Anthropology* 35, 270–1.

Moruzzi, J. F., Wyrobek, A. J., Mayall, B. H. and Gledhill, B. L. (1988) 'Quantification and classification of human sperm morphology by computer-assisted image analysis', *Fertility and Sterility* 50, 142–52.

Moss, H. A. (1967) 'Sex, age, and state as determinants of mother–infant interaction', *Merrill-Palmer Quarterly* 13, 19–36.

Muggeridge, M. (1972) *Chronicles of Wasted Time*, London, Collins.

Mulder, M. B. (1994) 'On polygyny and sex ratio at birth: an evaluation of Whiting's study', *Current Anthropology* 35, 625–7.

Myers, J. H. (1978) 'Sex ratio adjustment under food stress: maximization of quality or numbers of offspring?', *American Naturalist* 112, 381–8.

Norton, H. W. (1940) 'Note on Woods' paper on parental instinct', *Journal of Heredity* 31, 29–33.

Painter, T. S. (1924) 'The sex chromosomes of man', *American Naturalist* 58, 506–24.

Peippo, J. and Bredbacka, P. (1995) 'Sex-related growth rate differences in mouse preimplantation embryos in vivo and in vitro', *Molecular Reproduction and Development* 40, 56–61.

Perret, M. (1990) 'Influence of social factors on sex ratio at birth, maternal investment and young survival in a prosimian primate', *Behavioural Ecology and Sociobiology* 27, 447–54.

Purifoy, F. E. and Koopmans, L. H. (1979) 'Androstenedione, testosterone, and free testosterone concentration in women of various occupations', *Social Biology* 26, 179–88.

Pyrzak, R. (1994) 'Separation of X- and Y-bearing human spermatozoa using albumin gradients', *Human Reproduction* 9, 1788–90.

Rahe, R. H., Karson, S., Howard, N. S., Rubin, R. T. and Poland, R. E. (1990) 'Psychological and physiological assessments on American hostages freed from captivity in Iran', *Psychosomatic Medicine* 52, 1–16.

Ramanamma, A. and Bambawale, U. (1980) 'The mania for sons: an analysis of social values in South Asia', *Social Science and Medicine* 14B, 107–10.

Rawlins, R. G. and Kessler, M. J. (1986) 'Secondary sex ratio variation in the Cayo Santiago macaque population', *American Journal of Primatology* 10, 9–23.

Resnick, S. M., Gottesman, I. I. and McGue, M. (1993) 'Sensation-seeking in opposite-sex twins: an effect of prenatal hormones?', *Behavior Genetics* 23, 323–9.

Rhine, R. J., Norton, G. W., Rogers, J. and Wasser, S. K. (1992) 'Secondary sex ratio and maternal dominance rank among wild yellow baboons (Papio cynocephalus) of Mikumi National Park, Tanzania', *American Journal of Primatology* 27, 261–73.

Richards, S. (1972) 'Tests for behavioural characteristics in rhesus monkeys', Ph.D. thesis, University of Cambridge.

Ridley, M. (1993) *The Red Queen: Sex and the Evolution of Human Nature*, London, Viking.

Rivier, C. and Rivest, S. (1991) 'Effect of stress on the activity of the hypothalamic–pituitary–gonadal axis: peripheral and central mechanisms', *Biology of Reproduction* 45, 523–32.

Robin, M. (1982) 'Neonate–mother interaction: tactile contacts in the days following birth', *Early Child Development and Care* 9, 221–36.

Rose, R. M. (1974) 'Testosterone and aggression in man', *Psychosomatic Medicine* 36, 467–68.

Rose, R. M., Bernstein, I. S. and Gordon, T. P. (1975) 'Consequences of social conflict on plasma testosterone levels in rhesus monkeys', *Psychosomatic Medicine* 37, 50–60.

Rose, R. M., Bernstein, I. S. and Holaday, J. W. (1971) 'Plasma testosterone, dominance rank and aggressive behaviour in a group of male rhesus monkeys', *Nature* 231, 366.

Rosenthal, R. (1991) *Meta-analytic Procedures for Social Research* (revised edition), Newbury Park, Sage Publications.

Russell, J. A. and Mehrabian, A. (1977) 'Evidence for a three-factor theory of emotions', *Journal of Research in Personality* 11, 273–94.

Sackett, G. P. (1981) 'Receiving severe aggression correlates with fetal gender in pregnant pigtailed monkeys', *Developmental Psychobiology* 14, 267–72.

Sadalla, E. K., Kenrick, D. T. and Vershure, B. (1987) 'Dominance and heterosexual attraction', *Journal of Personality and Social Psychology* 52, 730–8.

Saling, P. M. (1991) 'How the egg regulates sperm function during gamete interaction: facts and fantasies', *Biology of Reproduction* 44, 246–51.

Sapolsky, R. M. and Ray, J. C. (1989) 'Styles of dominance and their endocrine correlates among wild olive baboons (Papio anubis)', *American Journal of Primatology* 18, 1–13.

Sawyer, R. (1993) *We are but Women: Women in Ireland's History*, London, Routledge.

Schuerger, J. M., Zarrella, K. L. and Hotz, A. S. (1989) 'Factors that influence the temporal stability of personality by questionnaire', *Journal of Personality and Social Psychology* 56, 777–83.

Seibel, M. M., Seibel, S. G. and Zilberstein, M. (1994) 'Gender distribution – not sex selection', *Human Reproduction* 9, 569–70.

Sheldon, W. H. and Stevens, S. S. (1942) *The Varieties of Temperament*, New York, Harper.

Shettles, L. B. (1960) 'Nuclear morphology of human spermatozoa', *Nature* 186, 648–9.

Shettles, L. B. (1970) 'Factors influencing sex ratios', *International Journal of Gynaecology and Obstetrics* 8, 643–7.

Silk, J. B. (1983) 'Local resource competition and facultative adjustment of sex ratios in relation to competitive abilities', *American Naturalist* 121, 56 66.

Silk, J. B., Clark-Wheatley, C. B., Rodman, P. S. and Samuels, A. (1981) 'Differential reproductive success and facultative adjustment of sex ratios among captive female bonnet macaques (Macaca radiata)', *Animal Behaviour* 29, 1106–20.

Simpson, J. L. (1979) 'More than we ever wanted to know about sex – should we be afraid to ask?', *New England Journal of Medicine* 300, 1483–4.

Simpson, M. J. A. and Simpson, A. E. (1982) 'Birth sex ratios and social rank in rhesus monkey mothers', *Nature* 300, 440–1.

Singh, D. and Zambarano, R. J. (1997) 'Offspring sex ratio in women with android body fat distribution', *Human Biology* 69, 555–66.

Small, M. F. and Smith, D. G. (1985) 'Sex of infants produced by male rhesus macaques', *American Naturalist* 126, 354–61.

Smith, E. A. and Smith, S. A. (1994) 'Inuit sex ratio variation: population control, ethnographic error, or parental manipulation?', *Current Anthropology* 35, 595–624.

Snowdon, C. T. (1994) 'The significance of naturalistic environments for primate behavioural research', in E. F. Gibbons, E. J. Wyers, E. Waters and

E. W. Menzel (eds) *Naturalistic Environments in Captivity for Animal Behavior Research*, New York, State University of New York Press.

Stern, C. (1973) *Principles of Human Genetics*, San Francisco, W. H. Freeman.

Stolkowski, J. and Lorrain, J. (1980) 'Preconceptional selection of fetal sex', *International Journal of Gynaecology and Obstetrics* 18, 440–3.

Tarin, J. J., Bernabeu, R., Baviera, A., Bonada, M. and Cano, A. (1995) 'Sex selection may be inadvertently performed in in-vitro fertilization-embryo transfer programmes', *Human Reproduction* 10, 2992–8.

Teitelbaum, M. S. (1972) 'Factors associated with the sex ratio in human populations', in G. A. Harrison and A. J. Boyce (eds) *The Structure of Human Populations*, Oxford, Clarendon Press.

Teitelbaum, M. S. and Mantel, N. (1971) 'Socio-economic factors and the sex ratio at birth', *Journal of Biosocial Science* 3, 23–41.

Thoman, E. B., Leiderman, P. H. and Olson, J. P. (1972) 'Neonate–mother interaction during breast-feeding', *Developmental Psychology* 6, 110–18.

Tomlinson, R. (1994) 'China aims to improve health of newborn law', *British Medical Journal* 309, 1319.

Trevarthen, C. (1993) 'The function of emotions in early infant communication and development', in J. Nadel and L. Camaioni (eds), *New Perspectives in Early Communicative Development*, London, Routledge.

Trivers, R. L. and Willard, D. E. (1973) 'Natural selection of parental ability to vary the sex ratio of offspring', *Science* 179, 90–1.

Udry, J. R. and Talbert, L. M. (1988) 'Sex hormone effects on personality at puberty', *Journal of Personality and Social Psychology* 54, 291–5.

Underwood, J. H. (1993) 'Secondary sex ratios in Micronesian populations', *Social Biology* 40, 200–6.

Van Schaik, C. P. and Hrdy, S. B. (1991) 'Intensity of local resource competition shapes the relationship between maternal rank and sex ratios at birth in cercopithecine primates', *American Naturalist* 138, 1555–62.

Van Schaik, C. P. and van Noordwijk, M. A. (1983) 'Social stress and the sex ratio of neonates and infants among non-human primates', *Netherlands Journal of Zoology* 33, 249–65.

Van Schaik, C. P., Netto, W. J., Van Amerongen, A. J. J. and Westland, H. (1989) 'Social rank and sex ratio of captive long-tailed macaque females (Macaca fascicularis)', *American Journal of Primatology* 19, 147–61.

Vandenbergh, J. G. and Huggett, C. L. (1994) 'Mother's prior intrauterine position affects the sex ratio of her offspring in house mice', *Proceedings of the National Academy of Sciences* 91, 11055–9.

Verme, L. J. (1969) 'Reproduction patterns of white-tailed deer related to nutritional plane', *Journal of Wildlife Management* 33, 881–7.

Verme, L. J. (1983) 'Sex ratio variation in Odocoileus: a critical review', *Journal of Wildlife Management* 47, 573–82.

Vom Saal, F. S., Quadagno, D. M., Even, M. D., Keisler, L. W., Keisler D. H. and Khan, S. (1990) 'Paradoxical effects of maternal stress on fetal steroids and postnatal reproductive traits in female mice from different intrauterine positions', *Biology of Reproduction* 43, 751–61.

Walby, A. L., Merrett, J. D., Dean, G. and Kirke, P. (1981) 'Sex ratio of births in Ireland in 1978', *Ulster Medical Journal* 50, 83–7.

Warren, M. A. (1985) *Gendercide: The Implications of Sex Selection*, Totowa, NJ, Rowman & Allanheld.

Watson, J. S. (1982) 'Parental manipulation of the sex ratio of offspring: a historical note', *American Naturalist* 119, 283–4.

Weinberg, C. R., Baird, D. D. and Wilcox, A. J. (1995) 'The sex of the baby may be related to the length of the follicular phase in the conception cycle', *Human Reproduction* 10, 304–7.

Wells, R. (1990) *Human Sex Determination: An Historical Review and Synthesis*, Tharwa, ACT, Australia, Riverlea Press.

Wertz, D. C. and Fletcher, J. C. (1992) 'Sex selection through prenatal diagnosis: a feminist critique', in H. B. Holmes and L. M. Purdy (eds) *Feminist Perspectives in Medical Ethics*, Bloomington, IN, Indiana University Press.

Westoff, C. F. and Rindfuss, R. R. (1974) 'Sex preselection in the United States: some implications', *Science* 184, 633–6.

White, E. M. (1980) 'Conceptual universals in interpersonal language', *American Anthropologist* 82, 759–81.

Whiting, J. W. M. (1993) 'The effect of polygyny on sex ratio at birth', *American Anthropologist* 95, 435–42.

Wiley, D. N. and Clapham, P. J. (1993) 'Does maternal condition affect the sex ratio of offspring in humpback whales?', *Animal Behaviour* 46, 321–4.

Williamson, N. E. (1983) 'Parental preferences and sex selection', in N. G. Bennett (ed.) *Sex Selection of Children*, New York, Harper & Row.

Williamson, N. E., Lean, T. H. and Vengadasalam, D. (1978) 'Evaluation of an unsuccessful sex preselection clinic in Singapore', *Journal of Biosocial Science* 10, 375–88.

Wilson, E. O. (1975) *Sociobiology: The New Synthesis*, Cambridge, MA, Harvard University Press.

Winberg, J. and de Chateau, P. (1982) 'Early social development: studies of infant–mother interaction and relationships', in W. W. Hartup (ed.) *Review of Child Development Research*, vol. 6, Chicago, University of Chicago Press.

Windsor, D. P., Evans, G. and White, I. G. (1993) 'Sex predetermination by separation of X and Y chromosome-bearing sperm: a review', *Reproduction, Fertility and Development* 5, 155–71.

Wolff, P. H. (1966) 'The causes, controls and organization of behaviour in the neonate', *Psychological Issues* 5, monograph 17.

Wright, D. D., Ryser, J. T. and Kiltie, R. A. (1995) 'First cohort advantage hypothesis: a new twist on facultative sex ratio adjustment', *The American Naturalist* 145, 133–45

Zuckerman, M. (1990) 'The psychophysiology of sensation seeking', *Journal of Personality* 58, 313–45.

NAME INDEX

SUBJECT INDEX

abortion, animals: selective 133;
spontaneous 130–3, 142
abortion, humans 162–3; selective
147, 184, 189–90; spontaneous 91,
93–4, 107
adoption 5, 186
aggression: in animals 113–14,
116–22 *passim*, 124–5; in humans
9, 41–5, 52, 56, 113, 177
amniocentesis 184, 189–90, 193–4
animal husbandry 3, 59, 70, 80
animals (cited in research on sex
ratio): alligators 89; baboons 127,
143, (olive) 115–16; bulls 82;
chicks 125; cockroaches 111; cows
(domestic) 95, 124; coypu 133;
deer (red) 118, 129–30, (white-
tailed) 136–7, 139; gerbils 104;
humpback whales 134; macaques
(bonnet) 128, (long-tailed) 134,
(pigtail) 131, (toque) 128; monkeys
(gelada) 114–15, (langur) 117,
(mouse lemurs) 78, (New World)
110, (Old World) 110, (rhesus)
113, 116, 117, 119–20, 121–2,
123, 130, 133, (squirrel) 124,
(talapoin) 46; mice 92, 102–3,
104–5, 125; opossum 133, 135;
rats 180–1; sheep 136; swine
(domestic) 134; toads 95; wolves
137–8
anthropomorphism 110–11
assortative mating 154, 165–7

babies' behaviours 5, 24, 54,
171–6, 179
body type: endomorph, ectomorph,
mesomorph 41–2, 166–7

captivity: effects of in animals 3, 78,
106, 112, 142–4; in humans 48
chance effects: likelihood of (in
literature) 11; (in research) 46,
59–60, 72–3, 77, 80, 88, 133,
146–51, 154–5, 163, 176
coin-tossing model 73, 146–7, 191
coital frequency 58, 68–9, 89, 160
competitive striving 166
conception 90; maternal hormones at
47, 66, 72, 74; ovum at 69–70; *see
also* primary sex ratio; timing of
intercourse
contraception 62, 66, 150, 162–3,
184, 185

demographic research 4, 62, 68,
73–4, 77, 146–59, 183–4, 194
developmental psychology 5, 7, 22,
56, 145, 168–80, 183, 186, 194
diet and sex selection 5, 95–7; *see also*
nutrition
dominance: acquired 19; in animals
2–3, 40, 110–25; biological basis
1, 3, 38–9, 40–57, 121–5; Cattell's
definition 13–15, 29, 76, 153–4,
178; comfortable 19–20, 123;
cultural influences on 8, 14,
18–19; decline with age 154;
definition 8–20, 51–5 *passim*, 76,

218